UNCOMMON FRIENDS

To Jimmie
Henry Ford.

To my young friend Jimmie
Thos A Edison.

To James Newton
a valued assistant in my office
Harvey S. Firestone

$\mathcal{U}$NCOMMON $\mathcal{F}$RIENDS

Life with Thomas Edison,

Henry Ford, Harvey Firestone,

Alexis Carrel, & Charles Lindbergh

JAMES D. NEWTON

With a foreword by Anne Morrow Lindbergh

A Harvest Book

HARCOURT BRACE & COMPANY

San Diego   New York   London

Requests for permission to make copies of
any part of the work should be mailed to:
Permissions Department,
Harcourt Brace & Company, 6277 Sea Harbor Drive,
Orlando, Florida 32887-6777.

The letter from Charles Lindbergh to Henry Ford
on page 267 is reprinted by permission of
the Henry Ford Museum, Dearborn, Michigan.
The letter from Charles Lindbergh to James
Doolittle on pages 323–24 is reprinted by
permission of the Yale University Library.

Library of Congress Cataloging-in-Publication Data
Newton, James D. (James Draper), 1905–
Uncommon friends.
Includes index.
1. United States — Biography.   2. Biography — 20th
century.   3. Celebrities — United States — Biography.
4. Newton, James D. (James Draper), 1905–   — Friends
and associates.   I. Title.
CT220.N48   1987   920'.073   86-26929
ISBN 0-15-192753-7
ISBN 0-15-692620-2 (pbk.)

Designed by Julie Durrell
Printed in the United States of America
First Harvest edition 1989
E F G H I

To Ellie

Contents

Author's Note

THE PURPOSE OF THIS BOOK is not to describe once again the accomplishments of five great men. This task has been achieved with brilliance and perception by others. My aim has been to try to set down what I learned about the deeply held convictions, the inner life, the humor, the values, and the faith of those men—and their wives—who came into my life (I never asked to meet any of them) and with whom I came to share close friendships. They were controversial figures. Others have described them differently, but I have written about them as they revealed themselves to me.

I have not had to rely on my memory alone to record the events, anecdotes, and conversations in which I took part with my friends over a period of nearly fifty years. Fortunately, during most of that time I kept a diary in which I noted times and places, key phrases, and vivid impressions. I also relied on publications by and about my friends, which jogged my memory.

I am grateful to many who have had a part: Basil Entwistle, who, at the crucial moment, with his insight and writing skills put the book together; to Anne Morrow Lindbergh, who encouraged me from the start; to Reeve Lindbergh Brown, for her warm-hearted dedication and perseverance; to John and Clare Hallward, for unceasing work and support; to Willard Hunter, for much of the research and story-line color; and to Dr. Theodore Malinin for his personal and scientific input.

My thanks also go to Richard Dennis, whose initiative got me going; to Kenaston Twitchell, Garth Lean, Lee Roddy, and Danny Cox, for their helpful advice; to Barbara Murphy, for her tireless organization of the daunting mass of material, and to Mina Creech, for her similar work with many photographs; to Judy Schiff, for her gracious access to the Lindbergh Collection at Yale University; to Robert Halgrim, Curator of the Fort Myers Edison Home and Museum, for making available rubber-related statistics of the Edison Botanical Research Corporation; and to Sharon Willis, for the typing of innumerable drafts.

To William Jovanovich, my publisher, who sight unseen accepted the project, for giving me the opportunity to share my memory of the friends in this book.

And finally, to Marie Arana-Ward, my editor, for her patience, inspired guidance, delicate tact and unceasing warm support.

Foreword

A BOOK ABOUT Jim Newton's friends is a paean to friendship itself. Our friendship with Jim goes back many years. My husband and I met Jim in 1938 when we were living on a rocky island off the coast of Brittany. We had spent two peaceful years in England, following the death of our first child, when Dr. Carrel invited us to visit him at Saint-Gildas, the Breton island on which he and Mme. Carrel lived in the summers. Carrying a baby in a basket in the cockpit of our single-engined plane, we flew from Kent, England, to a quiet field on the mainland of France, where we were met by the Carrels and driven to the wild coast of Brittany, not far from Mont-Saint-Michel. The Carrels' island of Saint-Gildas shared the gleaming sands, rocky outcrops, and galloping tides of the famous Mount. Soon we made the neighboring small island of Illiec our temporary home.

Illiec was hardly more than a gorse-covered pile of rocks, surrounded by surf. Above the rocks rose the stone tower of an old-fashioned, once-elegant house built by the nineteenth-century composer Ambroise Thomas. Romantic in appearance, it was not an easy house to live in. Sparsely furnished, no water but a brackish well, no plumbing or light, it was not only devoid of comforts but also difficult of access. It could be reached, depending on the tides; when high, by small boat, when low, over wet sands in bare feet, or at mid-tide, by a long, pebbly walk over a curved spit of land. The changing tides, however, were part of the beauty and mystery of the island. One was continually aware of the moon, the weather, and the seas. On windy nights, the storms tossed pebbles over the roof, but in calm weather and at low tide, one could walk across the sandbars to Dr. Carrel's island.

Saint-Gildas seemed to us quite civilized. A good-sized island, it contained an old stone house, an immense walled garden of vegetables and flowers, and a small, ancient chapel, as well as a functioning farm with chickens and cows. Milk for our baby came from these cows once a day at low tide—an hour later every day—carried by the farmer's son. Jim Newton, who was visiting Carrel, followed the same route to talk to us. He had made the journey from the United States to Brittany to visit Carrel after reading the Nobel Prize scientist's *Man the Unknown* and meeting him in New York. He had been impressed by the spiritual and moral aspects of Carrel's reflections on modern man. Carrel's point of view matched Jim's own conviction—that the world was ripe for a spiritual reawakening.

Jim came to see us, as I remember, by foot, climbing through the prickly gorse and wading across the tidal streams. But once on Illiec, with our backs sheltered by a giant rock overlooking the sea, we talked all afternoon. The tide crept up silently around us, making any escape impossible. Jim spent the night on a spare cot and began a fifty-year friendship—a double friendship after his marriage to Ellie.

At the end of the summer, the war clouds over Europe

caused our return to the United States, where the friendship ripened. All of us hoped war could be avoided, and Jim Newton shared our problems and cheered our spirits. He had an intuitive genius for appearing at the right moment. Arriving in Washington one weekend when my husband was about to make a speech urging nonintervention, I found that Jim was in a nearby library looking up quotations needed for the speech. "How like Jim," I recorded in my diary. "He never waits until someone asks to be helped, he is just there quietly in the place where one needs help."

Three times he suggested and planned escapes for my husband from his continuously publicity-ridden life. Jim arranged sailing trips to the many-streamed wilderness of the Florida Everglades, not yet a national park at the time. We found we shared a passion for wilderness and solitude. Opinions were exchanged and disputed on the slanting deck of that small boat. Jim could argue vigorously for his point of view, but he never became angry. He parried his opponent skillfully with humor.

One cannot think of Jim apart from his quality of humor. Humor is a difficult attribute to define. One is apt to think of it in trivial terms. At its best, it is a sense of proportion which implies an acceptance of the common bonds, failings, and endearments of one's fellow men. Delight leaps up in humor and compassion flows from it.

It is not strange that Jim's gift for friendship emerges in many episodes lit with laughter but probing deeply into the values which meant most to him. My husband once said of him: "To Jim, personal relationships come first." The priorities which are Jim's guiding stars illumine these memories of his friends.

—Anne Morrow Lindbergh

UNCOMMON FRIENDS

Chapter

ONE

I T IS TEN O'CLOCK on the night of October 21, 1931. The lights are going out all over New York in tribute to the man who lit up the city—and much of the world. President Herbert Hoover had asked that lights be dimmed in homes, in businesses, on city streets for a couple of minutes to mark the passing of Thomas Edison.

Henry Ford, Harvey Firestone, and I stand in silence at a bay window of the Firestone apartment at the old Ritz-Carlton Hotel, looking up Madison Avenue. In one area after another, across Manhattan, the Bronx, and beyond, the darkness is spreading. Street lights go out. The glitter of Broadway's theaters is dimmed. Out in the harbor, even the Statue of Liberty's torch is extinguished. From coast to coast, this pattern is repeated.

My mind is filled with memories as I stand in the darkness, and so no doubt are the minds of my companions. Henry Ford's thoughts flash back, perhaps, to a luncheon thirty-five years earlier, not far from where we stand, when

1

a rumpled, burly, electrical genius inspired him with the confidence that his great dream of a gasoline-powered automobile for the common man would come true. Harvey Firestone may be recalling those fabulous camping trips, begun fifteen years before, when time stood still in the company of one who was not only a brilliant thinker and doer, but also a carefree spirit. To all three of us, Thomas Edison was the most generous and inspiring friend any of us had known.

*   *   *

I can thank Edison Park for the start of my friendship with him and his wife, Mina. They had spent some forty winters in Fort Myers, Florida, and in 1924, when I arrived in town, he had completed many of his inventions in his laboratory there. He was already a world-famous figure. Across from their home on McGregor Boulevard was a property of raw land, which I was able to acquire for development. With the aid of friends, I formed a company and became its president. I was only twenty, and so my dad, a physician, testified in court to my legal responsibility. He also became vice-president.

The Florida real estate boom of the 1920s was at its height and I was determined to make the most of it. A brochure describing the property gives the scope of my ambitions:

> An exclusive, residential district where the natural advantages of the beauties of nature are enhanced, not spoiled by the hand of man. . . .
>
> Here are fifty-five acres of virgin land on which every kind of tropical shrub, flower and tree will grow (trees grow as much as fifteen feet in a twelvemonth) in this kindly climate where frost has seldom been known. . . .
>
> Investment in a home in Edison Park is first of all an investment in *living*. . . . Think what it means to see children's eager faces tanned as brown in January as in

2

July! To be able to sit in your patio in the evening, looking up at the stars while soft breezes from the Gulf stir the fronds of towering palms above your roof— and from your garden come the pungent odor of or- ange blossoms and the elusive breath of bougainvillea!

The lyrical description of the Fort Myers climate and beauty reflected my delight on first arriving there as a young luggage salesman from Philadelphia. I felt I'd reached paradise and decided to remain.

It was a "magnificent gateway" of Edison Park that led me to my first encounter with Mrs. Edison. Since their winter home was across the street from our entrance, I thought I'd better check my plans with her. I figured that she, more than her husband, was the one who would be interested in the cultural improvements of our property. I went twice to call on her, but she wouldn't see me. Mina Edison was known as a gracious, stately and slightly formidable character; de- voted to good works; a strict Methodist. Her father was a prominent Akron industrialist and churchman who had helped found the Chautauqua movement. She was a good mother to her daughter and two sons, now grown up; and protective of her husband, insofar as anyone could protect Thomas Edison.

One day, I was handed a telephone message at the office that she would like to see the head of the development. I walked over immediately, and went through the gate in the white picket fence. Ahead of me, across the lawn, was the unassuming two-story, Edison winter home—red roof, white walls, green shutters, spacious verandas—actually two houses, one in which the Edisons lived, the other—joined by a trel- lised walkway—a guest house where they entertained. It was one of the first prefabricated houses to be built—con- structed in Maine forty years before and shipped by schooner to Florida.

I sat in a wicker armchair on the porch and waited. As the minutes went by, I became nervous. Were the Edisons opposed to the development of the property in front of their home? Should I quietly fold my tent and slip away? Maybe it would be better to confront them with an accomplished fact. No, I decided, better to hang in there and make an ally of Mrs. Edison if I could.

The front door opened and she came out and stood looking at me sternly. I rose to my feet, and before I could introduce myself, she said, "I didn't send for you."

"Mrs. Edison, you wanted to see the person who is developing Edison Park?"

"I want the head man," she said.

"Well, here's my business card."

She was taken aback. She stared at my card and then at me. She was clearly surprised to find so young a man.

"I am disappointed about the park entrance. Some of the ladies of the town are unhappy about the fact that that statue doesn't have any clothes on."

I was amazed. How had they known? The sculptor, Helmut von Zengen, whom I had engaged, had been doing his work behind a heavy canvas tarpaulin, carving a Greek maiden of some two thousand years ago.

I asked, "How do you know the statue doesn't have clothes?"

"The ladies went with a flashlight one night and looked underneath the canvas."

"Mrs. Edison, it was the sculptor who designed it. He told me that the sculpted maidens of that time didn't wear clothes at the well. Does it offend you?"

"I don't think it should be that way."

"Well, what shall we do about it?"

She couldn't say.

I suggested: "We can't put street clothes on her—how about a veil?"

4

She thought a veil would be great. So I went to see the sculptor. He just about tore his hair out, but finally worked out a way to create a veil with powdered marble. From then on Mrs. Edison and I were friends. I asked her if she would do the unveiling—the entrance, not the statue—when the time came for the opening ceremony of Edison Park. She agreed.

During the twenty years that followed, she told the story again and again how, after our confrontation on the porch, I had gone downtown and described her as the "hard-boiled Mrs. Edison." It amused her to tell it and it embarrassed me. What I had said was she gave me the impression of being a formidable lady.

It was also through Edison Park that I came to know Thomas Edison. It took a great deal of hard work to transform the raw land—palmetto and swamp, home for six-foot rattlesnakes—into the handsome residential development pictured in my brochure.

Sometimes, instead of sitting in the office, I'd get into overalls and work with the crews, laying streets and sidewalks and sewers. One morning I was in a ditch on McGregor Boulevard, and as I threw a shovelful of dirt over my shoulder I looked up, and there was Edison, ten feet from me, sitting in his Model T Ford with his assistant, Freddie Ott. His fine head topped by unruly gray hair, his piercing blue-gray eyes, bushy eyebrows, prominent nose and jaw, broad shoulders and chest—all made him a striking, unforgettable figure. He stared at me for a long time and then drove on without saying anything. I had met him casually a few times, but from that moment on our friendship began. I later found out he liked somebody who'd spit on his hands and take a shovel. He was a worker and he admired hard work. I have a photograph that he signed for me: "All things come to him who hustles while he waits."

The Edisons began inviting me over for Sunday dinners—usually just the two of them and me, sometimes one or two others. Dinner was served in the guest house. Conversation was not easy because Edison was almost stone deaf, but Mrs. Edison showed me how it was possible to talk to him. She cupped her hand against his cheekbone and talked into her palm. The vibrations through his cheekbone permitted him to hear. I learned to talk to him this way.

As I got to know them better, the mutual affection, devotion and humor they shared became evident. I could see how Mrs. Edison bridged the gap between her husband's "inside" world of concentration on his work and the "outside" world of family and friends and relaxation.

Finally, my big day dawned—April 7, 1926—the official opening of Edison Park. We had lined up a distinguished group to participate, including the mayor and a New York state senator, who was also a big local land developer. The local school band would provide music and Pathé News, the national movie news company, would take pictures. But the biggest attractions, of course, were Mrs. Edison's unveiling of the entrance and Mr. Edison, who had promised he would appear.

On the morning of the ceremony, I had a bitter blow. News reached me that Edison was sick with flu, with a temperature of 101 degrees. I went over to see him, feeling anxious about his illness and also terribly disappointed that he would not be at my big event. As I approached his bedroom, I was astonished to see him fully dressed, sitting on the porch. Freddie Ott had driven the Ford over the lawn to the steps outside his bedroom.

"Let's go, Jimmie," he said, and climbed into the car.

"Are you really well enough to come, Mr. Edison?" I asked.

"Let's go." And we set off. He had given me his word that he would be there—and there he was, temperature and all, and close to eighty years old. I learned then what I saw on

6

many later occasions: he was a man of integrity; he kept his word.

*   *   *

Before long the Edisons were treating me like a member of the family. I would go over to the house midmornings after Mr. Edison had returned for a break from his laboratory, where he went to work very early. He'd be sitting in the living room, with the four New York papers he read every day scattered around him. He could read through a newspaper at astonishing speed, and he had a photographic memory, so he could repeat to me whole passages at which he had only glanced. That skill enabled him to read widely throughout his life, despite his long hours in the laboratory.

Occasionally we'd sit out on the lawn, and he'd talk. It was difficult to talk back to him because of his deafness—but he would talk and I would listen, just the two of us. I was having my troubles with mortgages and with the development of Edison Park—the Florida land boom had begun to bust. He told me the troubles he'd had with finances in the early years.

"I never understood the humbuggery of bookkeeping," he admitted. "I kept only payroll accounts. I hung a record of my payments on one hook and one of expenses on another hook. And I generally gave notes in payment. When I got notice that a note was due, I'd hustle around and raise money.

"The secret of staying afloat, Jimmie, is to create something that people will pay for. I didn't work at inventions unless I saw a market demand for them. I wasn't interested in making money as much as in being the first to invent something society needed. But if you do that, the money comes in. You're doing that, Jimmie, with your real estate. But if you find the market fades away, get into something else." He always gave me great encouragement, and a bond of trust grew between us.

I used to take Edison to the Arcade Theater in Fort Myers. He loved the silent Westerns: the ones starring William S. Hart, Tom Mix, and others. It was he who had made the first silent movies, short ones, hundreds of them. His company had made the first story told on film, *The Great Train Robbery*. Then he went on to invent himself out of his greatest pastime: he developed the talking movies. He could read the silent movie captions, but when the talkies came out he was lost. He couldn't hear the sound and had no titles to let him know what was going on. When he and Mrs. Edison watched a talking picture, she would tap out the dialogue in Morse code on his hand. Edison was very close to George Eastman of Eastman-Kodak. They had done a lot of work together, and Eastman felt that humanity, and especially the Eastman Company, owed Edison a debt of gratitude. So he reduced the new Westerns to 16mm film, had them titled, and sent them to Edison to play on his home projector. But the talkies were really less interesting to him. He thought that concentration on the voice weakened the acting, which, he said, a deaf person noticed more than others.

Later, when business took me North, the Edisons made me just as welcome in their New Jersey home, Glenmont. In fact, Mrs. Edison invited me to live with them. I had to keep all kinds of hours and felt it would have been an imposition, but I visited them often. Glenmont was a great contrast to their Florida home. Edison had bought it for Mina, his second wife, at the time of their marriage in 1886. He must have wanted to please her. It was a spacious, impressive mansion, painted red outside, with many gables and turrets. It had a porte-cochere, a great hallway, huge living rooms with chandeliers, carved furniture covered in heavy damask. Edison told me he had bought the whole thing furnished from its former owner. Mrs. Edison had settled in comfortably to make it her domain. He did not seem quite as much at home there as in Fort Myers.

One time, when I went there for the evening, it was Edison who opened the door for me and greeted me with a great smile and a wonderful sweeping bow of his hand and body—there was so much dignity and humor in that gesture. I was with them until about eleven o'clock that evening, and when I got up to leave, they insisted that I spend the night, rather than drive back to town. I hadn't brought anything with me. Mrs. Edison got me a toothbrush and one of her husband's silk nightgowns. It was very, very light and about three times as big around as I was. I remember being in a huge bedroom with a giant-sized bed in that enormous nightgown, and as I started across the room I had a sense of myself moving two or three steps before the nightgown began to move.

The Edisons' next-door neighbors in Fort Myers were Henry and Clara Ford. The two couples were close friends, though the Fords were much younger. They had joined the Edisons on McGregor Boulevard after they had known each other for a good many years. I asked Edison one day how they had first become friends.

"Oh, that was some thirty years ago at an annual convention of our Edison Illuminating Companies. We met at Manhattan Beach, outside of New York. When we sat down to dinner, Alex Dow, the head of the Detroit company, said to me, 'Over there's a young fellow who made a gas car.' That interested me because I was giving thought to the improvement of the electric car by designing a new type of battery. I had him come over and sit next to me and quizzed him. He drew sketches for me and I was very impressed. I told him to keep at it. And he did."

When I got to know Henry Ford, I asked him about it. His eyes lit up. "I should say I remember the day. It was a turning point for me. Mr. Edison listened to me very pa-

9

tiently. Then he banged a fist on the table and said, 'Young man, that's the thing. Your car is self-contained, no boiler, no heavy battery, no smoke or steam. Keep at it!'

"You can imagine how excited I was, the man who knew most about electricity in the world—my boyhood idol—telling me my gas car was better than an electric car! He was the first to give me real encouragement that my dream would work! Well, that boyhood idol became my manhood friend."

Their friendship developed over the years. One expression of it was Ford's gift to Edison of the first car off each Ford assembly line; the first Model T, the first Model A, the first V-8, the first Lincoln. They all stood in Edison's garage, and he loved nothing more than to drive around in one of them, especially the Model T. When Mrs. Edison was with him he was driven in his wide-open Lincoln by his chauffeur, Scarth.

The first time I caught a glimpse of Henry Ford was outside the Edison laboratory in 1927. My glimpse was of his lower half. His upper half was bending deep into a barrel. He bobbed up and down several times and then straightened up with a light bulb in his hand, looking very pleased with himself, and Mrs. Edison introduced us. He was formally dressed, as was the custom even in Florida in those days—gray suit, white shirt with a high, starched collar, and subdued tie. Bending over into the barrel hadn't helped his suit, which was by now badly wrinkled. He was as excited as a kid with a new toy. They explained what was going on.

Ford was having one of Edison's laboratories moved from Fort Myers to Ford's museum in Greenfield Village, at Dearborn, Michigan. Edison had just told him that three or four of his very early light bulbs were packed safely away in the bottom of this particular barrel. Edison had invented the electric light bulb in Menlo Park, New Jersey, but had been perfecting it in his laboratory in Fort Myers. When Ford heard about the barrel, he insisted on retrieving the bulbs himself. He had had the barrel brought out, and as I arrived, was exploring the contents, so that the bulbs could be rearranged exactly as they had been put there half a century earlier.

The Edison laboratory was being dismantled by experts, board by board, and each piece was being marked. All the bottles, all the jars, and every piece of equipment was taken off the tables and the shelves, then numbered and photographed, so that the laboratory could be reconstructed in Greenfield Village exactly as it had been in Fort Myers. Ford even insisted that a foot of Florida soil underneath the building go with it.

Ford asked Edison if he wanted the laboratory replaced in Fort Myers, or if he wanted other buildings in its place. Edison said he would like some simple buildings. Ford asked who could arrange that, and Mrs. Edison said, "Jimmie could get it done." That's when I became involved with Henry Ford. He told me to get everything done and to send him the bill.

I got in touch with Howard Wheeler, one of my closest friends and one of the best builders I ever knew. He built many buildings for me, and we never had a contract—just shook hands. Howard felt that he wasn't going to up his price in this case just because a millionaire was paying the bill. When I sent the bill to Ford, he sent me a check right off the bat. A dozen years later the superintendent of the Edison estate told me he had tried for a long time to come near Howard's price for similar work, and hadn't been able to do it. This piece of business was the start of my friendship with Henry Ford.

Ford never stopped thinking of ways to help Edison. I was over at the Edisons' one night, when the Fords came over from next door with some hearing aids that Mr. Ford must have gone to considerable trouble to obtain. They represented the very latest in technology. As usual, we sat around talking after dinner, and Edison reached for a book, being so hard of hearing and unable to take part in the conversation. He would rather do that than try to join in. After a while, Ford said, "I've brought these hearing aids for Mr. Edison."

Mrs. Edison stood up and, leaning over her husband, said, "Mr. Ford has brought some hearing aids for you, Dearie—three of the best in the world."

Edison smiled and said, "No thanks."

"Why?" Ford asked.

"Well, if one of them worked, I'd have to listen to what you folks are saying, instead of getting along with my reading."

Nobody would accept this; so then he said, "If one of them worked, Mina would make me go to church with her every Sunday."

He went on with several lame excuses. Then he admitted to us that when he was a young man running the Menlo Park plant, someone had prevailed on him to wear a primitive hearing aid. As he walked into the plant one day there was a crisis brewing, and the superintendent, a big Irishman who had been used to shouting at Edison for years, grabbed it and yelled into it. It just about took the top off Edison's head. He threw the instrument down and wouldn't have anything to do with hearing aids from then on.

This had made things difficult for him sometimes. I was at the opening of a national radio show at Madison Square Garden, waiting for Edison to come over from a dinner at the Astor Hotel with Will Rogers, Henry Ford, and Harvey Firestone, founder of the Firestone empire. Later, as they entered Madison Square Garden, the other three men moved ahead of Edison in the crowd. A policeman was trying to escort him, but couldn't communicate with him. Edison became confused, because in the huge crowd he couldn't hear what was going on. I walked up behind him and took hold of his arm. He looked around and said, "Jimmie," and relaxed.

Edison's deafness must often have been a burden, but he never spoke of it as anything but an asset. He could read and study and work quietly no matter how much conversation surrounded him. He said his deafness had given him an excuse to sit much closer to his future wife during their courtship. He taught her the Morse code when she was a teenager before they married, and they tapped out messages on the backs of each other's hands. Indeed, that was how he proposed and she accepted. He wrote in his diary, "The word 'yes' is an easy one to send by telegraph signal, and she sent it."

Being in Fort Myers was a working vacation for both Ford and Edison. Away from their pressures in Detroit and Orange, here they were in the relaxed climate of a small village, which in those days did not have many tourists. Mrs. Edison belonged to the Garden Club. Sometimes when she went shopping, Edison would wait for her, standing on the street corner or sitting in the car watching a building going up. Indeed, Edison was a booster of the town. He would say, "There is only one Fort Myers, and ninety million people are going to find it out."

When a small organization, the Civitan Club, wanted to honor the man, they brought a parchment to his house. Edison, who had been awarded just about everything, including the Congressional Medal of Honor, came out to greet the members, brought them into the living room, and made them welcome.

Among the Edisons' many friends were my parents, Dr. and Mrs. Robley Newton. They had moved down from Philadelphia, first to visit me and see what I was doing and then to make Fort Myers their home. They became close friends of both the Edisons and the Fords. Mother and Mrs. Edison often played golf together, and the two ladies decided that Ford ought to play golf too. He was not fully convinced, but he did go out with them and buy a set of clubs. They got a caddy—in those days they didn't have golf carts—and they started around the course. Ford kept missing the ball, and around the fourth hole he just gave up in disgust and threw the bag and clubs over a fence. A caddy showed up the next day with a bag of the best clubs in town and that was, to my knowledge, Ford's first and last experience with golf.

Thomas Edison had a youthful, unsophisticated side to his nature. He enjoyed "surprise" outings. I took him and Mrs. Edison on an unexpected outing up to Venice, Florida, fifty miles north along the gulf coast, in a Packard roadster I had received in exchange for one of the Edison Park lots. We had the top down, windshield open, the way they did in those days. Mrs. Edison and a niece, Mrs. Edith Potter, sat in the rumble seat! Edison and the ladies rode with the wind blowing through their hair. We started first thing in the morning, spent the day in Venice, and got back after dark. They had a blast. They were free people, having a wonderful time. "Venice All Agog as Edison Drives up in Sporty Car" was the headline in the Fort Myers paper the next day.

*　　　　*　　　　*

One day when I was working at Edison Park, one of the drivers arrived half an hour late with his Ford dump truck. He apologized and said he had been stopped just inside the Park entrance by a man asking questions.

"Some old guy came over to me and asked me everything under the sun about my truck," he said. "So I gave him some good points and some bad points, about what worked and what didn't. Never saw him before. He came right out of that little white gate across McGregor Boulevard."

"Well, that was Henry Ford checking on his product," I

told him. The man's jaw dropped. "No kidding! Well, he got the straight goods on his truck this morning!"

Ford liked activity. He liked to walk through Edison Park to watch our development work. Mother, who lived there, would sometimes go out and walk and talk with him. Then they would stand by the Park entrance and look across the boulevard at the Ford house, where sometimes there were people peering over the white picket fence, trying to get a glimpse of Henry Ford. They could have turned right around and seen him watching them. Eventually, he'd say good-bye to Mother, walk down the street, cross over and go into his house through the side entrance, still unseen.

One morning, when I went over to the Ford house, Frank Campsall, his secretary and assistant, was typing out jokes, each one on a separate piece of paper, as Ford dictated them. Campsall handed each to Ford, who slipped them one by one into his pocket. After he had half a dozen, we all went through the gate to see Edison. Soon enough, they were swapping stories. Edison was the best storyteller I've ever heard. He was a past master of timing. When he delivered the punch line he would explode with laughter and then we'd all double up. That day, Edison would tell a joke, we'd all roar, then Ford would draw out one of his slips of paper, open it up, and hand it to Edison—he couldn't talk loud enough for Edison to hear, unless he wanted to be heard all the way down in the middle of town. Edison would read, roar at Ford's joke, and Ford would take the paper back, tear it in half, and put it in another pocket. I guess he didn't want to "tell" the same joke twice.

A typical joke: One day a country boy, in a moment of mischief, pushed over the family outhouse. Next day at school they read the story of young George Washington being honest with his father about chopping down the cherry tree. In a fit of remorse, the boy confessed to *his* father that he'd

15

overturned the outhouse. His dad gave him a good beating. The boy complained that Washington's father hadn't punished his son. "Maybe not," said Dad, "but his father wasn't in the tree!"

The friendship between the two men intrigued me. I could see that on Ford's side it was based partly on his respect and admiration for the older man who had always encouraged him. When Edison and I were chatting one morning in his living room, I ventured to ask him, "What made you and Henry Ford such good friends? Was it the interests you had in common?"

"It goes back many years. Did I ever tell you what happened when my laboratory in Menlo Park burned down one night—back in 1914? I'd just gone home for dinner when they sent for me to hurry back to the plant. When I got there, everything except the main laboratory and the library was in flames. There was nothing I could do but watch. Charles [his elder son] was there and I said to him, 'Get mother and her friends over here. They'll never see a fire like this again!'

"I stayed up that night, telling the fire crews what machinery and merchandise to try to save. Next morning as we cleaned up the mess, I figured what it would cost to get started again. When people came to commiserate, I told them I was only sixty-seven, not too old to make a fresh start. But I said to Charles, 'I wonder what we'll use for money?' We'd thought the buildings were fireproof, and so they had been underinsured.

"Then Ford turned up from Detroit. Didn't say much, just handed me a check. 'You'll need some money; let me know if you need more.' When I looked at the check, it was made out for $750,000! He didn't ask for any security, and of course over the years I repaid the principal, though he would never take a cent of interest."

The following year, Edison told me, he and Ford and

16

Harvey Firestone, whose tire company had become a leader in the industry, journeyed to the West Coast, together with their wives. They visited the 1915 San Francisco World Exhibition, and John Burroughs, the great naturalist, took them up to visit the equally famous horticulturist, Luther Burbank. They had such a good time together that the Edisons, Fords, and Firestones set off next year on the first of their annual camping expeditions, along with Burroughs.

The Edisons had many distinguished friends, and not a few came to see them in Fort Myers. Edison would usually devote the day to them. He could talk with equal knowledge and ease with Barron Collier, a big advertising man who owned most of Florida's Collier County; President Hoover, who had been a mining engineer; or Emil Ludwig, the historian and biographer of Napoleon, Bismarck, and Lincoln.

Ludwig came with his wife to Fort Myers in 1928 and spent three days with the Edisons. I listened to their ranging conversations at the dinner table, and as their visit ended, Ludwig said to me, "We have been talking to the uncrowned King and Queen of America."

Dr. Hamilton Holt, president of Rollins College in Winter Park, visited the Edisons in 1928. After he left, Mrs. Edison told me that Holt had a "Walk of Fame" at the college and had asked celebrities to have their names engraved in stone and sent to him to put in his walk. Days later, Mrs. Edison said to me, "Dearie and I have thought this over and we've decided that we, too, would like to have one, only we'll make it a walk of friendship." I suppose Edison could have collected the names of enough famous people to have built a walk that went all the way to New Jersey. But the names of his friends, famous or not—local folks among them—went into the walk.

By that time I was working in Akron for Harvey Firestone. He and I went together to choose our stones from the estate of Mrs. Edison's father, Lewis Miller of Akron.

17

We had our stones engraved and sent them to Fort Myers to put into the walk. And there they still are; Firestone's is inscribed "Harvey S. Firestone." Mine says "Jimmie." Ford's is blank. He said he couldn't afford to have it engraved.

Edison's friends in Florida respected his need for privacy. He would go out to the end of his dock and sit and fish— but he'd fish without any bait on his line. Down there in snook country, when a man was fishing, you didn't bother him—and, of course, with no bait, the same thing went for the fish. They didn't bother him either. Edison was not interested in catching fish; he was after time to think. He used to say that we human beings use only about 10 percent of our mental capacities. He also said that there was no limit to how far most men would go to avoid the real labor of thinking. Harvey Firestone loved to quote that.

Mentally active though Edison was, he was not, like his friend Ford, physically energetic. He liked to sit and think, or sit and look out the window.

Edison had faith in hard work, but also in people. I got him talking once about the extraordinary range of his inventions, from the phonograph to the electric light bulb to the motion-picture camera. He stopped and shook his head. "People sometimes talk of me as a lone inventor. Nonsense! Where would I have been without Charles Batchelor and John Kruesi and all the others? We worked long hours together and nobody ever had a better time."

He rapped me on the knee. "Jimmie, you never saw such a mixed crew as we had at Menlo Park—my old-timers, bright young fellows who heard about what I was doing and came to work for me. And then there were more experienced men I hired for some research. We all worked as a team. When we were starting up at Menlo Park, I told George Beard [a noted physicist] I was organizing a workshop to turn out a minor invention every ten days and a big one every six months. He didn't believe me, but we did even better that that." Edison was granted 1,093 patents for his inventions—that is, a patent for every ten to twelve days of his adult life.

It was always Edison's intuitive spark that lit the fire. But often, he would turn over important projects to an assistant and give him full trust. He told me, for example, that when he returned with his wife from a European tour, his young assistant W. K. L. Dickson demonstrated a machine Edison had conceptualized—the kineto-phonograph—the first talking motion-picture camera.

Sometimes his trust in the young went too far. There is a story—whether true or a myth, it is characteristic of him— that when he was working on improving his first light bulb, Edison, to the astonishment of the onlookers, handed a finished bulb to a young helper, who nervously carried it upstairs step by step to the vacuum machine. At the last moment, the boy dropped it. The whole team had to work another twenty-four hours to make the bulb again, but when Edison looked around for someone to carry it upstairs, he gave it to the same boy. The gesture probably changed that boy's life. Edison knew that more than a bulb was at stake.

His son, Charles, told me about his father's handling of two young men that illustrates another side of his character—the simplicity that so often cut through academic approaches to solve a problem. Each year, for a while, Edison took on a couple of the brightest college graduates. One time he handed the new arrivals from the Massachusetts Institute of Technology an electric light bulb and asked them to figure how much water, by weight, it would take to fill it. At the end of the day, they returned—each with a different method of computing and a different answer. Edison took back the bulb, weighed it, clipped off its tip into the scale, filled the bulb with water using an eyedropper, and weighed it again, deducting one weight from the other.

"There's your answer," he said. "Now forget everything they taught you at MIT and get to the point."

Another thing that impressed me about Edison was the way he followed through on his inventions. He not only invented the electric light bulb, he went on to invent everything connected with it—the sockets, the switches, the wiring, the transmission lines, the meters—everything.

He also supplemented the work of other inventors. Although Alexander Graham Bell invented the telephone, its signal was too weak to be of general use. It was Edison who developed the carbon transmitter that made the telephone commercially practical. A telephone repairman looking at our phone recently said to me, "Yep, and that's exactly the same transmitter the old man invented. They haven't improved on it one bit."

It is fair to say that Edison invented the twentieth century. It's easy to forget about many of his inventions we use every day—wax paper, tin foil, the phonograph, right up to the "Edison Effect Tube," the forerunner of the primitive television tube. Without his inventions, modern life would come to a halt.

Today we focus on these triumphs. I was very conscious, however, of the seemingly endless "failures" that led up to them. After a thousand, or several thousand, experiments that did not produce the result he was seeking, Edison would just say, "Well, we're making progress—we know a thousand ways it can't be done. We're that much closer to getting there." He knew the answer was "out there."

*   *   *

By the time I knew him in Fort Myers, at seventy-eight, Edison was not in very good health. Later my dad was his Florida physician. I think Edison trusted him completely. Dad had been a great diagnostician in Philadelphia, so when he moved to Florida he brought a lot of knowledge and experience with him. When he first examined him, Edison was complaining of a stomachache. Dad asked, "How long have you had this ache?" Edison answered, "Oh, about forty years."

Edison was not by any means a passive patient. He wanted to know exactly what was prescribed and why. Dad would tell him what he thought was wrong with him and what should be done about it. Then he'd take *Gray's Anatomy* and tell him to read from, say, page 712 to 764. Invariably, when Edison had read the section he'd say, "Okay, Doc, I understand. I'll do it."

One time, when Mr. Edison had pain in his legs, Dad felt it was the result of a secondary infection from abscessed teeth. The only way they could prove there were abscesses was to have x-rays taken. But Edison didn't want to submit to x-rays. He had experimented with x-rays in the early days, before they knew how to protect people, and his men had suffered damaged hands and other injuries. So he said that if Dad thought the infection was due to his teeth, he'd just have them all pulled out. Dad was a little shocked, but he went along with it. He found four or five abscessed teeth pouring infection into Edison's system. After the extraction, the pain in his legs cleared up. The main casualty from the extraction, from Edison's standpoint, was that he could no longer chew tobacco.

Tobacco chewing was common in those days. I remember spittoons everywhere. One day, after noting the mess in the laboratory, Mrs. Edison said, "Dearie, why don't you get a spittoon in here?" He replied, "You can't always hit a spittoon, but you can always hit the floor." Years later, a television program on Edison's life was titled, "The Wizard Who Spat on the Floor."

Edison was against cigarettes, however. He felt that inhaling cigarette smoke was truly harmful, and he employed no smokers. "The roots of the tobacco plant grow right down to hell," he would say. Chewing tobacco, to his mind, was a different matter. Tobacco in this form, he thought, did less damage to the system. Ford was against chewing tobacco as well as smoking. He had all the corners of his factories painted white, even the stairways, so that culprits could quickly be identified and discouraged.

Edison's friend, Herbert Hoover, was also ahead of his time in campaigning against cigarettes. I learned about Hoover's feeling from his son, Herbert, Jr., when he came with his parents to visit the Edisons in 1929. He told me that the shortest conversation he ever had with his father took place after his father caught him smoking. Hoover told his son, "I want you to know that I have no doubt about the future of a young man who smokes cigarettes; he hasn't any."

The Hoovers came over from Miami on their yacht *Saunterer*. Hoover was a great fisherman and, while he was waiting to take office in March, was anxious to try for a West Coast tarpon in February. The yacht sailed up the Caloosahatchie River and it was touch and go getting the large craft alongside the little dock where Edison used to fish with his baitless hook.

Hoover had timed his arrival to coincide with Edison's eighty-second birthday, on February 11. The Edisons, Fords, Firestones, and local VIPs were at the dock to meet him. This was the first presidential visit to Fort Myers and the city felt it called for a parade through town as a joint celebration of the visit and of the birthday. Henry Ford provided five shiny Lincolns to head the parade, and I found myself riding with Mrs. Edison, Mrs. Hoover, and Herbert Hoover, Jr.

The annual celebration of Thomas Edison's birthday had begun as a spontaneous affair with family and friends. The celebration grew. By 1927 it had become a little chaotic around the Edison home, as national reporters joined the locals. So Mrs. Edison asked me whether I would like to organize things, be the official greeter, and make sure the guests were properly cared for. I stood on the Edison porch, greeted people as they came, introduced them to those they needed to meet, and got them to luncheons and dinners and back and forth from the Royal Palm Hotel.

As master of ceremonies, I was also involved getting an annual press conference into some semblance of order. Edison had decided to answer questions from the press on his birthday. Newspaper people were always wanting to see him, and he disliked having to stop his work. This way he could take on all the queries in one session. Because he was hard of hearing, he could only take written questions. The reporters would write and I would take the pieces of paper to Edison in order. Sometimes his answer was spoken and sometimes it was written. Many questions got no more than "Yes" or "No."

Mr. Ford declined to make any comments. "I am just here as Mr. Edison's friend," he would say. "This is his party."

In 1929, with the added presence of President-elect Hoover, there were more correspondents than usual, plus an army of camera people and newsreel photographers. The old gentleman, in his eighties, answered the questions with brevity and firmness, and often with his tongue in his cheek.

Q: Do you think Mr. Hoover's administration will result in greater national prosperity?

A: Yes.

Q: What are the dangers, if any, of the increasing stock speculations?

A: Ultimate panic. Loss of confidence. [The great crash came nine months later.]

Q: Is it advisable to appropriate an additional twenty-four million dollars at this time for prohibition enforcements?

A: Yes.
Q: Should the United States try to have the most powerful navy in the world?
A: It should build in parity with England.
Q: How will the approaching machine age affect the moral and physical living conditions of the so-called working class of people?
A: Very favorably.
Q: With the experience of yourself, Mr. Hoover, and Mr. Ford in mind, do you believe golf, tennis, and other forms of physical exercise advisable for the assurance of health, usefulness, and longevity?
A: No.
Q: Are any of your inventions brilliant intuitions?
A: None of my inventions came by accident. I see a worthwhile need to be met and I make trial after trial until it comes. What it boils down to is one percent inspiration and ninety-nine percent perspiration.
Q: What was the greatest invention ever made?
A: The mind of a child.

Then the Pathé News people had their turn. They arrived with a camera and huge microphones on a tripod. Pictures with sound were the latest thing and this equipment was among the first of its kind. A reporter asked Mr. Edison what advice he would give young men. The newsreel people wanted to photograph that one, but because the reporter did not look all that young, the cameraman swung around and drafted me to ask the question on camera. Edison laughed and replied, "I wouldn't give young men any advice, because they wouldn't take it anyway." That hit the newsreels across the country. The clip has been shown on television every few years for the last fifty years, and I am always being told, "I saw you and the Edisons." After the press conference I asked Edison what he really said to young men. The only really important piece of advice he gave them, he said, was, "Learn to be a good loser. Never be discouraged when things don't work out—keep at it!"

Edison seemed to enjoy the role of national oracle, but he did not like people to be too carried away with their praise. At one birthday ceremony it was arranged that he would press a button in Fort Myers and start a power plant in Bellingham, Washington, the northernmost plant in the United States at that time. They made quite a to-do over that, and the mayor of Bellingham sent a flowery cable of thanks. Edison's reply was:

I THANK YOU FOR PERMITTING ME TO START YOUR STATION. YOU WESTERN PEOPLE ARE QUITE SENTIMENTAL.

—EDISON

The year before, in February 1928, Mrs. Edison sent a cable to Charles Lindbergh, inviting him to her husband's birthday on his way home from South America, where he was finishing a tour in *The Spirit of St. Louis*. In 1927 he had made his historic Atlantic flight. He cabled from San Juan, Puerto Rico, that he had to be in Havana on the particular day, and sent his warm congratulations.

A few days after the birthday party, Mrs. Edison and I were in the yard and heard the sound of an approaching plane. In those days it was quite an occasion for a plane to fly over Fort Myers. There were no passenger planes, no airmail routes. I remember the bright sun as we looked up, and the hum overhead. Suddenly there it was—Lindbergh's silver-winged monoplane, flying quite low.

Lindbergh must have planned it carefully, the way he planned everything. Fort Myers was certainly not on a direct route from Havana to St. Louis. But he flew right over the Edison home dipping his wings. He didn't circle the house, which would have drawn attention to himself. It was a characteristic gesture for him not to want the spotlight on him, when it was Edison he was honoring.

*   *   *

I was in charge of the birthday parties each year until Edison died late in 1931. Even after leaving Florida to work with Harvey Firestone in the spring of 1928, I would come down for the occasion. Firestone encouraged this—he knew I had a commitment to the Edisons, and he honored it. We usually came together. The friendship of these three men— Edison, Ford, and Firestone—over the years made a great impression on me. Although each was a giant in his own right, Ford and Firestone were many years younger than Edison and regarded him almost as a father. On their side there was formality, respect. They always called him "Mr. Edison," as did I, while he called them "Ford" and "Firestone." Despite their age difference, they were very comfortable together. There is a photograph by Mike Gravelle of the three of them, with Edison in his favorite old suit with the patch on the pants. After Gravelle took the picture, he turned to me and said, "Look at them—they're just three old shoes!"

Edison had supported and encouraged Ford and Firestone as young men. They, in their turn, sustained him in his old age—especially through a great project in what was for him an entirely new field.

Long before I knew him, back in 1915, when the three of them visited Luther Burbank's plantation in California, he had told them that if the United States were to enter World War I, the enemy would be able to cut off our foreign supply of rubber too easily. It came from distant parts of the world—Malaysia, Java, and Sumatra. Ford and Firestone were only too aware of how dependent the country was by then on rubber for the transport of freight and passengers. Firestone told me later that Edison had obviously been very interested when he and Ford had suggested that he look into cultivating a strain of rubber or a substitute plant that could be grown in America. Edison had replied that he would look into it—someday.

That "someday" had materialized just at the time that I got to know Edison. Britain began restricting her empire's Far Eastern rubber exports in the mid-1920s, and Ford and Firestone again approached Edison to focus his genius on developing a domestic supply. When he responded by organizing the Edison Botanic Research Company, they supported him by covering the costs of the research from their companies, while Edison contributed his labor. It was the closest enterprise in which the three friends were involved, and I was sure that Ford and Firestone were motivated by more than their commercial concerns. They wanted to see their old friend involved in satisfying work.

While Ford stepped up the work he had already begun of developing rubber plants in Brazil and Firestone investigated possibilities in Liberia, Edison searched for rubber-substitute plants that would grow in the temperate zone of America. He tackled the job in characteristic style, with total commitment. Mrs. Edison said of those days, "Everything turned to rubber in the family. We talked rubber, thought rubber, dreamed rubber." Before the year was over, Edison reported to Ford that he had collected 3,227 wild plants and shrubs between New Jersey and Key West. He was making encouraging progress, he said, with his usual optimism.

I found myself in the middle of the hunt. On Sunday afternoons we'd go out driving, and when Mr. Edison saw some plant he wanted, Scarth would stop the Lincoln and we'd get out. Edison would cut a plant and I'd cut another and we'd put them in the back of the car and go on.

One day, to my chagrin, I tried to cut too tough a plant with his favorite lightweight knife and broke the blade. I apologized abjectly. "Don't worry about it, Jimmie," he said.

I remember the day he produced crude rubber—from different strains of goldenrod. He discovered that he could get up to 12 percent natural rubber—enough to make commercial production feasible. Edison had been up at 4:30 that morning, waiting on his porch for enough light to go across to the laboratory, and all day long he worked there and finally achieved his breakthrough.

I went over a little before nine in the evening to help him celebrate by taking him to the movies. The gardener had put up a rope over a square of grass that he was reseeding. As we crossed the lawn in the dark, we ran into this rope, which was chest-high. Edison, who was eighty years old, backed up and kicked his leg way up over the rope—he was so joyful at having produced rubber that day. Then on we went to the movies.

He soon got enough rubber to send to Firestone to make tires. Firestone sent him back four tires, made from the goldenrod, and Edison put them on the old Ford that Henry had given him.

Later, a process was developed in Germany at the same time for producing synthetic rubber from coal and petroleum. It proved more economical than the goldenrod solution. By the time World War II endangered national supplies of rubber, American industry was able to supply the country's basic needs with the synthetic product, mixed with a small amount of crude rubber. Recently, the University of Arizona has begun carrying forward Edison's rubber experiments.

During this time the inventor was often tired, often ill, and he could have been forgiven for retreating from his work entirely. These younger men offered him their excitement and he made it his own. They gave him new energy and commitment.

The last time that Edison, Ford, and Firestone were together was in March 1931. I took a picture of them sitting on the steps of Edison's laboratory in Fort Myers. In it, Edison looks like the cat that swallowed the canary, and the others are laughing. Mrs. Edison said about the photograph, "I think Dearie was telling a naughty story."

Those were happy days together. The three friends spent hours talking at a table in one of Edison's laboratories, and Roger Firestone (one of Harvey's sons) and I were included. Their talk ranged over business, philosophy, science, and personal affairs. They laughed a lot at each other's jokes and discussed seriously the deepening depression, with nearly five million now unemployed in the United States; the recent discovery through mathematical calculation of the planet Pluto; the first use of radio waves to detect aircraft.

Mr. Ford, I remember, held forth on one of his favorite themes—assistance to the needy: "Give a man a fish and he'll soon get hungry again. Teach him to fish and he'll never starve." He got no argument from his friends on that. When the conversation turned to management and workers, Firestone spoke out on the importance of treating workers as human beings, rather than objects, to get a job done.

Despite their enjoyment of each other's company and the relaxed atmosphere, away from the demands of their work, the three were very much aware of the serious state of the nation and the world. At one point they talked about the prospects for the future of a very disturbed world—Gandhi's civil disobedience campaign in India; Japan's military ambitions in Asia; the recent rise of the Nazi Party in Germany; deadlock in the League of Nations over disarmament.

But as they looked ahead, these men were no prophets of gloom and doom. Edison had faith in providence. He expressed the conviction I had often heard him voice in different ways: "When you see everything that happens in the world of science and in the working of the universe, you cannot deny that there is a 'Captain on the bridge.' "

Firestone's faith in God was more orthodox and conservative. He seemed to take it for granted that the Almighty was ultimately in control of man's destiny and that truth and justice would prevail. As for Ford—he was an unashamed optimist. He said with great conviction, "When fear seizes us, it's a sign that the body has taken over the soul." He summed up his attitude toward current troubles in the world thus: "There's enough goodwill in people to stop fighting, class war, and economic slump. Governments lack that kind of power. We have to find ways to turn our private moral convictions into public policies."

Sometimes they looked back at their eventful lives. Firestone spoke to Edison: "May I ask you a leading question, Mr. Edison? And please don't feel you have to answer it! The public thinks of you as 'The Wizard'—the genius out of whose mind leaped one invention after another. Some of my business friends think of you as a brilliant organizer, who built a team to work out the next steps in meeting the needs of society. How do you think of yourself?"

Edison couldn't hear Firestone well, and asked him to write the question down.

"Just like he does for the press," said Ford, with a grin. Firestone wrote, and after Edison studied the question, he said: "Firestone, I guess it's some of both. I use my eyes to look around and see what's needed and when I see something, like I saw the need to run several messages over one wire at the same time, I think it over and over and hope to come up with something. And often I'd throw it back and forth with my men."

Then he laughed, "But often, the solution jumped out at me from an unexpected direction—just like with the multiple message on the one telegraph wire. You know what gave me the solution? I stepped on the tail of a cat and an instantaneous screech came out of the other end."

The other men looked as mystified as I was.

"A screeching cat gave me the idea—an impulse! An impulse! That was the key. So you can call it intuition or wizardry or whatever! But along with it went hours and days of sweat by a great team."

Ford jumped in. "Mr. Edison gave America just what was needed at that moment in history. They say that when people think of me, they think of my assembly line. Mr. Edison, you built an assembly line which brought together the genius of invention, science, and industry."

Sometimes the three looked to the future. After they'd been discussing problems at home and abroad, the old man said suddenly, "We are like tenant farmers, chopping down the fence around our house for fuel, when we should be using nature's inexhaustible sources of energy—sun, wind, and tide."

Firestone responded that oil and coal and wood couldn't last forever. They'd been tackling rubber. He wondered how much hard research was going into harnessing the wind, for example. Windmills hadn't changed much in a thousand years."

Ford said there were enormously powerful tides—for example, the Bay of Fundy. Scientists had only been playing with the question so far.

Edison said, "I'd put my money on the sun and solar energy. What a source of power! I hope we don't have to wait till oil and coal run out before we tackle that. I wish I had more years left!"

It wasn't until forty years later I began to realize how attuned these men were to the waves of the future.

*   *   *

In their later years, the Edisons would rent a private railroad car for their journey to Fort Myers. Each year his friends

31

came to the railroad station to meet him. Sometimes there were a couple of hundred people when the train came in about dusk. One of the last times they arrived, Mrs. Edison got off the train first, to great applause.

Then came Charles Edison, their son, who became governor of New Jersey and secretary of the Navy. The group applauded him, too. Finally, Edison came out under the light, with his little top coat and his gray hair. There was silence. Even as he started down the steps, there was still no sound from the crowd. It was as though they had agreed not to applaud, not to break that silence. It was spontaneous reverence.

In 1931, my dad wanted to send Edison home to New Jersey early. He felt in those days that Fort Myers still lacked the medical equipment and expertise needed to keep Edison's health in balance, and he was failing.

Edison rested in his New Jersey home during the summer of that year, but by September he was seriously ill. Ford hurried to see him, and I went up too. By that time he was weaving in and out of a coma, but as I came into the room he seemed to know somebody was there. He looked up and said, "Jimmie," just like the time I had come to his aid in Madison Square Garden, and he wearily waved a feeble hand, with great effort. It meant a lot to me.

Thomas Edison died at eighty-four on October 18, 1931. For two days his body lay in state at the West Orange plant. Thousands of people walked past the open casket. I walked with Ford and Firestone. Harvey Firestone looked at Edison, and I looked at Edison, but Henry Ford would not look at him. He looked the other way, and later said to me, "I want to remember him the way he was."

Mrs. Edison told me that near the end her husband had come out of his coma. He looked straight ahead and said, "It's very beautiful over there."

Chapter

TWO

The day after Edison's birthday celebrations, in February 1928, I stepped out of the front gate at the Edisons' place and was heading down the sidewalk to get into my car for what I thought was a pressing appointment, when a voice behind me said, "Mr. Newton, do you have a minute?"

I turned around to find Mr. Harvey Firestone following me out of the entrance. I stopped. Certainly I "had a minute" for Mr. Firestone. We walked toward each other between the tall royal palm trees bordering McGregor Boulevard. He was a man of middle height, precise, vigorous, entering his sixties, the founder and president of the country's fastest-growing tire company, and one of America's best-known businessmen.

"What can I do for you, sir?"

"I just wanted a few words with you, young man, if this is a convenient moment."

The urgent errand I was on soon paled beside the opportunity.

"Congratulations, by the way, on the splendid way you managed these events. Not easy to take care of all those guests and the crowd and the press."

"Thank you, sir. I've really enjoyed it."

"Yes, I noticed that. Probably why everything went so well. But I wanted to talk to you about something else." He pointed across the street to the Edison Park gates and the Grecian maiden. Beyond the trees, a crew of my men were making a good deal of noise as they worked.

"The Edisons tell me you're the head of that company. I'm curious to know how you are able to keep on developing the property. I'm told that real estate in Florida has gone from boom to bust and prices have collapsed all over the state. How do you manage to keep selling lots, Mr. Newton?"

"Well, the truth is, Mr. Firestone, we aren't selling property for dollars. We're trading lots for paving material, labor, equipment, automobiles—anything we can get our hands on."

Firestone nodded his head. "I know very well what you're talking about. Eight years ago, the rubber industry plummeted and our company barely survived the slump. I know what it takes to streamline production and save on every cent."

He looked me up and down and went on to say that, nevertheless, by 1920 he'd already had a good deal of experience. I was still a very young man.

"Twenty-two, sir. But some good men, including my dad, have been pitching in with me, and putting up money."

"You took a big risk. Do you enjoy that?"

I paused. "I guess so," I admitted.

"But you must have learned something about running a business somewhere. Spend any time in college?"

I explained that my parents had planned for me to enter

36

Dartmouth when I graduated from high school. But I'd decided to get out and see something of the world first.

"Well," he said, "I didn't go to college myself, though I think college can help a man develop his business abilities. What work did you get into when you took off, then?"

Looking at Mr. Firestone's conservative appearance, I decided to skip any mention of my hoboing and cowboy careers. "I took a job as a luggage salesman."

"That must have taught you something."

"Yes, sir, I learned it the hard way." I told him that my boss at the Belber Bag and Trunk Company had sent me, as their youngest and newest salesman, to ride their toughest route—through New England, including Maine, in midwinter. I went on to say that "State of Mainers," where I started, were very conservative merchants and kept saying "No" to ordering any luggage from a new supplier. After a particularly discouraging week, I hit bottom. Early one morning I asked myself, "Are you a mouse or a man?" and decided never to move on out of a town until I'd sold some merchant something. And from that day I never did. In fact, it must have worked, for they promoted me to the Midwest, where I became their top salesman.

This story seemed to interest and amuse him. Loud hammering was coming from the Park. Firestone waved a hand in that direction and said he appreciated the way I'd managed to keep going over there. But he asked if it wouldn't be wiser to close down the development for a while until conditions improved—as they surely would?

"Mr. Firestone, when we sold those lots we promised to put in sewers, paving, street-lighting, and so on, to finish the job. I wouldn't feel right about breaking the promises I made."

There was a moment's silence.

"I respect that kind of integrity. That's the way I try to

operate my business. I believe fundamental honesty is the keystone of business."

He said it emphatically. I was to hear him repeat it often in the next few years.

"Well, I mustn't keep you," he said. "Congratulations again on how well you ran those birthday activities." As he walked away, he remarked on how difficult the press and the public could be. "It takes a lot of attention to detail, and you can't afford to make mistakes."

I grinned and assured him that mistakes were what I learned from.

He paused and laughed. 'I can't see Mr. and Mrs. Edison tolerating too many of those."

"No sir, I just have to watch I don't make the same ones again!"

A couple of weeks later I noticed a poster in the window of the local Firestone tire dealership. It showed Edison and Firestone together at the Edison birthday celebration. I was in the background. The poster was being distributed with the *Firestone Bulletin*, which appeared each month in Firestone stores all over the country. The local manager said he would let me have it when he was through with the display. When he gave it to me I asked Edison if he would autograph it. Then I sent the poster to Firestone and asked if he would be kind enough to do the same, as I wanted to have it framed.

Firestone sent the poster back with his autograph and a letter along with it. He wrote that he recalled our conversation and was "much impressed with your accomplishments and the way you handled your business and affairs." He went on, "As we are buying and building service stations all over the country and are active in the real estate business, I was wondering if you would not like to get into a larger corporation. . . ." He enclosed an application form and asked me to respond if I was interested in working for the Firestone Tire and Rubber Company.

The invitation was a big surprise to me. The opportunity to spread my wings was tempting, and Mr. Firestone's personal interest was flattering. But I had to consider leaving the Edison Park business, and I knew I would miss the Edisons and Florida. When I talked with my dad and business associates, they said they were prepared to carry on without me. Then I showed the letter to Mrs. Edison. She did not say much, but told her husband about it. His blunt comment was, "Why should Jimmie go up to Akron and leave Fort Myers, when he's got everything his own way here?"

He was concerned about my future. He knew I had an unusual amount of liberty where I was, and may have felt that Firestone would be a tough taskmaster. Mrs. Edison, perhaps at his suggestion, spoke to their son Charles about Firestone's proposal, and he came back with an offer of a position with the Edison Company in New Jersey. This offer was also totally unexpected and it, too, was a good opportunity. However, I decided to talk further with Mr. Firestone. His offer was welcome as my real estate business was slowing down and the part of Edison Park we were developing was almost completed. I sent Mr. Firestone a telegram expressing my interest and later drove to Akron for an interview.

He greeted me cordially as I entered his large, paneled, beautifully carpeted office, and waved me to a chair on the other side of his large desk. He was seated in an even larger chair, and when I knew him better, he pointed out the high cushion in it. Without it, he later explained, he'd be a few inches lower than most people sitting opposite him, and at a psychological disadvantage.

I sat down, still a little awed by the size and activity of the headquarters, which included two plants, one of them also the administrative building. People were coming and going at a brisk pace. I remarked that it must be a tremendous job running such an outfit.

He laughed. "After a while it sort of runs itself," he said.

I didn't believe him, but before long I began to understand that he had expressed one of his basic convictions: that the head of a big enterprise must pick men who can run day-to-day operations and leave him free to attend to policy. He had found one such man in J. W. Thomas, his vice-president, who had been with the company for many years.

Firestone sat back and looked out the window. He seemed as relaxed as he had been in Fort Myers. I just sat. He turned and asked, "Do you feel you can leave your business and come and work with me?"

I told him that my father would be prepared to look after things, that business had slowed to a degree that he could do this and keep up his medical practice too.

"Well, I appreciate that, and I look forward to your being with us."

It all seemed settled in his mind, but mine was full of questions.

"What kind of work do you have for me, Mr. Firestone?"

"I want you to settle in and help me personally. I have an office there for you, next to my secretary's."

I was startled. I had been expecting a real estate position, as he'd mentioned in his letter.

"What would my duties be, sir?"

"You'd be my personal assistant—though we'd better not tread on anyone's toes by calling you officially 'Assistant to the President.' For the moment let's call you 'Secretary to the President.' I need someone to follow through my instructions, travel with me, and be with me when I meet certain people; take care of all kinds of arrangements. Generally make himself useful."

Firestone leaned toward me. "In the old days I used to know everyone who worked for me. Of course, that's no longer possible. But I try to keep in touch with everything that goes on. That means moving around a lot. I'm not as young as I was and I need someone to move around with me as I go through our plants, meet with managers and dealers. Someone who—" he paused and stared thoughtfully at me; "someone who keeps his eyes peeled and can help spot problems and see opportunities."

I didn't grasp it at the time, but he was offering to teach me how the company was run, giving me the opportunity for an overall view of the operations. And, even more important, the chance to see how he worked and thought—his philosophy in action.

"That would be tremendous. I really hope I can be of help."

"Well, we'll see," he replied, and asked me what I thought my salary should be.

All I could say was, "Mr. Firestone, you don't know how much I'll be worth—and neither do I. Maybe we should hold up for a while—and then decide."

"No, I don't like that kind of arrangement. Let's figure it out. Work out how much it'll cost to leave your business without you. Then add your living expenses here, and say another 10 percent. Make that your salary to start with."

I agreed. Then he said, "If you like, I'll arrange for you to be made a junior member of the Portage Country Club and you could live there."

The club turned out to be the best housing for me in the area, and my expenses were modest. This consideration was typical of his care for me during the next years.

*   *   *

So began my employment with the Firestone Company. It was one of the most intense times of my life, but also a wonderful opportunity. In eight years I was moved around

41

to as many different jobs: everything from Firestone's personal troubleshooter, to production, real estate acquisition, construction, management, trade sales management for half of the United States. I used to tell him that I ought to be paying him for the experience I was getting, rather than his paying me. Some people in the company had a hard time, because for them it was a real pressure cooker. But I enjoyed the challenge. When I visited a doctor for an insurance examination, he took my blood pressure and then asked, "Did you say you worked for Firestone?" I told him I did. "You're the first one from there who not only doesn't have high blood pressure, but actually has low blood pressure."

My boss was definitely not a nine-to-five o'clock man. I used to come to work at eight o'clock in the morning and stay until six or seven in the evening. In the winter I never saw daylight outside the factory. Often I'd go home with him for dinner—usually just the two of us, with Mrs. Firestone. Then we'd work together until nine-thirty or ten o'clock. The company would work half a day on Saturdays, but often he and I would work right through that day.

On Sundays, Firestone would often invite me for dinner. That meal was a formal affair, a great contrast to those with the Edisons and Fords in Fort Myers. Everything about the house, which was named Harbel Manor (combining their first two names, Harvey and Idabelle), was formal—a great, long house with several levels and stairs and hallways and a covered swimming pool at one end. The family sat around a baronial table in a large, dimly lit dining room: Mr. Firestone and his wife and whichever of the five sons and one daughter were at home.

Mrs. Firestone, the former Idabelle Smith of Jackson, Michigan, was a quiet, but very pleasant person. She had fair hair, aristocratic features, and an engaging personality. One reporter wrote, "Idabelle Firestone doesn't need a grand mansion to be a lady. She'd be a lady in a shack." She was not involved in her husband's business and did not normally accompany him on business trips or attend his company functions except when they were held in their home. She had other interests: she was first and foremost a homemaker. Her husband and her six children were her primary concern. She took pride in the care of their large home, which she kept decorated with plants and flowers. Her other great interest was music. She played with distinction on the piano and organ, and she was the composer of a number of well-known songs. Two of them, "If I Could Tell You" and "In My Garden," were used as theme songs in the nationwide weekly radio program, "The Voice of Firestone." They were sung by the Metropolitan Opera stars, Risë Stevens and Richard Crooks.

The only occasion on which I can recall Mrs. Firestone taking part in one of her husband's business meetings was when she sat in on a conference, at which I was present, in which the future of the new radio program was being discussed. There was a strong sentiment, shared by Mr. Firestone, in favor of featuring comedy. Ed Wynn, star of the "Texaco Program," was one of his favorites. Mrs. Firestone believed that what was needed was a popular presentation of high-quality classical music. She convinced her husband.

We became good friends and each Mother's Day for many years I would send a message. Here is her reply in 1933:

Western Union
May 15, 1933

Jimmy Newton. Care Firestone T and R Co.
How very generous and thoughtful you are for others especially for me on Mothers Day. It was a greeting which warmed my heart and gave me inspiration. I find it difficult to fully express how deeply I appreciate it. With love to you and your mother, with the hope that I may see you both in the very near future. Wishing

you every happiness and success. And again let me thank
you for your thoughtfulness.

Idabelle Firestone

The two eldest boys, Harvey, Jr. and Russell, who was
known as Bud, were already out of college and working for
the company when I arrived on the scene. The younger ones,
Raymond, Leonard, and Roger, were still away at college or
prep school, so I didn't see much of them at that time. Some
years later, Ray's wife, Laurie, sat at those Sunday dinners.
She was, I believe, a Doheny, from the wealthy California
oil family, and not in the least awed by the formal atmosphere. She and I did more bantering back and forth than
the others.

I got to know Harvey Jr. and his family, and often lived
in the house when they were away on trips. I remember
bouncing his little girls on my knees—they would ask me
for "camel rides" whenever I came to visit. But the son I
knew best was Bud. He was about my age and we worked
together, necessarily spending a lot of time in each other's
company. We also went through a lot together over the years
and became the closest of friends.

Not long after I moved to Akron, Bud came to me and
asked me tactfully if I was happy with my automobile. I had
driven my old Ford from Florida up to Ohio. It was pretty
beat up, but I didn't care. For me, an automobile was for
transportation, not to impress anybody. I did still own that
long, streamlined Packard roadster, the one in which I'd
taken the Edisons to Venice, Florida; but I hadn't brought
it to Akron. Down home I had rarely used it, even when I
took a girl on a date, because I wanted to make sure she
was interested in me and not the Packard.

I told Bud that I was perfectly satisfied with my Ford. All
I did with it was go back and forth to work. It seemed to
run all right. It had brought me up from Florida.

44

"Well, you know," said Bud, "it's the only one in the executive garage that looks quite like that. Have you ever thought of getting a better car?"

"Not really."

"There's a Cadillac dealer who's a friend of mine, and I talked to him the other day. He said that if you'd go out there, maybe you'd be interested in one of his cars. The new models have just come in and he still has some of last year's at very good prices."

"But I don't want a Cadillac—I'm happy."

"At least go out and talk to him."

So I went out and talked to him and found that he had a beautiful Cadillac roadster, which he offered me brand new for half price. I suspect that Mr. Firestone was behind it, or maybe the manager of the executive garage had complained that my car lowered the standards of the place. It was an offer I couldn't refuse, so I bought it. I guess many at the company breathed a sigh of relief.

My first months were spent almost entirely with Mr. Firestone, or at his beck and call. I sometimes sat with him while he went over reports from his sales districts, talked with district managers, or studied some aspect of his rapidly growing company.

I also sat in with him on product board and committee meetings and watched how he handled his men. Although he was clearly the boss, he didn't come out like some people in his position and say, "Let's do this," or "We'll do it that way." He would sit in the meeting—whether it was the Products Board, Engineering Board, or whatever, and quietly draw out the various men with questions, listening intently to their answers. After a while they would come to a decision that seemed obvious to them all. Of course, if it came to the point that one person had to make a decision, Mr. Firestone would make it.

It was only many years later that I grasped the full significance of this way of doing business. It happened when Japan shocked this country by the quality and economy of its automobiles. When we looked for the reason, we found part of it was that the Japanese managed through the process of "consensus" instead of confrontation—what Firestone had been doing half a century earlier!

Another facet of successful Japanese management is their avoidance of a bureaucratic hierarchy. Here, too, Mr. Firestone had overcome the problem by cutting through four or five levels of management to ensure direct contact with his district managers. There were some forty of them across the country, and he regarded them as his vital representatives. He insisted that each of them send him a monthly report summarizing their activities. These reports went directly to him, bypassing all the intermediary management. I know how much he valued these reports in helping him keep his finger on the pulse of the business. While I was his assistant, one of my duties was to go through these reports and bring to his attention the significant details. He made sure he knew how each man was doing. It was his style of leadership. My boss was giving me priceless training in evaluation.

When I joined the company there were more than ten thousand employees and he had to have a good-sized nucleus of leaders to supervise all the departments. I quickly discovered another of his gifts—that he had a genius for choosing the right person for the right job. One evening at dinner I asked him what was the secret of his success in selecting his key staff.

He laughed. "Jimmie [as he soon began to call me], if I pick one out of two men who turns out well, I figure I'm a good picker. There's no set of rules that I know for selecting men. You just have to exercise your best judgment. But I have learned not to bring in men at the executive level, however impressive their credentials. I like to keep my eye on people as they prove themselves at lower levels and then promote them. My most valuable executives have picked themselves by their records."

I didn't raise the question of how come he had picked me.

The longer I worked with him, the clearer it became that the real keys to his leadership were his ability to delegate responsibility and, above all, to know men. He had a flair for putting the right men in the right place—and then inspiring them. They found his quiet enthusiasm contagious. He said to me one day as I went with him through a plant, "Jimmie, I can walk through the front door of any factory and out the back and tell you if it's making money or not. I can just tell by the way it's being run and by the spirit of the workers."

I think Firestone would have loved working at every job in his company single-handed. Perhaps that was one reason he was able to delegate so well—his plants were not run like the military, where someone is given responsibility and left to it and demoted if he fails. Firestone knew the man, knew his capabilities, and knew the job. He put them together and then watched them. If he found something wasn't going well, he would step right in and deal with it.

As a result, at the Firestone Company there was a tremendous commitment to getting the job done, but there was just as much commitment to Harvey Firestone himself. He made it a point to know the people who worked for him. He was concerned about their lives and their families. He would go through the factory and ask one worker how the new baby was, another one whether his wife was feeling better. He cared. He was one of the first in the country to offer company stock to his employees at reduced rates, so that they could be part of the operation.

When the unions came in, it inevitably got to be less personal. Some of the men began to talk to Firestone through a negotiator, rather than directly, as before. This was hard for him. He had watched the company grow from a handful of people with personal ties to each other, and I don't think he ever understood the unions. He was terribly disappointed to see the organization change the way it had to change. But when the tide is running, it is very difficult for an ordinary workman to stand against it; some of the men turned against Mr. Firestone, and that hurt him very much. When he died, though, I saw many of these same men coming to pay their respects with tears in their eyes. Many of them knew they had lost a friend.

*   *   *

His company was the history of his life. Some evenings I would encourage him to relax by telling me about its early days. It had grown up among the giants—Goodyear, Goodrich, and U.S. Rubber, which were older and much more powerful when he started the Firestone Company in 1900. He had many stories about the fierce competition. One time I asked him how he happened to meet Henry Ford.

"The first time was even before I started our company. I was a salesman for the Columbus Buggy Works in Detroit." He said that one day a young man came in with a plan for building a low-priced car that the farmers and the workers could afford. The man said he was building it in a shed behind his house, and he needed four tires. He was looking for solid-rubber tires—the old carriage tires that were in use then—but Firestone recommended trying a new type, pneumatic tires, with air in them. His company had just ordered a few. He took Henry Ford back to the warehouse stockroom to see if he could find them. He did, and Ford bought them. As he left, Ford said, "I may be back for more." And a few years later Firestone went to him with many more.

"By then I was running my own business, making tires. I had bought an old tumbledown factory in Akron. In 1905 I heard that Henry Ford was going to build two thousand cars—big business in those days. He would need eight thousand tires. I hurried to Detroit with a few sets of our pneumatic tires. Ford wasn't manufacturing his own tires. All he was really interested in was the car's engine at that time."

Ford had said to him that if Firestone's tire was as good as he said it was, Ford would use it. Then, as was typical of him, taking nobody's word for anything, Ford had Firestone fit a couple of his cars with his tires and had them driven around the streets for sixty days. The tires passed the test and Firestone left with an order for two thousand sets of tires.

"But that was just the start of the challenge," my boss said. "We only had one man making pneumatic tires and the expansion of the department and its financing nearly bankrupted us. But we made it. It was the start of a big deal. We've made half of the tires for Ford cars right along." At that point we were making about twenty-five thousand tires a day for Ford.

Shortly after that conversation I accompanied Firestone to New York. While we were in the office of the branch manager there, he mentioned to Firestone that he was having a little trouble leasing a property in Flushing.

Firestone turned to me. "You've had some experience with leases. Take a look at this one. I have an appointment." And he left.

I went over the lease and made a number of suggestions that saved the company money. On the train back to Akron, Firestone said to me, "I hear you fiddled around with that lease and came up with a more favorable agreement." The train rattled on for a while, then he said, "Jimmie, we're figuring on going into real estate in a big way, starting our own stores and warehouses all over the country. How would you like to take over the real estate department?"

I'd almost forgotten that real estate was the original reason for Firestone's offer of employment. I'd always loved real estate, and I wasn't afraid of the hard work it would take. But then I thought of his son, Bud, who was at the moment in charge of that department.

"Mr. Firestone, I'd be happy to take that on—but what about Bud?"

"No problem. The two of you will just switch jobs. He can be my assistant. I don't think Bud is all that keen on real estate anyway."

I soon found I'd stepped into a far bigger job than I'd realized. When I took over the department, it employed only twelve, secretaries included. I thought at first we'd be buying properties in maybe a dozen cities, but during the next few years the numbers mounted into the hundreds. When Mr. Firestone went after something, his was the hardest hitting outfit in the business. Before long we got into one-stop service stations, with not only tires, but also other auto supplies and more and more services and stores.

Soon we found we weren't just leasing existing properties, but having to buy properties and build new buildings to meet our needs. After I'd been in charge of the real estate department for a few months, Firestone called me into his office one day and said, "We need to have our own building program. I want you to supervise the construction of these buildings."

I was taken by surprise. "I've had no experience. I'm not an engineer, Mr. Firestone, or a construction man. All I've done is to let a few contracts down in Florida."

"Don't worry. Hire the best engineer and construction man you can find. Help him find the supervisory men. Then put that department under you and go ahead."

I took him at his word and hired an architect, an engineer, some good construction men I knew in Florida, and an equal number of construction superintendents. I had already hired a dozen real estate men to look for property across the country and analyze it, and we were in business.

We gradually took on four hundred cities and towns: in each one we located property, negotiated purchases, handled the closings, designed the buildings—usually through local architects—let the contracts, supervised construction, and finally completed and equipped the buildings before turning them over to the sales department. I was soon running not a real estate department, but the "Firestone Realty Company." There were times when we had fifty buildings under construction in that many cities, and in the peak years we were finishing on the average one every forty-eight hours. In the process, I was getting architectural experience, building experience, even legal experience. I had my own legal man, although when we went into a city we did business through local law firms and real estate firms. We didn't try to do everything ourselves, but we always liked to be equipped to supervise.

Construction is a tough industry, and Firestone's advice to me then was to be prepared to be as firm as the opposition. He had in mind competitors in the tire business, lawsuits, price wars, and so on. Before long I ran into situations that demanded even more muscle. We found ourselves up against real gangsters, and our supervisors had to be tough to deal with them. We had a field construction supervisor working for us in an area that included Chicago, a man named Platt. He was a rough, football player type, rangy looking. He began to have problems with a Chicago gang. He refused to knuckle under to their "protection" demands. He had also become friendly with one of the big ward bosses. When he was threatened by one gang that something would happen to him or to the building if he didn't pay them off, the ward boss came right down to the building, got between Platt and the gang men, and told them to get lost. They never bothered Platt again.

I had been afraid that in taking on real estate I would lose the close association with Mr. Firestone. I soon found

51

that he was as interested in real estate as I was. During all this activity, I communicated with him regularly, either in person, since my office was still in the headquarters building, or, when I was on the road, by telephone to him at his office, or in his home. It astounded some colleagues that I was able to get Mr. Firestone to decide on things without delay. I found that I could walk in to see him or J. W. Thomas, the vice-president, and clear up policy matters with them first thing in the morning. It cut through a great deal of the red tape that plagued so many big companies, even Firestone at times.

The direct touch with Mr. Firestone was very helpful, because the company's expansion across the country could not have come at a more difficult time. I started with the real estate department in 1929. In October of that year came the great New York Stock Exchange crash—the start of the Great Depression of the early 1930s.

Five days before that "Black Friday," Mr. Firestone sold preferred Firestone stock that realized sixty million dollars—something like half a billion today. He always said, "My only stock is Firestone. All my eggs are in that basket." It was not a question of his seeing the crash coming. He was looking ahead to securing the capital he knew the company would need, especially for the real estate and construction development for which he had made me responsible. Intuitively, he knew it was the right time to sell. Had he not done so, the stock would have been impossible to sell, and the company expansion could not have taken place.

Shortly after that, I was with him in an elevator in the Wall Street district. Also with us was the president of the National City Bank of New York, which I believe had handled the transaction for Firestone. He said to my boss, "The good Lord must have had his hand on your head." Mr. Firestone grinned over at me: "I hope you heard that, Jimmie!"

Every cent of that money was precious during the following months and years. It provided the means to acquire commercial land at depressed prices and to build hundreds of retail outlets, and so helped stimulate economic activity in those cities and provide desperately needed employment.

In the middle of all this austerity, Mr. Firestone had the imagination to encourage me in some bold strategies. For example, my first move, when we entered a city to establish a store, was to analyze possible locations. We always tried to find the "100 percent corner," the prime real estate spot in town. We figured that the place where the most business was going on already would be the place where we stood the best chance ourselves, and then we'd back off a few blocks till we found a site that was affordable.

As we moved into one fair-sized city, I had the idea of flying over it in a plane during the morning and evening rush hours to look for traffic patterns to pinpoint the maximum traffic flow, so as to be sure our store location was where we could best capture it. When I asked Firestone for the use of the company plane to do this, he saw the point and agreed at once. So I'd go up, spread out our real estate man's traffic map and reports on the floor of the plane, and check the whole thing out. Despite the economies, my boss went right along with me on things like the use of the plane, and also on buying store sites, once we'd established the most promising ones. Of course, as real estate values came down during the Depression, it was easier to acquire them. When I returned from a trip I'd walk into the comptroller's office and he would groan at some big outlay, but it would go through anyway because he knew that I already had the boss's okay.

There was only one time when Mr. Firestone and I had a real disagreement on a location. It was at 13th and K Streets in Washington, D.C. I told him that if we bought it, whatever we built on it would never make money. It just was not a profitable location. He told me to forget that. "I want to see 'Firestone' in neon letters right there near downtown Washington," he told me. That was in 1930, and it stood there for more than fifty years.

I valued the close relationship with Mr. Firestone because it gave me support when problems had to be dealt with quickly. For example, we got one of our first building construction permits from a city hall through a local law firm. Soon after, they sent us an unusually large bill. When we questioned it, they indicated that they had had to pay off certain officials to obtain the permits. That was the way it was always done, they said. I wrestled with this for a long time, but the building was already under construction and we finally had to pay the bill. From that time on, though, I let it be known that we would never authorize or countenance in any way that method of obtaining permits. I sat down with Firestone when I got back to Akron and told him what I had run into and the decision I had passed on to my staff.

"You are absolutely right, Jim. This business has grown on honest deals—a good product and good service. I want that honesty maintained in all our activities. Any time you run into that kind of monkey business, don't yield to pressure. I'll back you all the way, even if it means losing opportunities. Our reputation is more important."

One of the things I appreciated most about working with Firestone was his flexibility. He could be rough and tough one day, but the next day seem to lean over backward in his consideration for someone. And he expected us all to be equally sensitive about how to deal with people. I had an opportunity to practice that sensitivity when a crisis blew up in a construction project in Kansas City. It was probably the first time a full-service center like ours was being located in the heart of a heavily developed business district. There were questions arising about traffic congestion, parking problems, the ultimate appearance of the building, and so forth. We ran into serious opposition. The *Kansas City Star* took up the issue editorially, and there were two or three pages of news and comments in the course of a few weeks—all against our project.

Eventually we were sued by a local business association that took encouragement from the news items in the paper, and one night our man phoned from Kansas City and said, "You've got to come out! This thing's about to explode in our faces. It's already exploded!" I caught a plane early next morning, and as I flew I thought about the controversy over the building, and the *Kansas City Star*, and the local position and Firestone's position and the job ahead. I decided that, as Mr. Firestone's representative, I should go and talk to the opposing attorneys alone, instead of taking company people with me; simply go in on my own and lay everything on the table in a very straightforward way. I thought if I did that, I might be able to get it across to the community that we were not a big company trying to push our interests through without regard for anyone else. We wanted to do what was right for the local community as well as what was right for Firestone.

This idea of mine was not very popular with our man in Kansas City, or with our attorneys. They said that I was crazy; that I should have at least one of our attorneys along as a witness. But I had an intuition about the way the problem should be handled. I insisted that I wanted to carry it out alone. And that's just what I did. The first thing the opposing attorneys said to me when I walked in was, "You're alone?"

"Yes. I'm going to lay our cards on the table, because I feel there is a right answer in this situation. It might be Firestone's answer, or it might be yours, or it might be neither. It might be something else entirely. I believe that in all honesty on both sides we can find what is right, not who is right. I'm just here to tell you exactly where we are at Firestone, what's important to us, and what we feel will hurt us. Then I hope you'll do the same."

The attorneys were stunned. They were probably wondering just what kind of strange bird I was. But when I finished, they asked me if I would go over the same ground with their clients on the following day. I agreed.

At the second meeting, a dozen powerful men from the business association gathered around a table. I said what I had outlined the day before about trying to find what was best for both Firestone and the community. Then I asked if they would go around the room and have each man tell us honestly what he felt was the difficulty with the proposed project and exactly what he was afraid of. When it came to my turn I would let them know the Firestone point of view, what points in the project were important to us, where their position came into conflict with ours, and where we might be able to agree.

By the time the discussion came around to me, it was clear that their real objections were not obstacles to our plans. In their zeal they had pointed out every possible objection, but many of them were not crucial. By a slight modification in Firestone's building plans, and a clarification of our company's objectives, we were able to ease the minds of the townspeople and work things out together.

The construction of the building went ahead. In fact, when the building was completed, the business association gave a dinner to welcome the Firestone people to the community.

I had had to move so quickly there had been no opportunity to consult with Mr. Firestone. But when it was all over, he was delighted by the outcome.

"What gave you the idea of going in alone and getting everyone to put their cards on the table?" he wanted to know.

"I guess it was a kind of intuition."

"Nothing wrong with intuition, if your motives are right. I often depend on it, as you know."

"Mr. Firestone, you know that I try to start off each day with a few minutes of quiet. I need any help I can get from the Almighty to throw some light on how to deal with people and the job. Well, it sure paid off this time."

Firestone nodded. He was a regular churchgoer, and I knew he had a firm belief in God that he tried to apply in his own life. He was not a man to talk much about it, though every now and then he would come out with a remark that revealed his convictions. He was a strict Republican, but before one presidential election he said to me, "Elections don't make much difference any more. We've gotten away from things that matter in this country. We need a much deeper moral and spiritual change than politics can give us."

*   *   *

By the time I had been president of Firestone Realty for nearly three years we were busy in the last third of those four hundred cities and my staff had grown to seventy-five—engineers, architects, draftsmen, real estate analysts, construction supervisors, and so on. One morning in January 1931, after one of my reports, Firestone said to me quietly, "That's fine. You've done well with real estate. Now it's time to move on. Things will ease off a little from now on with store openings. I need you to be freer to travel with me and represent me."

With time, the Depression really took hold and we felt the pain in Akron as did everybody everywhere. It almost killed Mr. Firestone to lay off faithful and loyal employees. But he had no choice. If there wasn't enough money coming in, there was no way he could pay them. He tried in many cases to make work as long as he could.

There were no welfare facilities as we know them today. There was no unemployment compensation to tide people over. Soup lines were all the welfare there was, and proud men set up rickety boxes and sold apples on street corners.

One of the first things Firestone said to me when I became his assistant was, "You don't know anything about cutting costs, Jim. I learned in '21, and I'm going to teach you." He got tough and went to work on all kinds of expenses, cutting back everywhere. Even executives had to get permission from the comptroller's office to make long-distance phone calls. Everyone took a 10 percent cut in salary, right across the board, including Mr. Firestone. Later, we took another 10 percent. But in this way, the company was able to reduce layoffs to a minimum.

In January 1931, Firestone asked me to join him in his winter home on Miami Beach. There, he conducted most of his business by telephone. I was back and forth for a while, troubleshooting for him in some of the newly developing districts around the country, winding up real estate business. Then, when the winter was over, I set out with him on what had become one of his annual trips across the country. He liked personal contact with his managers and dealers, and this year, especially, he had many to see, since we had expanded so rapidly. He would cross the southern states, go up the West Coast and back across the North.

Our headquarters was a private railroad car, a symbol of power in that era. Men of Firestone's stature leased them not only for their own transportation, but for sales and public relations. It carried a staff of two—a cook and a steward. And there was plenty of room for sleeping, eating, conferring, and working.

Since Mr. Firestone used a private car, and the company shipped freight all over the country, the railroads were most cooperative about hitching his car onto any train convenient for him. When we were hitched onto a major passenger train, we'd sometimes be hitched to the observation car, and the regular passengers would look into our kitchen windows—which neither they nor we enjoyed!

The journeys were hectic. Firestone wasted no time. He'd invite the dealers in one city for dinner in his private car, be off to breakfast in another city with other dealers and local managers, and then have lunch with a third group somewhere along the line.

The troubleshooting part of my job gave me the latitude to do whatever needed to be done. If there was a problem in El Paso, I'd get off the train with a small overnight bag and fix it. Sometimes it took a while—not like fixing a leak in the sink. I would find out where Firestone was going to be a day or two later, and take a shortcut to meet him.

But our most memorable train ride was in the Northwest. Firestone got a telegram calling him to Akron immediately. There were plenty of trains going East, but they took their time getting over the mountains. We called Northern Pacific to see what they could do—did they have an express train perhaps? It turned out they could do better than that. They offered to hitch Firestone's car to the "Cherry Special." It was leaving that night. I didn't know what the "Cherry Special" was, but I said fine. I soon learned that the train was the one that carried freshly picked cherries from the Northwest orchards all the way to Chicago. Its refrigerator cars were packed with cherries, and several locomotives were set up to speed them over the mountains without slowing down, before the cherries spoiled.

They hitched our car to the caboose, and the "Cherry Special" began taking us up over those mountains as if they didn't exist. Coming down a straightaway, before they took off the extra engines, we'd move like a bullet. We'd go through those little flat towns and see nothing but a swirl of dust. When we hit the long, straight stretch of track around Medicine Bow, Wyoming, the train was going over a hundred miles an hour and the end of the train, where we were, started vibrating. When the speed went up, the vibrations got worse. Glasses and silverware started rattling; so did the pots and pans—even our private cook was hopping up and down.

Our teeth began to chatter. As the train hit its stride, Firestone turned to me and said, "JJJim, can't wwe sstop the vvvibrations?" I pulled the alarm cord for the conductor.

When the conductor came in from the caboose, I asked him, "Cccould you dddo sssomething to ssstop the vvvibrations?"

"I thought you wwwanted to ggo fffast."

Firestone said, "Well, not ththis fffast."

They slowed the thing down a little and we got to Chicago in one piece.

In Jacksonville, Florida, we didn't have a private car and there were eight or ten of us aboard a passenger train. Firestone addressed a meeting, met the mayor and city officials, and we all waited for him in taxis until the last minute. We finally got him and rushed to the train station just as the conductor was calling "All aboard." We had barely put the senior officers on and started putting luggage on the train before it began to move. Soon it was going too fast to cram all the baggage into the right car, so as the next car came by, two of us and the porters threw in a couple of cases; car by car we flung more in, until the last bags went into the last car and we jumped in with them.

There were no dull moments. Sometimes I made it to three or four cities a day on trains and in automobiles and overnight sleepers. I went for one whole week sleeping every night in a Pullman berth. And then there were the sudden changes of plans. We had a policy meeting one evening at the Ritz-Carlton Hotel in New York, where Mr. Firestone leased an apartment. Under discussion was whether I should go West or not, to handle a problem there immediately. It was decided I would go, so I rushed to my room and threw my stuff into a suitcase. Then Firestone came in and said, "No, Jim, we'll do it later." I started to unload—but before long he was back again saying, "Yes, go." I threw everything in again, and shot out of there.

Another highlight of my travels with Mr. Firestone was our annual attendance at the country's greatest automobile race, the Indianapolis 500. The Firestone Company had been deeply involved in the event ever since its beginning in 1911. Most Memorial Days would find Harvey Firestone seated in his box above the first turn of the track. Sometimes I sat with him and shared his enjoyment.

Firestone was not there, however, just for the pleasure of the spectacle. Participating in the event had an important twofold purpose for the company. It was a major test of our tires and the biggest advertising opportunity: from 1920 to 1966 every winner came in on Firestone tires. Many years, almost every car ran the race on our tires. Needless to say, our advertisements stressed that if the daring driver trusted his life to Firestone, the family driver would do well to do the same. Out of Indianapolis many an improvement was developed, from low-pressure tires to shock-resistant tires for the new airplanes.

As fascinating as these trips were for me, they had their embarrassing moments. On one trip West, Firestone stopped in Arizona to see Mr. Paul W. Litchfield, the president of Goodyear. Goodyear and Firestone were great competitors waging constant price wars. When we arrived at the Litchfield ranch all of the family and guests were swimming in the family pool. Mrs. Litchfield asked me if I would like to swim while her husband and Firestone talked. I said yes, but that I didn't have my bathing suit with me. She offered me her husband's.

Mr. Litchfield was a great, big man—very wide and very tall. His suit was the one-piece contraption worn by men in

those days. I got it on and it was a little broad on the side
and quite low down the middle. Had I had any sense I would
have stepped gingerly into the pool. Instead I dived in. I
felt as if a parachute had opened up. The shoulder straps
stayed on, but the water got in everywhere and I could feel
the suit down around my knees as I swept through the water.
I didn't dare surface until I had everything rearranged, and
by then I was completely out of breath.

Mr. Litchfield invited my boss to take a ride in the Goodyear blimp. I didn't go along, but Firestone told me later
that it had occurred to him there might be a trapdoor in
the floor, and a lever that Litchfield might easily have pulled
to get rid of his chief competitor!

Firestone wasn't too fond of that blimp. Once in Miami
Beach at a formal evening party a man came up to him and
said, "I've been wanting to meet you for years, Mr. Firestone. I think of you everytime I see your blimp overhead."

One positive result did come out of that Arizona visit,
however. The price war disappeared all over the country,
for the time being.

Then there was the time in St. Louis in 1932. I had been
district manager there for a couple of months and we had
taken over the Allweather Tire Company dealership. Allweather was already a standard name for Goodyear tires, so
it was a piece of good fortune to have a Firestone dealership
with that name. I was supposed to show J. W. Thomas and
some other Firestone executives around this prize dealership, but I couldn't find it. We drove up one street and down
another, and all the time I could hear Thomas in the back
seat, laughing.

Another time I was driving Firestone around in New York
and I somehow started too soon through a light in Manhattan. A whistle blew and a cop came over and demanded to
see my license. I gave him some pretty good conversation
and finally got off. I heard my boss chuckling and saying to

the executives with us, "I was wondering how Jim would get out of that one."

*   *   *

Between all the hectic events, there were spells of quiet train travel and relaxation, when Firestone enjoyed talking about anything but business affairs. On our first western swing he was peering through the window as we passed cattle grazing on a ranch. He had grown up on a farm, had traded horses, and owned polo ponies.

"Jim, Mrs. Edison told me you once spent some time riding herd as a cowboy. Tell me about that."

I told him that as soon as I had graduated from high school, I had headed West on a hoboing trip. I was watching some men load cattle onto freight cars when a guy asked me if I'd like a job tending an engine out in the salt licks.

I didn't know what a salt lick was, but I figured I could run an engine well enough. And I needed the dough.

We made a deal at a dollar a day plus grub and headed off in his truck. He dumped me at a ranch twenty miles out. Very early the next morning, a guy brought up a horse, pointed to the horizon, and told me to ride out and round up twenty horses.

Fortunately, the horse he left me with was saddled. All I knew about horses was what I'd seen in movies, but I figured some of that technique had sunk in. I scrambled on and did fine, until we came to a rushing stream. I pointed the horse at the water and prodded him; between his inching forward and my prodding we got literally up to our necks in that stream—only his head and mine cleared the surface of the water. He was swimming, and I was swimming above him, clinging to the saddle horn.

Firestone, who had been chuckling as I told the story, was really laughing now. "And you came on twenty horses, I hope."

"Oh, yes. More than twenty. More than I'd ever seen in my life."

"And you managed to cut out twenty?"

I said *I* hadn't; my horse had gone ahead and rounded up a dozen or so and had headed them back toward the ranch. All I had to do was hang on. But as we recrossed the stream, he lunged up the bank so fast, I slid backward into the water. The horse drove the others into the corral, but as he didn't know how to shut a gate, they moved right out again.

The rancher arrived exactly at the same time I trudged up, soaking wet.

"You're fired!" he roared. But the truck that could give me a ride out of the place wasn't due back for a week, so he sent me out with a two-horse wagon to cut maize. Out in the field, I moved through the maize, chopping it and throwing it into the wagon. But just as things were going smoothly, something spooked the horses and they bolted, spilling a trail of maize through the wagon's open tailgate all the way back to the ranch house. I was fired again, but the truck still wasn't due back, so the rancher had me mending fences for a few days. Later, I moved on to southern Arizona, hired on as a pearl diver (dishwasher) at a ranch near Tombstone, gradually worked up to ranch-hand status, and didn't get fired!

"Jim, I can see I've been pampering you," laughed Firestone. "I'll have to think up something really tough for you to do!"

It wasn't in connection with that remark, of course, but Firestone eventually began to lay on me some heavier responsibilities. He sent me to meet on his behalf with Rufus C. Dawes, one of the great businessmen of the day. Mr. Dawes was in charge of arrangements for the upcoming Chicago Century of Progress Exhibition. It was an important assignment because Firestone was eager to secure a prominent site there. We happened to obtain an excellent one. My boss told me later that Mr. Dawes had been pleased with the way "the young kid" had handled the discussion.

Firestone said to me one morning, "We need to develop and sell a full line of automobile supplies in our stores. I want you to look into that, Jim. Get the whole thing going. Pick the most promising items, design the displays, help select the operating personnel."

Again, he had handed me a major responsibility and some busy days followed. The hardest job was figuring out the thousand most marketable items—everything from seat covers to windshield wiper blades. In due course, despite miscalculation on some items, we established the automobile supplies department and began a rapid expansion.

In October 1931, when J. W. Thomas, who was in charge of day-to-day operations of the company, was due to leave on a trip to our West Coast plant, he and Mr. Firestone told me to move into Thomas's office and follow things in his absence. Thomas said to me, "Jim, if questions come up, you make the decisions you are comfortable with. The tough ones we can handle when I call in each night."

I was in a sensitive spot and was careful to step on as few toes as possible. For example, a certain tire suddenly began causing serious problems. I called our chief engineer and scheduled a meeting right away. When he asked where it would be held, expecting me to use Thomas's office, I said, "How about your office?" That gesture would make it easier for both of us.

Chapter

THREE

IT WAS A PLEASANT SPRING DAY in 1932 and I was feeling at peace with the world. I'd just finished eating a good Sunday dinner with J. W. Thomas, Mr. Firestone's able right-hand man. The two of us were walking along the road near the country club. J. W. was a great walker. He strode along, talking, looking straight ahead. In the middle of a conversation he broke off, then said casually, "Did you know we're transferring Trawick out West?" Trawick was one of three national sales managers; he had been in charge of the eastern third of the country. "That leaves quite a job to be filled," I said. Then I asked out of simple curiosity, "Who will you put in Trawick's place?"

"You," he said.

I couldn't believe my ears. I'd never been in sales. I'd been in real estate, with which I'd had a good deal of experience before joining the company. And I'd learned a lot about the company's operations working with Mr. Firestone. But I knew very little about the sales end of the business.

I started to protest, but J. W. stopped me.

"If you have any questions, Jim, talk to Mr. Firestone."

I was in Firestone's office the next morning.

"Mr. Firestone, I do appreciate your confidence in me. But you know I've had nothing to do with sales. I really don't know the first thing about the operation, and you're asking me to start off by taking charge of thousands of dealers!"

He looked at me with a twinkle in his eye. "Aren't you the young man who sold suitcases to those hard-boiled State of Mainers?"

"Sir, a few dozen suitcases a day is one thing. Hundreds of thousands of tires is something else!"

"Jim, you've been with me now for—what is it—four years. I know what you can do. This may be a big step for you, but you've already taken some big ones. I have confidence in you. And you know you can reach me any time you need help."

I tried one more shot. "Mr. Firestone, you've said to me many times that a manager should know all about his product. Well, I've sat in with you at the product board meetings and been with you when you talked to our district managers. But I really haven't handled our tires or our other merchandise, nor do I really know our service work. . . . And I—"

I could see a frozen look come over my boss's face. I knew I was getting nowhere fast.

"Don't underestimate yourself, Jimmie."

"Okay, sir. I'll give it my best."

There was no more to say. I moved into my sales office and got to work. Within a couple of months, though I knew I was managing reasonably well, it became clear that I needed a more solid footing in sales. I needed the surefootedness of knowing I could do any job I asked my men to do. All I wanted was a few months in one of our stores, so that I could really get the feel of the business from the ground up.

I knew it was no good going back to Firestone, so I talked to his son Bud, by now a close friend. Would he please persuade his dad to demote me to managing a store for however long it took? Bud went to bat for me. Although Firestone wouldn't settle for a store, he did give me the St. Louis district. That was plenty big—an area that included half of Missouri and half of Illinois.

But I got my way. On Saturdays I would put on overalls and go down to work at our city store, selling and mounting tires, grease work and all the jobs. I got to know all our products and the work.

It was still during the years of the Depression and I had to apply myself to keep our volume of business growing. I was responsible for four warehouses, twelve stores, and three thousand dealers. During my months in St. Louis, from the end of 1932 until late 1933, I learned a lot about markets, disgruntled dealers, our whole line of tires, and the other products we sold.

I also quickly learned that being a district manager involved much more than selling tires. One of the first things I had to handle in St. Louis was a lawsuit I had inherited from the previous manager. It was brought against us by a big dealer who no longer handled our tires. Firestone was upset about it. The dealer had hired a powerful law firm whose senior partner was a Mr. Hensley, later a U.S. senator. I made it my job to get to know him. We settled out of court on the basis of what was right, not who was right, and he got to be one of my best friends.

Firestone kidded me about that: "You should have been a lawyer yourself, Jimmie. You have a golden tongue."

"Mr. Firestone, it took more than quick talking to turn Mr. Hensley around. He's a smart cookie. No, the truth is, it was like that trouble we had with the new center in Kansas City. I got some direction from the Man Upstairs. I talked with Hensley on the basis of what was right for each of us, and he responded."

Another time, one of the toughest dealers I ever had told me he would sue Firestone under the Federal Trade Commission Act because of something I'd done, something that I'd thought was right, but evidently he didn't. He said that before he sued, he was going straight to Akron and report me to J. W. Thomas, our vice-president. I couldn't stop him, and off he went.

I sweated it out for a couple of days. Then I got a telephone call from Thomas, with Firestone on the extension. J. W. said, "Mr. Firestone's right here, and we both thought you'd like to know that this dealer came in and we told him the situation was totally in your hands."

His encouragement on this occasion helped me later when I was offered fifty thousand dollars' worth of business—the equivalent of at least half a million today—by a neighboring state. It was the middle of the Depression, after all, and we'd just lost our biggest dealer and were down in sales volume.

The state representative came to see me, saying he wanted to make arrangements.

"What arrangements?" I asked.

"I'll see that you have the state's business, on one condition. Just put my man on the local Firestone store's payroll for full-time work. He'll show up and do an hour or so's work a week. That way we'll keep it legitimate."

This stunned me, but when I consulted some of the local men, they said that was the way a lot of state business was obtained. You didn't get it just by having a better tire than the other guy. And they pointed out that if we didn't do this, somebody else would. It was a lot of business and I needed it very badly. I remember I didn't say no right away. I walked around the block and walked around the block and thought about it. But my gut said "No," and finally I said "No" too. So, of course, we lost the contract. Firestone backed me up. "You lose some and you win some," he said, "but stick to honesty no matter how much you need the business. Keep pitching, Jimmie."

He was more right than he knew. Weeks later, a large tire dealer who had been doing business with another brand for years came to me out of the blue. "We're dissatisfied with our manufacturer," he said, "and we'd like to go with you." The amount of business he gave me was almost exactly the amount I'd turned down from the state.

Firestone had drummed into me that we should never allow a competitor to undersell us. "We're not out to cut our prices by lowering the quality of our product or our services. But we will shave our prices when we have to—by streamlining our operations and tightening our belts. No one is going to beat us over the long run that way."

So I was always on the watch for sudden moves by our St. Louis competitors, and I would check the newspaper advertisements regularly for clues. I'd been out in the territory until about nine one evening, and bought the bulldog edition of the *St. Louis Dispatch*, which had just come on the streets. There, to my surprise, was a full-page ad by Sears, our fiercest competition, announcing a Fourth of July "two for the price of one" sale. It was July 2, and Sears assumed they had scooped everybody. Our procedure on prices at Firestone was for district managers to telegraph the home office for an okay on price changes, and it sometimes took two or three days to get an answer. I had reversed that policy by telegraphing "Unless I hear from you by tomorrow morning, I will go ahead with such-and-such." This time it was too late even for that. I could imagine the streams of people heading for Sears next morning from miles around St. Louis for new tires before their holiday trips.

I called up the newspaper's advertising man and asked

71

him to meet me right away at our offices. We were big clients of the paper, so he came.

"What's the game?" he asked, as he walked in.

"I want a full-page ad in all tomorrow morning's editions, and I want it beside the Sears one."

He just laughed. "You can't have it. The bulldog edition is on the streets and the early morning edition is on the presses now. Absolutely impossible."

I made him go with me and root out the assistant manager of the paper. He gave me the same answer.

"Who's your boss?"

"The manager."

We reached the night manager, but he only said, "Look, you're too late. The paper is all set up."

"We've got to have a full-page ad. Who's your boss?"

"The publisher."

"Get him on the phone."

That produced some action. He didn't pick up the phone, but he grabbed the copy for my ad, raced down to the composing room, and told them to tear out some type. I waited while they put in the ad and started up those great *Post Dispatch* presses, then headed for home and bed. Next morning, there was the ad announcing our half-price sale. We made record sales that weekend over the states of Missouri and Illinois.

When Firestone got me to tell him how I had managed it, he laughed about as loud as I'd ever heard him.

"For someone who said he knows nothing about selling tires, you're learning fast, Jim. I should have sent you to a really tough district like New York!"

I assumed he was kidding, and maybe he was. But a few months later, I became the district manager for the Newark, New Jersey area—and a tough district it was. There were three brothers who were good dealers, but chiselers. They controlled a big part of the New Jersey market and

72

were always demanding better prices from Firestone. One of the brothers was the senior spokesman, another was the hatchet man, and the third came along as reinforcement. Our switchboard operator called me one day, saying, "Those brothers are on their way down the corridor to see you." Sure enough, the three of them came filing in, and I knew it was going to be kind of rough. One of them, Izzy, gave me the word.

"Mr. Newton, we're here to talk business. We like Firestone—but when a truck breaks down at 2:00 A.M., who's out there in the snow and sleet? Who's under the truck, looking up and changing the tires? Is it Firestone? No, it's us. We give a service; we make Firestone what it is in this area." And on and on.

"What do you want?" I finally asked.

"A bigger discount."

"How much are you thinking about?"

"We thought 5 percent was, umm, fair."

Well, a 5 percent additional discount is a lot in the tire business, and it was a no-no, strictly against policy, even back during the Depression.

"Five percent is all you want?" I said to them.

All six of their eyes lighted up. "You might as well think big and ask for 15 or 20 percent—because you have just as much chance of getting 20 percent as you do 5 percent."

Then trouble set in, and the brothers and I went round and round. But they got no further discount. Firestone was tickled by my report. "Well done, Jimmie," he said. "You have all the makings of a top-notch negotiator!" Then a faraway look came into his eyes. "It takes all kinds to make a world, doesn't it?" I had the feeling that he was a little jealous of my forays into the rough-and-tumble of things. He had plenty of fights of his own to contend with, but the people he met were a bit smoother than my Newark brothers.

Newark was home territory for the many cutthroats who

muscled in on the market. There was a colorful character named Frenchie, who always wore a beret. His game was to pick up our expensive forty-by-eight tires off scrap heaps and turn them in to our adjustment department as defective tires for rebate. I put a stop to the whole thing, which did not sit well with Frenchie. He asked me for a private talk. "We ain't gonna stop doing what we been doing," he said.

"It has to stop."

"Then you may find yourself in *real* trouble."

He made some colorful threats, but we continued our legitimate business. Later, he asked me to come by his tire store and meet his partner. Frenchie's partner had achieved fame during Prohibition by selling a carload of watered-down booze to a Philadelphia mob. They had responded by giving him a good "lead poisoning." Somehow he recovered.

After some hesitation, I accepted the invitation and the three of us ended up by becoming quite good friends. When Firestone next came through New York, he invited me to dinner and I told him about Frenchie.

He laughed, but quickly grew serious.

"I appreciate your keeping these fellows straight, but, Jim, look after yourself. Don't take unnecessary risks."

From Newark I was promoted to the New York district, a territory of many opportunities. I had an unusual experience with Firestone over one of these. While I had been in St. Louis, one of our bigger dealers, Saul Cohen, pioneered time payment in the tire industry. He charged customers who couldn't put down the full amount an additional percentage but gave them time to pay in easy installments. He did a very big business that way.

When I moved to the New York area, I soon saw that there were thousands of potential customers for time payment in the tire market, people who during the Depression didn't have the cash for a set of new tires. They had to resort to buying cheap, poor-quality ones. I found a dealer in Newark, New Jersey who was eager to try out time payment, so I asked the Cohens to come East from St. Louis and show him how to work it. Meantime I talked to Mr. Firestone and tried to sell him on the idea.

"Jim, I've never been one to cut corners. Maybe I'm conservative, but I believe a man should only buy what he can afford to pay for. It's no kindness to lead him into debt."

"I understand that, Mr. Firestone. But we are forcing people to buy inferior stuff, and you know that's no kindness to them. They're paying a lot more in the long run, because they go through those tires so fast. But they can afford good tires if they pay by the week."

"I'll think about it, Jim."

That meant no, for the moment. But before long my Newark dealer was doing such a volume of business that my boss became interested. On his next trip to New York I said casually, "You might like to go see the Newark man." He agreed, and his chauffeur drove us over.

He walked in quietly, as was his habit, dressed in his brown suit—a favorite color—homburg hat, neat shirt and tie, with a cane in his hand. He greeted the secretary, asked how she was and how the work was going, and had a word with an overalled workman lifting a tire from its rack.

Then he walked over to the dealer, shook his hand, and congratulated him on the pace of his business; the place was a beehive, cars lining up to have their tires changed. He looked at the dealer's records and finally said to me, "Jim, why don't you come to Akron as soon as you can and we'll see about starting up this system across the country."

So I spent a week there writing a manual on time payment and the company used it nationwide with good results.

During the two years, 1932–1934, that I served as district manager in St. Louis and New York, I learned a great deal about selling. And I came to appreciate the wisdom of my boss, whose favorite sayings I still remember:

"The sole reason a business exists is because it meets a human need."

"The only way to compete with bigger companies is to make a better product."

"You must always be able to believe in what you sell."

In other words, Mr. Firestone set a high priority on quality, and everyone in the company knew that. When Henry Ford first introduced his V-8 engine early in 1932, for example, it caused a crisis at Firestone, which was producing half of Ford's tires. The new engine was so powerful that the car's "jackrabbit" starts sometimes separated the treads from the tires and left what we called "snakes" on the highway. Firestone told Thomas to shut down the plant and tell the engineers to come up with a tire within forty-eight hours that would stand the traction and not separate. They met the deadline and restarted the plant, but came up with a tire at almost triple the cost. Then Firestone gave them a couple of days to bring the cost down to what Ford had been paying previously. Somehow they managed to accomplish that.

One day I was in J. W. Thomas's office when two men came in and proudly put on his desk a blue and orange package. It was the new Firestone brake lining, just in from production. J. W. picked it up and looked it over.

"Beautiful packaging," he said. "How will it stand shipment?"

The men looked surprised. "I don't know."

"You mean you haven't tested it yet?"

"We'll get the engineers on it right away and let you know."

"Don't bother the engineers." J. W. raised the package over his head and hurled it down on the office floor. It broke apart, brake lining and paper spewing all over the office.

"It will never stand shipment. Go off and make a package that will."

We used to call it "the direct approach." And it was typical of the standards Mr. Firestone demanded.

There was a theory in the tire industry in those days that if you improved the quality of the tire too much you would be forced to cut back on production, because it would last too long. Built-in obsolescence. Firestone would have none of that. His company policy was to make the best tire at the best possible price, and to work constantly on improvements.

I used to take a hacksaw in my car on my sales trips. I would ask a prospective dealer to take any tire made by one of our competitors out of his stock, and then a Firestone tire of the same size. I'd pay him for them. Then I'd produce the hacksaw and cut a section from each and have him compare them. Ours was always superior—in number of layers, thickness, and construction.

I also learned the power of understatement and "soft sell." Dealers would ask me whose tire I thought was best—expecting the obvious answer. I'd often say, "I don't know which is best. But I do know whose is second best."

"Did you say *second* best?"

"Well, if you ask a Goodyear man which is best, he'll say, 'Goodyear.' Then if you ask him which is second best, he'll say 'Firestone.' You'll get the same kind of answer from Goodrich, General, and Seiberling people. Theirs is best, but Firestone is always second best."

Mr. Firestone's pride in his products was inherited by his sons. Many years later, in 1947, I attended the wedding in Akron of Harvey Jr.'s daughter, Martha, to Edsel Ford's son, William Clay. The groom's party drove from Detroit in new Lincolns, which were duly parked in the Firestone executive garage.

I was standing with Harvey Jr. when the manager of the garage asked if Harvey had noticed that all the Ford party Lincolns were mounted with Goodyear tires. Would Mr. Firestone like to kid Mr. Ford about this?

"No," said Harvey Jr. with a big grin. "Say nothing to Mr. Ford. Just jack up all the Lincolns, take off the Goodyears, and put on ours."

As the manager hurried off to do just that, Harvey Jr. turned to me with a twinkle. "I'm not going to have a daughter of mine married on Goodyear tires."

Over the years, the loyalty of some dealers to Firestone was due to regard for the man, at least as much as the tire, as happened with the products of Edison and Ford.

Marcel Wagner was just such a loyal executive. He was a colorful character, a brilliant linguist, something of a scholar, and a great admirer of Mr. Firestone. He had been born in Alsace Lorraine and had come to America as a young man. He scoured the *Saturday Evening Post* ads, picked out a dozen companies, and wrote each a letter, Firestone among them. He sold himself and within a few months became our representative in the Near East.

On his arrival in Alexandria to set up his office in Egypt, Marcel got off the boat and walked up and down for a while, looking over the taxis waiting there at the dock. He told the drivers, in their own language, that he was going to walk to his hotel because not one of them had Firestone tires. Firestone was little known in that part of the world before Marcel got there—the market was cornered largely by Dunlop of England. But when Marcel started walking that day, a decrepit old taxi came thundering along and stopped and the driver pointed out that there was in fact one Firestone tire on his vehicle, so Marcel hopped in. From then on, whenever he emerged from a building anywhere in Alexandria, taxi drivers would all point to their Firestone tires, and the one with the most Firestones got the fare. This proved to be a dramatic way to enter the tire market in Egypt. Marcel soon became known in one country after another, and before long he was doing business with their sheiks, extolling not the tires, but Mr. Firestone—his character, his standing and leadership.

*   *   *

Looking back now on my time in St. Louis, then Newark, and finally New York, I can see that Mr. Firestone had intended for me to manage the tough areas that needed a clean-up man. There was no better way to learn the business. But they had been a strenuous two and a half years, and by the end of 1934 I was happy to be given notice from Akron that I was due for reassignment.

J. W. was again the man delegated to break the news.

"Jim, Mr. Firestone has a job for Leonard back in the East, and he wants you to take over from him."

Leonard, Firestone's fourth son, had been in charge of the sales division that included eleven western states. J. W. and I discussed what my responsibilities would be. The territory included six districts with twenty warehouses, one hundred retail stores, and seven thousand dealers. I was with the headquarters in Los Angeles.

When I got up to leave, J. W. stopped me. "You may not realize it," he said, "But you should be made aware. You're being groomed for the presidency of the company some day."

I remember standing in the doorway looking at him and not knowing what to say. It was a new idea, and as I thought about it, I assumed he was preparing me for the possibility way down the line. Everyone assumed that J. W. himself would take over as soon as Mr. Firestone felt the presidency was too demanding for his age. Then would come probably L. R. Jackson, with Harvey, Jr., next in line. I was not yet thirty years old—plenty of time ahead.

I'd visited Los Angeles many times before, but I was im-

79

pressed again, as I was driven along Firestone Boulevard to the magnificent building that housed our western head-quarters and tire plant. I looked forward to working in an area less pressured than New York, but I ran into an un-expected problem. I was accustomed to having friendly and cooperative associates, but there was one man who was a difficult character from the start.

George Bateman was the credit man in our headquarters, and credit men and sales managers are often on opposite sides of the fence. Salesmen want to stretch credit points to make sales. Credit men regard themselves as ordained to rein them in. But there was more to it than that. I felt he resented my coming from Akron, and I soon found he was trying to sabotage my efforts. Before long, without realizing it, I was starting to make things as difficult for him as he was for me.

One morning in the summer of 1935, before I went to work, I was sitting in my apartment and two thoughts came very clearly into my mind. The first was: "You resent Bate-man." Well, nothing surprising about that. But the second one pulled me up short: "It's your own fault." I realized all of a sudden that, no matter what he'd done to me, my re-sentment and bitterness were my fault. I asked the good Lord to forgive me for my bitterness. By the time I got to the office, it was gone and I was fine. But for three days another nagging thought stuck in my mind: "Go and tell Bateman." I said to myself, "If I do this and it doesn't work, it will be worse than before."

Finally I made a deal with myself—if his secretary wasn't at her desk in his office—and she was there just about all the time—I would go in and do this. So I went to his office, and she wasn't there, but I didn't have the nerve to go in. So I went to the washroom and had a little conference with myself, and I decided that if she still wasn't there I'd go in. And she wasn't there! So I went in and I said three sentences to him. I remember it as clearly as if it were yesterday:

"Bateman, I've had a deep resentment against you, and it's my fault. It's gone and I'm sorry about it. I just want you to know it doesn't agree with the way I'm trying to live."

I looked at him, and his eyes were as hard as flint. I knew I'd made a terrible mistake. It seemed an hour later, but was probably only a minute or two, when something happened in his eyes. They softened and he said, "Newton, I never knew you were like that inside. When I was a lot younger, I was hurt deeply by somebody, and I decided then and there that I would get the other fellow before he got me."

We talked for an hour—I can't remember what about—but in that hour he became a different person, so different that not only did he start being more sociable generally, but the secretaries would watch him come in each morning with a smile on his face.

Bateman and I were responsible for six hundred people, between us, in the eleven states, and they had been at each other's throats, his men and mine. I don't think he ever wrote them a letter about it, and I know I didn't. But a month later you could feel the tension begin to leave.

Firestone, who kept his ear to the ground, somehow had heard about the reconciliation when I next met with him. In the middle of our talking about other business matters, he said, "I hear you've been taking some of my advice to heart. Do you remember when you started with me, you asked me the secret of my success? I gave you a two-word answer. 'Know people.' And you've heard me say that many times since. Our company is built on people—those who work for us, and those we do business with."

I nodded, wondering what he was leading up to.

"You and Bateman are hitting it off these days. I know Bateman and I know you, Jim, and I'm not so sure Bateman was the peacemaker. It must have been you who put 'know people' to work."

"Believe me, Mr. Firestone, the change in Bateman is more than I can take credit for. The good Lord did it, in spite of me!"

"Speaking of the good Lord," said Firestone with a smile, "let me tell you what happened the other day in New York. I had a meeting with Taylor [Myron C. Taylor, New York banker] and his men. Mr. Baker [head of the First National Bank] joined us as we sat around the table. Taylor pointed me out to him and said, 'Meet a man who made five million dollars in the rubber business last year while all his competition lost money!' Baker beamed at me and said, 'You must have had God for a partner.' "

"I said, 'I did!' And I went on to tell him, so he'd know I was serious: 'We try to run our business on the level, honestly, and with consideration for other people.' "

I was impressed, not just by what Baker had said, but by how articulate and direct my boss had been about this principle with his business friends. At a meeting of our executives right afterward, he told them the story and added, "And don't think it's been easy. The way of the pioneer is rough. You fellows know the temptations to give in to our animosity about our competitors. It's hard to have God with you as a partner all the time."

It wasn't the first such conversation we'd had. True, he had a remarkable intuition about people who worked for him and was very patient and determined in their training. But his efforts were focused on their growth within the framework of the Firestone Company.

So much single-minded concentration on business can be a liability in other ways. It can make a man blind. When I came to him, the company was expanding so fast that he was away from his family a good deal, and his wife did not seem to share in his business life. She raised the children, pursued her interest in music, and left the Firestone Company to him.

As they grew up, the sons did become involved in the company—first Harvey Jr. and then Bud, then the others, as they came along. From birth, the boys were expected to follow in their father's footsteps and I believe there was a sense of pressure, though he may not have realized it.

In those days, businessmen rarely talked about their personal concerns; family and business were kept on separate levels. If there was a personal problem, it wasn't talked about.

It became quite obvious in the company after a while that one of his sons was having serious trouble. Bud was already a director by the time I came to the company, head of a big department and responsible for a lot of people, but there were days when he wouldn't show up on time and days when he wouldn't show up at all. Yet he was a keen businessman, with his father's abilities for negotiation. You could tell there was great love between father and son, and Bud was breaking his father's heart. None of this was talked about. It was one of those things everyone tried not to see. I don't know to whom Firestone would have talked about Bud, even if he'd wanted to. Nevertheless, Bud's capers were the talk of Akron.

Bud and his wife, Dorothy, and I were good friends from the time I first started at Firestone. We were all of the same age, and as I was unmarried, I would often go over to their house, which was very near where I lived at the Portage Country Club. I found out about Bud's problem from Bud himself. He was a hard drinker. One day he told me that he had been in and out of institutions to "dry out." His father had sent him in great hopes, but by the time I came into the picture I think Firestone had about given up on Bud's alcoholism. It was tearing him up, but he just didn't know what to do.

Bud and I talked often about his problem. When he decided to go into yet another institution and try another cure, I went to his father and asked permission to join Bud, to share the experience with him. In spite of the tremendous business pressures, Firestone was grateful and made arrangements for me to leave work.

The institution on the Hudson River I attended with Bud was run like the army. I'd been sitting at a desk for a few years by then and was not prepared to be awakened at dawn and made to run all over the countryside. They were intent on drying these guys out and drying me out right along with them. I got more exercise than I'd had for a long, long time. The place did help Bud, and our talking helped. I shared with him the times I had found myself unable to handle things and told him that in my experience there was always an answer. The God who made us would have an answer for us if we only gave him the chance. Bud was somewhat receptive, but he didn't really believe anything could change—not for him, anyway.

Several weeks after we'd returned to Akron, I invited Bud to go with me to a conference in Denver where he would meet people I knew who were involved in what was then called the Oxford Group. It was an informal association of men and women, started by an American, Frank Buchman, who were committed to creating sound homes, teamwork in industry, and unity within and between nations, based on moral and spiritual change.

On the train to Denver we agreed that I would carry his liquor for him. He had been drinking a fifth of whiskey or more a day. That arrangement we made put a small barrier between himself and the alcohol, and it slowed down the consumption some, but it wasn't enough.

The conference marked a turning point in Bud's life. After we'd been there a few days, I could see that he was wrestling with the choice before him. Finally I was able to get him together with a friend of mine, Sam Shoemaker, a skilled counselor, who helped him make a decision to let God deal with the stresses that had driven him to alcohol.

While all this was going on in Denver, Mr. Firestone called me to discuss a company problem on the West Coast. The construction of our San Francisco building was running into trouble. He needed to cut costs substantially and wanted me to go right out there and do it. The problem was one I was used to handling, but I did not feel it right to desert Bud at this moment. Very few people bucked Mr. Firestone's orders. I took a deep breath and said, "Well, Mr. Firestone, if you absolutely insist, I'll go out there. But I think there's more involved right now than the San Francisco building. I think your son's life is at stake. I don't know if I'm all that necessary to him, but I do think I'm a bridge between him and some people here who could help him. I think I should stay."

He thought that over for a while, and I waited. It took him some time to shift gears. He finally said, "Okay, Jim, you stay there."

Bud's decision to put his life into the hands of a Higher Power, to trust and obey him, had an extraordinary effect. His whole life changed. It was visible right away; his face relaxed, some of the lines were gone. He had come to terms not just with the drinking, but with the underlying cause that was making him drink.

Bud went to stay for a few days with some friends of mine, Jack and Connie Ely, in Cold Springs Harbor on Long Island while I went back to Akron. Then I accompanied Mr. Firestone on a visit to his son. At the Elys', we walked together up the slope of a lawn to where Bud was standing. I will never forget the look of wonder that came over Firestone's face. The father could scarcely believe what he saw— a son come back to life. He had come to believe that the situation with Bud was hopeless, something he couldn't control.

Bud went home and started taking his responsibilities to the company seriously. He became a real husband to Dorothy and a real father to his two sons. Dorothy had been trying as hard as she could, but the alcoholism had put a terrible strain on their marriage. There were times when she had thought she would have to leave him. All of that soon changed. The family doctor called the transformation a medical miracle. He had thought withdrawal would take much longer.

Not long thereafter, I was with Firestone for a weekend at his apartment in the Ritz-Carlton in New York. On Saturday evening after dinner, the two of us went to his room for a talk. He had been uncharacteristically silent and I could tell he had something on his mind. Suddenly he said, "Jim, I'm not as young as I was, and I need to plan ahead. I've been going over in my mind what I should leave to my children."

I was used to long conversations with him about business, politics, news of the day, but this was different. He wanted to talk about things close to his heart.

"I've been thinking, ever since Bud's change, of what I can leave the children, more than just the material things of life. I blamed Bud for his drinking and his poor showing at the company. It never really dawned on me that it might have had anything to do with me."

I didn't have much to say. I didn't need to. He just wanted an understanding listener.

"I'd always felt that Mrs. Firestone and I had brought the children up well. We had a solid family life. I sent them to good schools. We brought them up to go to church. I thought they'd want the opportunities that our company could give them. Now Bud has told me a little of how he felt. It makes me wonder about the other boys. Most of them seem to be doing pretty well. Jim, what do you think? Do they talk to you?"

"Mr. Firestone, I know it must have meant everything to Bud to talk about these things with you. Maybe Harvey Jr. and the others would appreciate it just as much. Maybe you need to spend some time together, apart from the business."

"Ah, that's difficult. Hard to know where to start. . . ."

We went on talking about the family, the company, about hopes and fears he had never spoken of to me, perhaps to anyone. It got to be eleven o'clock, and I got up to leave. He said suddenly, "Why don't you come in and have breakfast with me tomorrow before I take the train to Washington at ten?" We talked through breakfast Sunday morning, and when it came time to go to the train, he said, "Jim, let's keep this up. You don't have anything to do here in New York until Monday morning. How would you like to ride down on the train with me?" So we proceeded to talk through the four hours to Washington. I said good-bye to him at the station and returned on the next train to New York.

During those long conversations Firestone seemed to be looking at himself with fresh eyes. He was battling his own life. Bud's honesty had made him take a hard look at all his children. He seemed to feel that a distance had grown between him and his sons—maybe it was his fault. Was it his inability to communicate with them? Or was it that he was often too preoccupied with his business? Or did it have something to do with his enormous determination to control not only the company, but the lives of his own family? He was realizing that material wealth was not enough of a legacy. He wanted more than anything to draw the boys to him—but how to show it and what to do for them?

And he was thinking about the company, into which he had poured all his energy, his life. He knew that he had built with his own hands a company that stood for quality and integrity, virtues that often seemed to be disappearing from American industry; but, he was asking himself, was he building into his sons the desire and will to continue the best of what he had begun?

After that weekend, I saw a deepening of the relationship between Bud and his father. Firestone spent more time with Bud; he relied on him much more, and Bud became a real part of the business. Firestone's involvement with the community also took on a new dimension. In fact, Bud's change and his father's response to his son surprised Akron. Mr. Firestone, Bud, and Dorothy headed a civic committee, which invited a team from the Oxford Group to hold meetings in the city over a ten-day period. The local interest became front-page news. Bud and Dorothy spoke at public meetings, and so did Mr. Firestone. He was known as an impersonal and tough businessman, but he stood before the crowds and announced that his family had been brought closer to God and that he himself had been brought "a very great happiness." He did it, perhaps, because he felt that his son's life had been handed back to him.

This visit to Akron was the start of a chain of events that led, among other things, to the birth of Alcoholics Anonymous.* Bud was in a sense indirectly responsible for a great deal more than the personal decision that reunited him with his wife and father.

One of the first people to hear from Bud about his change was Henry Ford. They were at an evening gathering of the Ford and Firestone families at New York's Ritz-Carlton. After dinner, I was standing with Bud when Mr. Ford came up to him.

"I've been hearing some interesting things about you, young fellow," he said.

---

* "Dr. Bob" Smith and "Bill" Wilson, whose life was transformed in New York through the same man with whom Bud made his decision, met with a group of Bud's friends in the homes of Henrietta Seiberling and T. Henry Williams, following the Oxford Group meetings in Akron. The two men decided to focus their energies on the needs of alcoholics—the start of AA.

Bud responded without hesitation. After describing his decision and his new lease on life, he said, "Each day's a fresh start, Mr. Ford. I wasn't much of a Bible reader, but now I find it's a great help to read it every morning. I use the Weymouth translation."

Ford said he wasn't familiar with that, only the King James version.

"I'd be glad to send you a copy."

Ford thanked him and added, "Congratulations, Bud. Keep at it. Nothing is more important in the world. I'll tell you what—if you and your brother Harvey, and Jim here, would like to come out to Dearborn to see the museum for a day or two, I'll stack my time against you young fellows' time any day you say."

*   *   *

In the summer of 1935, Mr. Firestone sent Bud and me to Spain. The company did not have many plants in Europe, but because Spain had such a high tariff on imported tires, Firestone had decided to build a plant there, in Pamplona. Now a problem had arisen because the plant was becoming profitable, but the government would not allow us to take our profits out of the country. So Bud and I were sent to look into whether the blocked funds should be used to enlarge the factory by adding a battery plant.

We went into the question in great detail with our Spanish partners. We found that the local work force of some five hundred men—mostly Basques from the nearby mountains—had developed into excellent craftsmen, trained by a cadre from Akron. We figured production rates, current demand, market prospects, our financial assets, cost of expansion—all the mathematical and material statistics. And we came to the conclusion that the company should go ahead with the addition to the plant.

Bud and I had hardly set foot in the United States when the first violence of the civil war broke out in Spain. In the early waves of revolution, the Communists took over our plant and held it as a fort. Our Spanish manager barely escaped with his life.

It taught me a lesson, one I felt the Firestone Company and American business needed to learn. We had to take into account more than technical and financial considerations in reaching our decisions. There were human, political, and ideological factors that could prove to be more important. I felt that here I had not applied in the realm of business what I had learned in my personal life—that it was essential to look beyond the material to the moral and spiritual for a wisdom greater than my own intelligence. When I voiced these convictions to Mr. Firestone, he agreed with me.

I was closer now than ever to Bud and the other Firestone sons. Firestone had given me extraordinary training during the eight years I had been with him, and he had come to lean on me much as one would on a son. But just as he was becoming truly united with his family, I was beginning to think seriously about my future in the Firestone Company.

By the time I was managing sales for the western part of the country, I was thirty and a glutton for work. J. W. Thomas would say, "We could use a dozen Newtons around here." But he would also say, "We've got to slow you down, Jim." The fact was, I loved the work, and yet it had become an endless race, an all-consuming life.

The business was moving so fast and the decisions were so urgent that I seemed to be on call constantly. Once, when I was hunting in the Everglades, Mr. Firestone told L. R. Jackson, the Firestone vice-president in charge of sales, to get hold of me immediately. He called my mother in Fort Myers, but she said I couldn't be reached. He kept persisting. Finally my mother told him that if it was really important she could probably get a Seminole Indian to track me through the Everglades. That was one too many for Jackson.

In 1935 I collapsed from overwork—just passed out completely. In several weeks I recovered, but it made me think. I had little doubt I would be making more money and wielding more power, and ultimately reaching the top. But was that what I really wanted in life? Was I being honest with myself? I needed time to breathe and sort things out.

The completion of my West Coast assignment brought matters to a head. I returned to Akron, where I suspected I would find myself in a yet more responsible position. I remember walking down the corridor to Mr. Firestone's office, passing colleagues who looked up at me from their desks. I knew they must be thinking, "What will Jim be getting into this time?"

As I entered the familiar office—the same desk, couch, and chairs—I said to myself, "Now is the moment to tell him honestly what's on your mind, before he lays out his plans for you." So, after giving him my report on our company's activities in the West, and answering his questions about business conditions out there, I said, "Mr. Firestone, I want to ask for a year's leave of absence."

He looked shocked. "What is it, Jim? Do you need a vacation? Is money a problem? How about a change of pace?"

"No, it's none of those things. The truth is I just need to get away for a while. You know I love the work, and you have been great in everything you've done for me. I just need time to think things over. I need time to let my soul catch up with my body."

He nodded, got up, and took my hand. He didn't say more, nor did I. He seemed to respect the fact that I was responding to something deep within myself. And he may have felt that I would not be returning. Now that I'm older, I know how much it must have hurt him. Maybe it was like losing a son. And I'm sure he was depending on me to take a lot of the load off his back, but I couldn't escape my conviction.

The night I left, Mr. Firestone and I had dinner at Bud and Dorothy's house, just the four of us. At the evening's end, he walked me to the door. There were tears in his eyes. And in mine.

*　　　　*　　　　*

From Akron I headed down to Florida. As I walked the sands of Fort Myers Beach two thoughts came together in my mind. I looked around at the business and industrial scene in America, which seemed to be in increasing turmoil, and I thought back to my experiences in the Firestone Company and how I had applied my convictions about seeking what was right, rather than who was right—the reconciliation with Bateman on the West Coast and resolving the conflict over our Kansas City center, and so on. Could the solution that had worked for smaller problems be applied to the larger concerns of industries?

I was encouraged by news from my friends in the Oxford Group about the startling moral and spirtual impact that had been made on a national level in the Scandinavian countries.

In March 1937, after I had started my leave of absence from Firestone, I embarked on a journey with an Oxford Group colleague which led me to Mr. Firestone's winter home in Miami. Charles Haines, of Philadelphia, had worked for some years in steel companies, but now, like me, was free to pursue wider concerns. The two of us had decided to embark on a bold project.

This was the decade in which organized labor in America was undergoing a major expansion. Until then, the unions had been built around crafts—carpenters, metalworkers, electrical workers, and so on. A tough, militant character, John L. Lewis, head of the United Mineworkers, was changing all that. He was determined to build unions whose workers of whatever skills formed a cross-section of the great mass-production industries—steel, automobile, rubber, and the like. His Committee for Industrial Organization (CIO) was already a force, and it was confronting the American Federation of Labor (AFL), the old craft union concept, splitting organized labor in two.

The creation of industrywide unions was also having an impact on the great companies like Ford, Firestone, and General Motors. Henry Ford and Harvey Firestone and the other free-enterprise pioneers did not take kindly to sweeping their labor force into these new and powerful industrial unions. They found themselves confronted by a united organization. Understandably, they felt resentful at seeing many of their workers accepting the militant leadership of union officials.

Haines and I and some of our colleagues had given a good deal of thought to the direction in which industry and labor were headed. Would it be growing confrontation, with strikes and lockouts, violence and class war? Or could a new teamwork be developed in industry, with management and unions recognizing each other's rights and dignity? We understood that labor in the mass industries was finding a cohesive leadership in the CIO. Why shouldn't there be, Haines and I figured, a similar, united leadership in the management of these industries? Its purpose would not be organized opposition to labor, but teamwork with the unions to achieve the harmonious expansion of industry, for the benefit of all.

Between us, we had a number of contacts with presidents of large companies in the United States and Europe, as well as with heads of labor unions. We planned to go from one to another to sound them out, and if possible to build a network of positive leadership. Our plan called for moving up through the mushrooming textile industry of Georgia and the Carolinas and through the midwestern steel and machine-tool companies. Frits Philips, a senior officer in the giant Philips electrical companies, was giving us introductions to heads of major concerns in the Netherlands, Germany, France, and Switzerland.

Our first call was on Harvey Firestone. He welcomed us to his wood-paneled study, with its familiar heavy, comfortable chairs. He had aged considerably in the twelve months since I had last seen him. I asked about his health.

"I'm slowing down, Jim. Leaving more of the work to J. W. now. And the boys are pitching in well. We miss you, though. Tell me what you're doing."

We outlined for him our hopes and our plans, not only for creative teamwork in industry, but for multiplying a change of motive in men and women that could affect government policies and international relations.

He listened. Then he said, "Go right ahead and let me know how it goes."

"Thank you, Mr. Firestone. It means a lot to have your backing." And then I remembered my leave of absence. I thought perhaps it would be an embarrassment to him. My year was up. I asked him if he didn't think it was time to make an official resignation.

"Nonsense, Jim. You're part of Firestone and always will be."

Then he picked up a copy of one of his favorite books, Emerson Fosdick's *The Meaning of Faith*, and inscribed on the flyleaf,

> To Jim,
>
> You have my very best wishes
> in the great work you are doing.
>
> With best regards
> Harvey S. Firestone

As we left, I thought of how much I'd learned from him, how much of a father he'd been, how generous, understanding, and affectionate.

*   *   *

On February 7, 1938, I was in Fort Myers when Bud Firestone called me to say his father had died. He was the only one of the family there in Miami Beach. Could I come over? I jumped into my car and hurried to be with him until some of his brothers arrived.

After a brief memorial service, the casket was placed aboard a private railroad car and we all made the journey North.

In Akron the casket was carried first through the silent Firestone plant and then to his home, Harbel Manor. Thousands of mourners—executives, workers, citizens of Akron—filed past, paying their last respects. The next day, we took him to his final resting place in Columbiana, Ohio, near the farm where he had been born and spent his childhood.

Chapter

FOUR

DURING MY JOURNEY with Charles Haines through the Midwest, I had a brief encounter with Henry Ford in the spring of 1937. I had not seen him since my departure from the Firestone Company one year earlier, but at that time he had sent me a Bible in which he had underlined a favorite verse which we had often discussed: "Now faith is the substance of things hoped for, the evidence of things not seen." —Heb. 11:1

I met him at a lawn party at the home of a mutual friend. As I came up to him, he said, "Jimmie, how are you? Mr. Firestone told me about your leave of absence."

"I'm fine, Mr. Ford. Yes, I had to get away from the treadmill and figure some things out for myself—some of the deeper things of life."

He stood looking at me out of his piercing blue eyes. Then he nodded.

I said, "I'm grateful for my years with the company. I

don't know what lies ahead. I just feel I have to be available to work with others to do what the Almighty wants done in the world."

Ford stepped over to me and clasped my arms in his hands, something he'd never done before. We looked deep into each other's eyes and I felt for the first time as if I was looking straight into the man's soul. He nodded again and said with great conviction, "Jimmie, you did the right thing."

Early in 1938, at the Firestone funeral, I decided to get in touch with Henry Ford. I phoned him in Ways, Georgia (now named Richmond Hill), and he asked me to come right down. There, in Ways, just north of the Florida border, he had purchased many thousand acres for an experimental plantation and a winter retreat. After Edison's death in 1931 the Fords never returned to their Fort Myers home. Perhaps Mr. Ford felt he could not face the memories.

As I stepped off the train that morning at the little station, the familiar solitary figure stood awaiting me. Ford greeted me warmly and showed me to his car, where his driver was waiting. When we reached the fence at the edge of the plantation, he stopped the car.

"Come over here, Jim. I want to show you something." He slid back three crossbars in the high fence and showed me how he could drive through the gap. "This is a shortcut, which I can take to the house instead of driving all the way around." Then he grinned, "And I can slip through here away from the press and people who try to stop me as I go through the front gate. I have other ones like this around the estate."

It didn't surprise me. Ford had always been a private person, just as determinedly as he was a maverick, going his own way.

We spent the entire day together, walking and talking. He showed me a different face from the one I was used to.

The death of Harvey Firestone had hit him hard, and he needed to talk to someone who felt the same loss.

"How old was he?" he asked.

"Sixty-nine."

"He was too young to die, too young." Ford was then seventy-five. He went on to ask about every detail of the funeral, and how each member of the Firestone family had faced and was handling the loss.

"He was a fine man," said Ford. "During all those years we did business, I knew I could trust his word all the way. And I think he felt he could trust mine."

We stopped by some tree stumps and Ford sat on one of them, pulled out a pocket knife, broke off a branch, and started to whittle—a habit of his I'd seen many a time in Fort Myers.

"Firestone and I went through many of the same experiences," he said. They had fought many of the same battles. Firestone wasn't afraid to close down a plant when he felt a new tire was urgently called for—like the time the V-8 engine became a sudden challenge to his tires. And neither was Ford, though switching from one auto to another was a big job. It took him longer to decide, longer to change over.

He talked about abandoning the Model T in 1927, largely because of Chevrolet competition. "Maybe I should have done it sooner," he said. After nearly a year he surprised the world with his Model A. At the thought, a smile brightened his somber expression.

"I fooled people with the Model A, and five years later I really made them sit up with the V-8. The experts said it couldn't be done. Cadillac had tried it in 1925, but it hadn't been a success. But I knew the eight-cylinder engine block would be better balanced, if we could just cast it in one piece. I had some fun with you and your boss over that—remember?"

I remembered well. It had been in early 1932, when I was with Firestone at his winter home in Miami Beach. Ford had called him from Fort Myers to say that he had driven down from Dearborn. He knew I was planning to visit my parents in Fort Myers that weekend, and asked whether I could bring along a certain reporter who had asked him for an interview on Ford's philosophy of life.

When the man and I arrived at Ford's home, I noticed that there were two Model A cars in the driveway. Ford said he had driven one of them from Detroit, and his assistant, Frank Campsall, had driven the other.

The interview had begun with Ford and Campsall standing; the reporter sat on a running board, taking notes. I sat there with him while Ford expounded his personal philosophy:

"A business ought not to drift. It ought to march ahead under leadership. The easy way is to follow the crowd and hope to make money. But that's not the way of sound business. The way is to provide a service. Try to run a business solely to make money and the business will die.

"The rock on which business breaks is debt. It owes a divided allegiance—to the public and to the financier.

"Profit is essential to business vitality. But a business that charges too high a profit disappears about as quickly as one that operates at a loss."

And so on.

When the interview was over, the reporter expressed his thanks and left for the bus depot. As soon as he was gone, Ford turned to Campsall and said, "Should we show Jimmie what he's been sitting on?" I got up and Frank opened up the hood of the Model A. There it was—the new V-8!

Ford had wanted to test the engine himself: that was why he had insisted on driving the car from Detroit. He explained they had used the two cars so that if the V-8 engine broke down, they would not have had to take it to a garage

100

and "spill the beans." They would just hitch it up to the standard Model A and tow it.

The reporter had probably had the biggest scoop of his career within arm's reach, but Ford had kept the news secret, no doubt because he wanted a dramatic occasion to make the announcement. And I had the fun of seeing what the world would see a month or two later.

As he whittled away sitting on the tree stump, Ford started talking again about the Firestone funeral. "You said some of his workers were crying as they walked past the casket. I wonder whether any of mine will do that at my funeral. Probably not. Bigness and the unions have broken up the closeness there was between boss and worker. Maybe Firestone coped with it better than I have, though I know he was hurt by them, too. Even without unions it's hard to have personal contact with the men any more. The plants have grown so big."

I had seen Ford making the rounds of the small satellite plants around the area, talking with the older workers, whom he seemed to know from simpler days, although it was the assembly lines which had made him famous in the eyes of the world.

He whittled in silence for a while, then looked across at me. "You know, Jimmie, it's a strange thing. I was the one, back in 1914, who doubled the workers' wages to five dollars a day. It upset most of my colleagues, and the bankers." People talked a lot of nonsense about his coddling the workers. He did it for a very simple reason. Of course the higher wage drew a more productive worker. But that wasn't the real reason. The fact was, it was no good mass-producing a cheap automobile if there weren't masses of workers and farmers who could afford to buy it.

Twenty years ago there was a big gap between the wealthy and the poor. Big industry had to follow his lead, and look how the life of millions had improved. The Communists and Socialists don't want to face that. He gave the working man an incentive to work hard. And he made it possible for industries like theirs to grow.

He was whittling again, and his knife seemed to throw off not only wood shavings, but his familiar old-fashioned truths:

"Some people thought I took a big risk when I started paying that high wage. But I felt the money the company was making wasn't mine. It was meant to be shared with those who created it. That's sound philosophy.

"The purpose of money is to provide more opportunity to perform more service. Short-sighted businessmen think first of money, but service is what really makes or breaks a business; without it, customers soon go elsewhere.

"True happiness comes from the realization of accomplishment."

He got up, and we started to walk again. "Firestone and Mr. Edison and I used to talk about these things, as you remember—when we weren't cracking jokes, or worrying about the supply of rubber, or something."

"Yes," I added, "Mr. Edison's first concern wasn't in making money. What really interested him was inventing things the world needed."

"He wasn't afraid of getting into something new, that's for sure," Ford agreed. "He was unique. Most people were turning out the same old stuff. Or just trying to improve it a little. He changed the world completely.

"Yes, Jimmie, the old world's gone, and it's not coming back. I suppose we should be glad of that. But, as I get older, I miss some of the old ways."

His spare frame was striding out now, and I had to stretch my muscles to keep up. After a while I said, "You haven't slowed down much, Mr. Ford."

"Jimmie, I just walk now—no more running." My mind went back to the first time I'd seen him run. Late one evening I was driving him home from downtown Fort Myers.

As we reached the edge of the business district in my Ford roadster—no Packard for him—he said, "Jimmie, will you let me out? I want to run." He started off down lonely McGregor Boulevard in his suit and ran the mile to his house. I stayed about a block behind him, so my headlights wouldn't disturb him. He jogged all the way and waved good-night to me as he went in his gate.

And then there was the square dancing. Back in the Fort Myers days, Mr. and Mrs. Ford had surprised me with their expertise. One particular evening when I dropped in on them, Mrs. Ford decided she would teach me to dance.

Ford got up, put a record on the phonograph—an Edison phonograph—and wound it up. He did the calling and she showed me the steps very patiently. A-one, two, three, this way and that. We went on for an hour or two. Mr. Ford turned out to be a real square-dance buff. He did his best to revive it as a national pastime. He even started a national contest for fiddlers and put up prize money. I guess it was part of his nostalgia for the past, or maybe an attempt to encourage wholesome social activities.

My heart went out to him now as I walked beside this energetic old man. What an enormous responsibility rested on those slight shoulders. His empire was made up of sixty American, nine Canadian, and twenty overseas manufacturing branches; vast experimental farmlands in Michigan and Georgia; hundreds of thousands of acres of timberlands in Michigan and Kentucky; a fleet of Great Lakes steamers, an entire railroad, sixteen coal mines, a glassworks—and on and on. And of course his River Rouge plant, that extraordinary complex where all the raw materials came together and automobiles rolled out the doors—an industrial wonder.

Yet, the genius of Henry Ford was his ability to cut through complicated problems. He said to me one day in Florida, "Jimmie, I feel that life is an obstacle course, and what we're here for is experience. That's what's going to count in the end." The direct approach. He and Firestone shared an ability to "cut through the cackle and get to the corn."

Thomas Edison's son Charles told me a couple of stories about Ford's way of doing this in the early days. He had been at the River Rouge plant one day with Ford, whose concern at that moment was the fenders on a current model of automobile. He thought they needed to be changed. A week or so earlier, Ford had instructed his engineering department to make the alteration. A few days later he was told they hadn't been able to work it out. Days later still, the same story.

The following day, when the younger Edison was there, Ford showed up at the plant unannounced. He went directly to the section where several huge stamping machines were still pressing out the old fenders, ordered the machines stopped, called over two of the biggest mechanics and asked them to remove the molds and put them on the floor. "Get your sledgehammers and break each one of them," he said. And then he walked out.

Two days later, the new fenders were in production.

Charles also told me about the time there was an electric power emergency at one of Ford's plants. There was not enough time for the power company to put up poles and string their cables, so Ford ordered his men to string company powerlines along telephone company poles. Do it, he said. We'll settle with the phone company later.

Despite Ford's contempt for men who made money their main motive, he had a nose for finance. He would say things like: "If money is your only hope for independence, you will never have it." Or: "It's our first duty to do the right thing, and this will earn us the right money." But he was savvy in money matters. He had outfoxed Wall Street and kept his company from being taken over by big bank creditors during the serious 1920–1921 recession.

He was producing a great many cars even at that time.

Demand was down, and he had dangerously high financial obligations. He saved himself and the company by shipping his cars with the bill of lading and sight draft attached. The dealers had to pay for them on receipt or they lost their dealerships. This was serious business in a small town, where having the Ford dealership gave a person considerable financial and social status in the community.

Most dealers had to borrow from their local banks to pay for the cars. In the end it was the small banks that were providing the cash to pay off the big ones. In this way, Ford was able to wrest control from his eastern creditors and was never again without large reserves of cash. I remember, once many years later, when I asked a bank president in Jacksonville, Florida if he had any Ford money on deposit. "Yes," he said. "We have a couple of million dollars." "I bet you're happy with that," I said. He replied, "Not too happy—it's on a one-day withdrawal, so I can't really put it to work." Ford had money stashed away like that in banks all over the country. While driving with Edison one day, he told me that Ford had $326 million on deposit in banks.

As the day went on—walking, whittling, sitting, talking, thinking—Henry Ford's mood lightened.

As we sat down to a luncheon presided over by the every-motherly Clara Ford, he leaned over me and asked to look at my glasses. I handed them to him and he examined them carefully, then handed them back with a mischievous grin.

"They must have cost you plenty, Jim!" He reached into a pocket and pulled out a slightly battered pair of wire-rimmed spectacles. "I picked out this pair at a store. Nothing fancy. Just plain magnifying glasses. Does the job fine."

A billionaire with an incorrigible habit of thrift!

The time finally came for me to head for the train station, and he said, "Jimmie, we've talked about almost everything except what you're doing." I told him, as I'd told Firestone, about my new work—the efforts by me and my friends to create teamwork in industry and to apply moral convictions in public and private life, instead of just depending on our material strength.

He listened with interest. "As I told you before, Jimmie, you did the right thing. It's good, your work. I'm sure it wasn't easy to leave Firestone. People may remember Mr. Firestone because he put the farms on rubber tractor tires instead of those steel lugs. Or because he did away with those phony patents that were controlling the use of the demountable rim. Or just because he built a great tire company. But you and I can be grateful for him as a man who encouraged the best in a lot of people."

As I traveled home on the train, I thought about my friendship with the three men. My relationship with Henry Ford had been very different from those with Thomas Edison or Harvey Firestone. Edison, when I knew him, was an older man with leisure time. I was a young fellow, a listener, a helper, more like a grandson. Firestone had been my employer, often a hard driver, and I had been his right hand, a loyal employee available during long working hours, ready to take on sudden emergencies. But I had been a listener with him, too—and off-duty something of a son. Ford was, despite his years, still ruling an industrial empire. My times with him were far less frequent, and I was in no way involved in his enterprises. Perhaps my common link with all three was that I had a good pair of listening ears and a sympathetic spirit. And no ax to grind.

*　　　*　　　*

During the next few years, from 1938 through 1942, before I joined the Army, I traveled widely in the United States and in Europe. From time to time I was able to get to Detroit and would call Mr. Ford—he had given me his closely guarded private number—and I'd go out to Dearborn. We talked as we drove, or walked through one of his plants. Two encounters were different from the rest.

106

In January 1940, one of my colleagues, Kenaston Twitch-ell, and I were invited by Ford to stay for several days at the Dearborn Inn. This was during the "phony war," before the devastating blitzkrieg of the Nazi forces across Europe and the furious air battles over Britain. Henry Ford was chafing to do something to promote peace. In 1915, during World War I, he had conceived the idea of a Peace Ship that would sail from America to Europe to intervene in the hostilities and persuade the warring states to end the fight-ing and "get the boys out of the trenches by Christmas." The effort had failed.

In the midst of our talk with him, Ford startled us by saying, "I have an idea how the hostilities might be stopped before they escalate. Of course, the key to it is Hitler. I think it's possible he might listen to my suggestions."

We must have shown our astonishment.

"It's not just a wild idea out of the blue. You know, he's following my example of producing a car for the millions. He got his engineers to come up with a cheap 'people's car'— Volkswagen. I think I just may have his respect, the door may be open. Now, I think you two men are just the people to take him a message from me. You have experience of peaceful mediation work."

Ken and I just sat and stared. He must have taken our silence for encouragement, because he went on to outline his plan seriously. "Of course, I'll finance the whole thing. I know it won't be easy, but we'll find a way to get you in there."

His plan was to get across to Hitler the conviction that Germany was leading the world into a global war and, in such a conflict, that he and everyone else would suffer. Ken, a Princeton man with more diplomatic skill than I, said, "That's a most interesting proposal, Mr. Ford. It's one we'll need to think over very carefully." Then we moved on to other matters.

The idea was never raised again, neither by him nor by us. Despite his genius in other fields, Ford was often naïve in politics and world affairs, though there were plenty of men in public life who underestimated Hitler's fanaticism. Even Winston Churchill was quoted in the *Times* of London at that time as saying, "I have always said that if Britain were defeated in war I hope we would find a Hitler to lead us back to our rightful place among the nations."

Ford's deeply held convictions about international peace-making seemed to spring from a genuine desire to create a better world. He hated to see suffering. In any case, Ken and I were agreed that if anyone should take Hitler on, Henry Ford himself would have to be the one.

The second unusual meeting with Ford was as different as it was down-to-earth. It took place six months later, in June 1940. The German military invasion of Western Europe had made spectacular progress. Paris had just fallen, and great pressure was being quietly exerted by the Roosevelt administration to step up war production, although as a nation the United States was claiming neutrality. Ford had been asked by the government to look into the assembly-line production of Rolls-Royce aircraft engines. He wished to do nothing to promote war by making offensive weapons, so he received the request with reluctance. While his people were highly skilled in manufacturing ground vehicles, airplanes were something else. He talked the matter over with Charles Sorensen, his production chief, his son Edsel, and others, and they all agreed that the best man to advise them was Charles Lindbergh, who, beyond his intrepid transatlantic flight, had proved himself a brilliant aero engineer with wide experience of aircraft capabilities.

Ford had first come to know Lindbergh after the historic flight, when Lindbergh brought *The Spirit of St. Louis* to Detroit and offered to take Ford up in it. Until then, Ford had resolutely refused to fly, even in the trimotor plane his company was manufacturing. But he accepted Lindbergh's invitation. After that, they put their heads together to develop air transportation, and their consultations led to the formation of an airline that later became TWA. For a while Ford had been excited about manufacturing an air equivalent of the Model T—a "flying flivver" for the family. But when his favorite test pilot, Harold Brooks, was killed on an experimental flight, Ford never took up the project again. It was an example of how his humanity could irrationally control his business policies.

When Ford decided to secure Lindbergh's help on the Rolls-Royce engine, he asked me to phone Lindbergh, since Lindbergh and I had become close friends. Lindbergh was already in the Midwest. He readily agreed to come to Detroit, where he stayed with his mother, a chemistry teacher at Cass Technical High School. I picked him up next morning and drove him out to Fair Lane for breakfast. Then Ford took us by car on a tour through some of the satellite plants around River Rouge. After lunch, we were joined at a meeting by Charles Sorensen and Edsel Ford. We looked over the parts of the Rolls-Royce engine. Sorensen was the genius who had been with Ford since 1904 and had masterminded the technical details for manufacturing the Model T and every successive car.

In the conference room we were met by Alvin Macauley, president of the Packard Motor Car Company, to whom Ford intended to give the Rolls-Royce project. Ford called on Sorensen to outline his plans for mass production. Sorensen did so energetically and brilliantly, explaining how the construction of the Rolls engine could be simplified without loss of quality.

Then Lindbergh was asked for his comments. Very quietly he said he thought it would be wise to obtain the advice of an expert on the performance of German fighter planes, since any American plane would have to be at least their equal in capabilities. He went on to say that he had been talking to a French flyer, Captain Michel Détroyat, who had that information. Détroyat was in Washington, but about to return to France.

Détroyat had come to the rescue of Lindbergh the night he had landed in Paris and been mobbed by the crowds. He and a few other French officers had slapped Lindbergh's helmet on the head of another young man and so diverted people long enough for him to get away. Lindbergh reached Détroyat in Washington and persuaded him to come to Detroit for a meeting the next day.

The next morning, Détroyat gave Ford and his men precise information about the combat capabilities of German aircraft. It was clear from what he said that the Rolls engine was only half as powerful as those the Germans already had. That settled the matter for Ford. After the United States got into the war, Ford sent Sorensen to Hartford to study Pratt and Whitney engines, and these ended up being the power plant of the Ford mass-produced Liberator bomber.

This meeting between Lindbergh and Ford was followed by another in which I took part after Pearl Harbor. As soon as America declared war, Ford plunged into the work of creating "the arsenal of democracy." The bomber was one of his most important projects, and again he asked Lindbergh to meet with him.

Lindbergh, too, had immediately abandoned his campaign to keep America neutral and set out to offer his services to his country. He ran into opposition from President Roosevelt, who resented Lindbergh's earlier antiwar activities. When Lindbergh applied for active duty in the Air Corps, Roosevelt intervened. The president also sabotaged a major aviation company's attempt to hire him as a consultant.

In March 1942, Lindbergh and I went to Detroit at Ford's request. Together with a number of Ford's men, Sorensen and Harry Bennett among them, we went out to the giant factory at Willow Run, in a farm area thirty miles west of Dearborn; it was there Ford was to produce the Liberator bomber. On the way back in the car, Ford asked Lindbergh if he would help them as a consultant in their aviation program. Lindbergh answered that he would like to help, but perhaps it would be advisable to talk to the White House first.

Ford leaned back over the front seat of the car, looked hard at him and said, "You have not answered my question, Colonel."

Lindbergh repeated that he wanted to help. That settled the matter, as far as Henry Ford was concerned. Ford was not on cordial terms with the White House and had too much clout for Roosevelt to interfere again.

Our visit to Willow Run gave me a further insight into Ford's complex character. It was there I met Harry Bennett.

Over the years Bennett performed thousands of difficult chores for his chief. A former prizefighter who packed a gun and seemed to understand the ways of the street, Bennett was utterly loyal. Whatever Mr. Ford wanted, Mr. Ford got. Ford counted on this complete loyalty and seemed to prefer not to know the details. His attitude was: "Don't bring me the labor pains, just the baby."

In the early years of growing conflict with the unions, Bennett's responsibility was to know everything that was going on in the plants. When I asked Bennett why relations between the company and the union were so much tougher at Ford than ours had been at Firestone, he gave me two reasons. First, they had to guard against industrial espionage by the other auto companies. "I never allow my men to write anything down. I make them memorize names, numbers, everything. Then, if they are kidnapped or arrested, they have no notes on them."

Second, according to Bennett, Mr. Ford was concerned

111

about designs the underworld might have on him, his family, or his industrial empire. Although Ford never said so, I assume he felt that Bennett understood how criminals operated and could deal with them. He simply slept better at night with Bennett around.

Henry Ford has been critized for allowing Bennett such a free hand. I never asked Ford why he had employed the man, but I believe it had a lot to do with his unwillingness to deal directly with human unpleasantness.

*   *   *

I saw Ford a number of times before I went into the Army in 1942. On one occasion I was astonished, on arriving at the train station in Detroit, to find Mr. Ford there to greet me and drive with me to Fair Lane for breakfast.

On another visit he invited me to lunch in the executive dining room. One of the executives came over to our table and gave him a package. He opened it, smiled, and passed it around. It was the original contract between him and the Detroit Automobile Company, which he had founded in 1899 together with some local businessmen. The relationship did not work out, and Ford was replaced by Henry Leland, who reorganized the company under the Cadillac name. Later it became a part of General Motors. As I remember, the contract showed that this man, now a billionaire, had originally been paid one hundred dollars a week. There was plenty of laughter as it was passed around. A top official at General Motors had unearthed the document in the archives. Ford appreciated this gesture from a competitor.

On my visits, I would sometimes meet with him at Fair Lane. It nestled in a clump of trees in the midst of a thousand acres of open land bordering the River Rouge. The house was not ostentatious, but it was much larger than the plain clapboard Florida home where I had first met him. Just as on his Georgia estate, Ford would set off on his bi-

My "big day," the official opening of Edison Park, April 7, 1926, with Thomas and Mina Edison before the entrance statue.

All things come to him who hustles while he waits

...my young friend ... ue Newton

Thos A Edison

The photo Edison autographed for me in 1927.

Mina Edison, as I first knew her in 1925.

Mrs. Edison enjoyed fishing.

Henry Ford and Thomas Edison on a dock at Fort Myers.
Sometimes they sat and talked, and sometimes they just sat.

On their last visit together, in 1931, Ford (left), Edison (center),
and Firestone (right) pose for an official photograph.

Sometimes Edison baited
his hook, and sometimes
he left it unbaited and
enjoyed the quiet to think.

A cavalcade of cars
followed Edison and
Herbert Hoover when the
president-elect visited Fort
Myers on Edison's eighty-
second birthday, February
11, 1928.

I lead Mr. Firestone to join the Edisons on Edison's eighty-second birthday.

I hand Mr. Edison a written question during his annual press conference, February 1928. Pathé News microphone stands in the lily pond.

Edison (center) leads Harvey Firestone (right) to his Fort Myers laboratory to show him the results of his rubber experiments, 1928. I am behind Mr. Edison.

The Edisons relax before a press interview on his eighty-first birthday.

Edison presses a telegraph key to open the most northerly power plant in the United States, as I watch behind the screen.

Ford (left) and Firestone (right) look over Edison's shoulder as he checks out an experiment.

Left (l. to r.): Harvey Firestone, Thomas Edison, and his secretary, Freddie Ott.
Below, left: Ford, Edison, and Firestone laugh at each other's jokes, March 1931. I snapped this photo as Edison delivered his punch line.
Below, right: At their last meeting, 1931: (seated) Ford, Edison, and Firestone; (standing) Frank Campsall (Ford's secretary), Freddie Ott, Roger Firestone, and me.
Bottom: "I made this tire from your rubber for your Model T," says Firestone (right) to Edison (center).

Left: Corporate Man at ease.
Below: Bud Firestone was
one of my closest friends. At
Firestone's winter office,
Miami Beach.

Above: Mr. Firestone relaxed
and laughed on our train journeys.
Right (l. to r.): Harvey
Firestone, Jr., Harvey, Sr., and
"Bud" (Russell) Firestone in Texas.

With the Fords at their Fort Myers home during their last winter there in 1931.

Above: Sometimes Ford sat and whittled. Sometimes he just sat and did his thinking.

Left: An early meeting with Henry Ford. Behind us is Edison's Fort Myers laboratory, which Ford moved to Greenfield Village.

cycle or on foot first thing in the morning for exercise and to clear his mind for the business of the day.

But our most frequent meeting place was the Martha and Mary Chapel (named for his and Clara's mothers) in Green-field Village. I would find him in the balcony, attending the eight o'clock service. Below him were the children of Ford employees from the McGuffey-type school he had started. (The *McGuffey Reader*, of which more than 100 million copies were in use in schools around the turn of the century, em-phasized teaching of the "three Rs," along with moral and patriotic values.) This time of worship and watching the children meant much to him. When I telephoned to say I was in town, Ford would usually say, "meet me at the chapel." He would often revise his day's schedule so that we could spend time together.

I particularly remember one morning in the chapel. The children below us were singing their last verse, when Ford turned to me and said, "Aren't they wonderful? They're what life is all about. Their future—that's why I have to turn out those tanks and planes. Sometimes over there at the plant I look at those weapons rolling out and I think we've gone plumb crazy, killing each other off like this. Then I come here and watch these youngsters and I know it's worth-while. We've got to win this war, so they can grow up in a free world."

We think of Ford today as a giant industrialist, but like his friend, Thomas Edison, he was also concerned about man's stewardship of the Earth's resources, especially met-als. He'd say to me, "Jimmie, I've been making progress with those soybeans." And he'd chuckle. "My men can make a really strong steering wheel out of soybeans, you know. Be-fore I'm through, we'll build an entire automobile out of them—think how much metal that'll save!" Unfortunately he didn't live long enough to accomplish that dream.

*　　　*　　　*

One moment stands out in my mind from my visits to Fair Lane.

"People often talk about business as if it was lower than other human activities," Ford said to me. "If a plant is producing something worthwhile, it's just as sacred as a home." He said he'd tried to make what the world needed, to anticipate the future. And of the future he said, "It'll be different from the past. We ought to think of our country as a servant of mankind. A trustworthy, righteous nation, whose joy is to help all people toward peace and progress."

He was standing as he said this, his spare body leaning into the wind, gray hair blowing, sharp jaw clenched. Faith in the future and a respect for the past; these seemed to sum Ford up best. "Except for idealists there would have been no United States," he said to me once.

The next time I saw him was when I was on an Army leave; Ford had put his son Edsel—his only child—in charge of the whole Ford organization. Sadly, disagreements developed between the older and younger Fords. Henry and Clara were extremely strict in their social life, and they disapproved of the company kept by Edsel and his wife. The younger couple had friends in Grosse Pointe with whom they enjoyed cocktail parties and dinners. Edsel was very disciplined in his drinking, but to his parents his "fast social life" was abhorrent.

Edsel's unselfish nature was a tribute to his upbringing. At the same time, it was often difficult for him to live under the shadow of such a father. The stress may have contributed to his untimely death of stomach cancer in the summer of 1943. It was a terrible blow to Mr. and Mrs. Ford. My military duties prevented me from going to see them, but Ellie, my bride of five months, and I telephoned and wrote to them.

Mrs. Ford replied in a characteristic letter:

We have received your several messages, with consolation and much help, after such a shock and grief that has been given to bear. The reason that it has been so hard is that we did think, until a few days before Edsel went, that he was going to get well, but the undulent fever was so severe, he lost so much strength and weight, he could not get over it. His face did not show his nearness to death, and he was making plans to take a boat trip with his wife. We have none of us quite been able to give him up, but time will help. We have come up here to our cabin with Lake Superior in front and pine woods up to our back door, where a mother deer comes, and sometimes brings two babies. She eats from our hands. . . .

Henry Ford, now eighty, immediately stepped back in and picked up the company's reins. Soon afterward, his grandson, Henry II, was released from the Navy to help carry the load.

While I was with the Army in the Philippines, I heard that Ford was in poor health. Shortly after my return to the States at war's end, Ellie and I tried to reach him by phone at his home in Georgia. A few days later, at the end of February 1946, we received another characteristic letter from Mrs. Ford:

I was *so* sorry we did not know you called a few nights ago until the next morning. There was no one in the back of the house where the telephone is, but the cook, and why she did not tell us, I can't understand, as we were there, and quite alone. She said she had not heard your name before and thought it was a stranger.

This morning the little souvenir from the Philippines came. Thank you very much for it, and for thinking of us, and even if it is late, I want to congratulate you for your rank of Major. You must have had a wonderful experience, both in the work you were doing and the countries and sights you have seen. You also had hardships, I am sure, and hope you came through without a scratch. . . .

Last year of the war was very hard, trying to turn out the bomber and airplane the best possible, and to contend with government officials who were not mechanical, and strikes, and not enough rest. A younger man could not have stood it and he was 82.

The war is over, but what a turmoil the world is in. We will be here as long as we can, and if we are still here when you come through, we would be glad to see you. We came January 21st and have had such a nice, quiet time.

Friendship with Mrs. Ford meant a great deal to Ellie and me. Few great men have been blessed with a more devoted wife. Through the years of struggle, success, and fame, she remained the same sprightly, warm, responsive little lady. She was not involved in her husband's business world, but she did share his social interests—square dancing, the school for his employees, Greenfield Village, and his fascination with the past.

For our wedding they gave us an antique silver skewer. Accompanying it was a handwritten note from her:

In case you do not know the history of this skewer, the English in the early days used them to hold together the huge roast they used at that time. Then they went out of style, perhaps because they did not eat so much beef. Since then they have been used for paper cutters. I use one every day to open letters.

After the war was over, I spent a day with Ford at River Rouge. He was an aged man. The years of coping with the urgency of armaments production, the red tape of bureau-

116

crats, the sudden changes of priorities, and not least the ignorance of engineering among some military officers—all these had drained him. But his welcome to me was as spontaneous as ever, and his concern for my affairs just as thoughtful.

He asked me if there was anything he could do for me. I mentioned that I was having a problem getting a car from my Ford dealer in Florida as there was a long waiting list. He asked what model car I was looking for—what color, two- or four-door, and so on. When I left that afternoon he said, "There's a car waiting for you at the end of the assembly line." It was exactly the kind I had described to him.

"Now that the fighting's over, your real work lies ahead," he said to me. "While the war was on, most Americans pulled together to get the job done. Now we have the free world we were fighting for. But it could become every man for himself. We need universal training in teamwork. That's what you and your friends in the Oxford Group must give."

I saw him only a few more times. Just over one year later in early April 1947, Ellie and I were at Mackinac Island in northern Michigan when we heard the news that Henry Ford had died. We immediately drove the three hundred miles down to Dearborn. We drove up the long lane to the house, where Mrs. Ford greeted us affectionately, and with a graciousness that touched us deeply.

She talked about her husband's passing the night before. "Henry was bending over to untie his shoelaces and just keeled over. He was gone." Later in the evening she told us that that day there'd been a power failure and Fair Lane was blacked out. They'd had to use candles all over the house. I thought then, as others soon noted, that this great man, who had entered the world eighty-four years earlier by candlelight, had left it the same way.

Mrs. Ford did not dwell on his passing. She wanted to

know how we were and asked about our mutual friends and my parents in Fort Myers. Despite her personal grief, there was no self-pity.

Henry Ford's automobiles had transformed communities, work patterns, life styles. His empire had reached out to alter forever the economic life of nations. Yet, with it all, he remained an unspoiled, vulnerable man.

He said to me more than once, "Jimmie, I would not have made it without Clara." It was easy to see why. Her courage supported him when the blows came. Her faith in God and in him renewed his own faith when problems loomed too large. They remained to the end a united, dedicated couple in a world where many of the marriages of the wealthy and famous were falling apart.

Chapter

FIVE

IN THE AUTUMN OF 1936, after I had begun to catch my breath following my departure from the Firestone Company, I came to know a man who had as profound an effect on my life as Thomas Edison, Henry Ford, or Harvey Firestone.

He was Alexis Carrel, a French surgeon who lived in America and who had been awarded the Nobel Prize in 1912 for his work on the suturing of blood vessels and the transplantation of organs. He was also credited with the development of cell and tissue culture. During World War I, Carrel pioneered the successful treatment of infected war wounds. His popularity as a scientist was great, and he was frequently quoted in the press. In 1935 Carrel published *Man the Unknown,* an international best seller about man and his environment. This book made a big impression on me, and it also sparked the attention of Ed Moore, a businessman engaged in financing natural gas enterprises.

Here was a distinguished scientist who was reaching out

to explore the fundamental nature of man and his place in the universe. Moore responded to Carrel's ideas, and he wrote to ask if he might meet him. Carrel invited him to his office at the Rockefeller Institute for Medical Research. Moore told me about their first encounter:

"I said to Dr. Carrel, 'Before I leave, would you glance at my notebook and see whether I think somewhat as you do?' He quietly turned a few pages and noticed some definitions, including the word, *God.* I'd forgotten what I'd written, when he pointed his finger at me and said, 'Mr. Moore, what is your idea of God?' I looked directly at him and said, 'The creative force that permeates everything in the universe.' Carrel said, 'Mr. Moore, that's right. Will you have dinner with me at my club next Monday evening?' "

Shortly after that, in January 1937, Moore said he wanted me to meet Dr. Carrel. "I think you and he are on the same wavelength." Carrel responded to the suggestion and invited the two of us to lunch in the dining room of the Rockefeller Institute. So began my friendship with a fascinating character, different from anyone I have ever known.

To a young American like me, Dr. Carrel, sitting across the table, was the very picture of a Frenchman. He was solidly built, dapper, in his early sixties. His movements were quick; he waved his hands as he spoke, and he talked quickly. His eyes gleamed behind pince-nez glasses and twinkled with humor. They were a soft brown. He had a high, broad forehead, thin nose, wide generous mouth, and a square cleft chin. His head was nearly bald, except for a tuft of closely cut hair on top. He gave the impression of a man brimming with energy.

Ed Moore gave him a rather flowery description of my career with Firestone and went on to say that I'd given that up to seek something deeper and more rewarding.

"And have you found it, Mr. Newton?"

I told him that, much as I loved business and had been

comfortable with the demands of a big company, I felt that the world today needed a moral and spiritual counterbalance to materialism, especially if we were to prevent a disastrous war. I was trying, with other friends, in whatever ways I could, to wake up America.

"Remarkable. And how old are you?"

"Thirty-two."

"Half my age, and you've already learned a great truth."

"What is that, sir?"

"You understand that man does not live by bread alone. Nor does society. It needs equilibrium between material and spiritual nourishment."

It was an exhilarating opening to a relationship that grew over many meetings at the Institute, over meals at the Century Club and in his apartment on 89th Street, and later on his lonely island of Saint-Gildas. My conversations with Edison, Ford, and Firestone had been tremendously stimulating, but talking with this man was dizzying. I felt as if I were stepping into one of those express elevators. One moment we'd be discussing the likelihood of war in Europe, the next the dangers of specialization among scientists, and then suddenly on to telepathy or whom he looked forward to talking with in the afterlife.

Early in our acquaintance I said to him, "Dr. Carrel, when I talk to people about you, they often ask me just exactly what you do—I mean, your work at the Institute. Could you tell me in one-syllable words?"

He laughed. "I may have to use some two or three syllables now and then." When he worked as a young surgeon in France one big problem was that blood vessels could not be repaired or brought together without obstructing them. He worked on the problem and developed a method for suturing blood vessels which everyone now uses. He started using fine silk sutures which he placed in the walls of the vessels. He also designed some vascular instruments with which he could handle tissues without injuring them. Later, when he came to the Rockefeller Institute, he began to study cells and tissues, the basic structures of the body. He learned ways to make tissues and cells grow and how to change their rate of growth.

Carrel went on: "These experiments with cell and tissue culture gave us a great deal of information about how cells behave, what nutrients they need, what can kill them. We've also learned how, under some conditions, normal cells in culture can be changed into malignant ones." He believed that tissue culture work might be the beginning of understanding the nature of cancer.

Carrel's work had been interrupted by World War I. He went into the French army and spent the war near the front lines treating the wounded. Carrel said he witnessed the Great War firsthand: it was unnecessary, did not solve any problems, but produced many more. When he arrived in France the death rate of soldiers from infections of war wounds was appallingly high. He wanted to do something about it and after many frustrations was allowed to set up a military hospital in which he could devise methods for preventing and treating wound infections. This he did by leaving the wounds open, irrigating them with a mild antiseptic (Carrel-Dakin solution), and studying the bacteriology of the wounds. His treatment of infected wounds was very successful, and he received wide acclaim for devising it. When America entered the war, a War Demonstration Hospital was set up on the grounds of the Rockefeller Institute to teach the surgeons of the U.S. Army and the U.S. Navy his method of treating war wounds.

When he returned to New York from France after the war, he wanted to develop methods of studying isolated organs in the laboratory. He knew that since much was learned from studying tissue, much more could be learned from studying organs. Then he said that for a long time he was

124

prevented from doing this because there was no way to circulate blood or fluids artificially to keep an organ alive outside the body without its becoming infected. He needed a pump which would act like the heart and which would maintain the sterile environment around the organ. About ten years after Carrel resumed his laboratory studies, Charles Lindbergh joined him and designed a perfusion pump which did all that. This allowed him to do research on various intact living organs—thyroid glands, ovaries, and hearts and kidneys of animals.

My grandfather and father were doctors, so I'd grown up with an interest in medicine. I asked him what, exactly, this capability could mean for medicine.

"It means we are discovering the specific chemicals each organ needs for its growth and function. It could lead to building artificial parts for the body—even an artificial heart—and also to replacing organs for those that must be removed."

It all sounded most impressive to me, but it was not until many years later, with the development of the heart-lung bypass and the transplanting of organs, that I grasped the full significance of Carrel's pioneering.

I asked him to tell me more about his work together with Charles Lindbergh. They seemed an unlikely pair.

"How did you run across Lindbergh?" I asked.

"Oh, he ran across me," Carrel said. "He sought me out at the institute back in 1930." He said his wife's older sister Elisabeth had died of heart disease, and Charles had become very involved in that tragedy. When he learned that his sister-in-law had developed a defective heart valve as a complication of rheumatic fever, he asked her doctor why surgery wouldn't help. The doctor said there was no way the heart could be stopped long enough to permit an operation on it.

He told me that Lindbergh soon found that none of the

doctors he'd talked to had seriously thought about the construction of an artificial heart, until an anesthesiologist, attending Anne Morrow Lindbergh at the birth of their child, had told him about Carrel's research.

"Lindbergh came to see me at the Institute and I talked to him about organ perfusion and showed him the devices we were using. He said he would try to build a better pump, and so of course I warmly accepted his offer."

Like Thomas Edison, Lindbergh had then tried seemingly endless experiments. And like Edison, he kept trying until, five years later, he perfected the all-glass perfusion pump in which Carrel could keep organs alive and free of infection for his studies.

"So you might call it a marriage of his mechanical genius and my scientific research," said Carrel. "And the offspring was the beginning of—who knows what? The fountain of renewable, replaceable youth?"

But I'd read that Lindbergh had taken his family to live in England in 1935, when the invasion of their privacy had become too painful after the kidnapping and death of their first son. I wondered whether his leaving meant the end of this remarkable team.

"Oh, no," Carrel assured me. "He's putting his mind to building other things for our work together. He'll be back. Over these years we've become close friends as well as partners."

"Wasn't it amazing that he turned up just when you needed him!"

"Yes, but he needed me, too. I certainly benefited from his mechanical genius. And I could offer him the facilities he needed to do his work. But, beyond that, the atmosphere at the institute was just what he needed to protect him from the demands of the press and the public. Our staff here was very understanding and they guarded his privacy fiercely."

Carrel liked to shock me if I showed signs of falling away

from his line of intensive reasoning. He was off on one of his favorite topics one day—that man's mind operates not just through the brain, but with all the organs of the body—when he turned and said, "Do you realize, Jim, what a powerful influence your testicles exert on your mind?"

I'm sure I looked startled. Carrel had some definite ideas on sexuality, which I remembered from *Man the Unknown.*

"He said we know that the removal of the genital gland changes a person's mental state. All great artists and poets were great lovers. I don't mean they had one affair after another. Often the opposite. Do you think Dante would have written the *Divine Comedy* if Beatrice had ever been his mistress?"

I hadn't read much Dante.

"Well, the point is, she wasn't his mistress, and instead Dante expressed his sexual longings in literature. When love can't always attain its object, it seems to stimulate the mind."

He went on to develop his theme that mental activities depend on physiological activities. Human personality is modified by diseases of the liver, stomach, and intestines. The whole body is the cradle of man's mental and spiritual energies. He leaned forward in his chair and wagged a finger in front of my face. "Man thinks, loves, suffers, creates, prays with his brain—and all his organs."

"Does that mean we should concentrate more on our arms and legs and stomachs?"

"No, no. But look after them. If you think too much about them, they get disturbed. No, the point is to concentrate your attention on something beyond the self—then comes inner peace. Man integrates himself by meditation and by action. And most of all by bending all his energies in a moral and spiritual quest."

Carrel was a good many years ahead of the Zen and "Inner Game" philosophies that would surface decades later.

One day he allowed me to watch him perform an experiment at the Institute. I wore a black gown and mask just like Carrel's and those of his assistants. The walls and ceilings of the operating room were also black, so that nothing reflected the light coming in from the skylight. That day he was removing the minute organs from the fetus of a pig and placing them in the apparatus perfected by Lindbergh.

He told me later about his experiment with tissue taken from the heart of a baby chicken, which he had kept alive and growing inside a flask for many years—seemingly immortal. This had stirred continued interest from the newspapers, and he went on to discuss man's age-old quest for eternal youth and pointed out the danger of achieving longevity in quantity (senescence) instead of quality (youthfulness).

Lingering over the dinner table at the Century Club—as we often did—he expressed typically firm convictions about education: "Few people seem to recognize the supreme importance of education in early childhood, when growth is so fast and impressions leave a lasting mark. The waste of this period can never be compensated."

As for aging, he felt there should be no retirement. Inaction and leisure are more dangerous for the old than the young. The days of the elderly should be filled with mental and spiritual adventure.

People ask me to summarize what I found so stimulating in Dr. Carrel's converstions. It's a difficult question to answer, because when I put a label on it—philosophy, religion, science, faith—I narrow it down. Or if I say life, the nature of man, the universe, God—it's all too vague.

He was truly a universal man. His interests were all encompassing. He was also very enthusiastic about the topics he discussed, and his enthusiasm was infectious. It seemed there was nothing that would not interest him, but when something was on his mind he would try to analyze the matter, and if at all possible, would try to do so scientifically. This, at times, had produced some difficulties in the Institute, for if somebody interested Carrel in a topic such as parapsychology, he would attempt to design experiments to study it! His talk would swing through great regions of thought, one idea leading to another, all surprisingly connected in his mind.

He was telling me one evening about something he'd learned about bone marrow. What interested him was that the more he studied one part of the body—like the skeletal structure—the more he found intimate links to every other part. Bones don't just hold the body together. Through their marrow they manufacture leucocytes and red cells, so they became part of the circulatory system, the respiratory system, the nutritive system.

"I could take you all through the body and show you how marvelously complex it is in its structure, and yet how unified it is in its function."

"And it all goes on without our being in the least conscious of it."

"Exactly. There you are, scratching your ear. Do you have any idea how many millions of little pieces of you are getting together, sending along chemical messages and electrical impulses and muscular movements, to run from your brain to your fingertips?"

I was pondering that, but he leaped ahead. "The trouble is that we have lost sight of the oneness of life, not only within the body, but in the world at large. We've become so specialized—we give the mind to the educator, the body to the doctor, the priest takes the spirit—and they all ride off in different directions."

Modern life, he explained, would not be possible without specialization. The immense growth of knowledge had imposed it, and it had brought about marvelous results—better clothes, food, machines—all the things we'd come to depend on. But if specialization had been what created modern civilization, it could be what could destroy it.

His gentle brown eyes were flashing now. We'd become so overspecialized, he said, that we neglected most of our natural capacities. Man was not meant to be just a shoe salesman or a mail carrier or a physician. A week had 168 hours in it. Work absorbed 40 or more. Sleep, 56. That left more than 60 hours. What did most people do in that time? Eat, drink, drive a car, dance, play cards, look at absurd films, and listen to ever more absurd radio. (This was before television!)

What he meant was that these pastimes did little to help us overcome our specialized lives. The only way people can grow is to broaden our personalities—think, develop our character, our moral strength, aesthetic feeling, religious sense, power to love.

"So, character is the key to a full life?"

He agreed it was a very important part. But there were other, more significant questions, according to him. Man was so isolated from his environment that he'd come to think of himself as a self-sufficient, independent being. And look what a mess he was making of the resources of this planet, which he thought he could run just as he pleased. We'd forgotten that we are surrounded by scores of things that influence us, not only the chemical elements—air, water, soil—but also our social environment—our dwellings, schools, hospitals, churches. In this room, right now, he said, thousands of radio waves, talk and music, are floating through us. But so are ideas, and maybe their impact is as physical as that of cosmic rays. They come at us from books and radios, movies, conversations.

I looked around the room where we were sitting, a nook on the second floor of the Century Club and a favorite haunt of Carrel's. Secluded from the sounds of New York's traffic and little used by club members, it was a place where we could talk undisturbed. Our deep armchairs, drawn up facing the fireplace, the thick carpet and book-lined walls gave the room a reassuring atmosphere. Cosmic rays looked out of place here, I thought.

Carrel was leaning back, his stubby fingers tapping on the arm of his chair to emphasize the point he was making.

"Who knows what their effect is?" he said. "It's a subject that has never been systematically studied. But you can be sure that the flood of commercial and political and social and religious propaganda does shape us."

Carrel went on to develop what I came to understand as a central conviction of his philosophy: man needs to conform to the laws of nature, but must also seek ways to know the will of God. When I asked him to explain that more concretely, he said:

"Jim, we must find the balance between adapting, which leads to serenity of the spirit, and freedom, which involves liberating the spirit from the demands of the body. Adaptation lies beneath healing. As a surgeon I can bring the edges of a wound together, or the ends of a broken bone; then the cells of the body get to work to regenerate the tissue. Modern surgery and all medicine is really just learning how to work with the natural processes of the body."

The same holds true, he went on, in the sphere of the spirit, although modern man lags far behind in his study and understanding of it. Today, anything in the way of spiritual endeavor is regarded with great suspicion by most scientists and intellectuals. But the real obstacle to following that path is the strict discipline it requires. Just as an athlete has to go into physical training, someone who follows the road to the mystical and spiritual must accept a discipline of the physical appetites. Only then can his mind begin to escape from space and time and enter the realm of intuition and illumination.

*　　　　*　　　　*

131

Carrel had expressed many of these views in his book, *Man the Unknown*. He told me one day how he had come to write that best seller.

His friends kept pushing him to put these convictions on paper. But his work at the Institute took all of his attention, and he didn't want to be interrupted. However, an opportunity came when his laboratory had to be closed four months for repairs.

Later on, Mme. Carrel told me that the French publisher to whom Carrel submitted the manuscript had said that it was magnificent, but there weren't fifty people in France who would read it, and returned it to him. Carrel was discouraged and ready to put the manuscript away. When they returned to the United States, it was put into the hands of Harper's, who published it. Mme. Carrel told me with glee, "The book was published in nearly twenty languages, including French, and it sold thousands of copies in France!"

Man the Unknown made Alexis Carrel's name known far beyond the scientific circles that had honored him for his medical research. It also brought violent criticism from scientists who felt it was improper for a fellow scientist to write about matters beyond his specialized knowledge. They attacked Carrel's search into the mystical, spiritual, and extrasensory realms. To him, everything in the universe had seemed a subject fit for study. He had been extremely careful in reaching any conclusions, but he was impatient with those who refused to open their minds to exploration. "Audacity," Carrel used to say to me, "is one of man's most precious qualities. If he lacks that, he'll never amount to anything." And, indeed, his own life exemplified it—risking his surgeon's career in France to seek freedom of research; reaching into unorthodox fields; braving the untried and the unknown.

One evening Carrel got to talking about time. As a normal, corn-fed American, I had assumed there was just one kind of time—the one my watch told me. Not so, said Carrel, there are several kinds. There is solar time, which we measure by the hands of the clock, and it corresponds to the earth's rotation on its axis and around the sun. It is a convenient standard by which we measure duration, just as it is convenient to measure spatial dimensions by comparing them with the surface of the earth—a meter is the forty-millionth part of the meridian of the planet.

But there were other kinds of time. Did a dog, who lives for fourteen years, regard time the same as a man who lives for eighty? Or a mosquito who lives for a couple of days? And how about the day in the life of a young child, which may seem like an eternity compared to a day in the life of his grandfather, who feels the years hurrying by?

Inner, individual time is of two kinds—physiological and psychological. Physiological time is quite different from physical time. True, age is an organic and functional state. It has to be measured by the rhythm of the changes in this state, and that rhythm varies according to individuals and differs in different organs of the body. He told me that he had published an article on physiological time in *Science* in 1931.

I felt at bay in this conversation and interrupted: "So you mean that that kind of time is different for different individuals?"

"Not only that, but it varies with different parts of the body. Your heart may be relatively young and your liver relatively old."

Psychological time, he said, is another matter. Its nature, like that of memory, is unknown. Memory is responsible for our awareness of the passage of time; but it is composed of other elements. Personality is partly made up of recollections, but it also comes from the impression made on all our organs by every kind of event in our life. This estimation of time by our tissues may be responsible for the deep feelings

133

we have that are not identical with those of our childhood selves, and yet we and our former selves must be considered the same being.

Later, I was better equipped to follow Carrel's far-reaching ideas when he gave me copies of his unpublished articles.

Carrel told me about an experiment he had conducted at the Institute with the help of his wife. Mme. Carrel had the capacity to see things beyond the abilities of most people. One thing she could do was see light waves beyond the upper and lower scales visible to ordinary eyes—just as a dog hears sounds beyond the limits audible to human ears. Further, he said, she could detect an aura around the heads and hands of some people. She said the purer, more dedicated the person, the brighter the aura. So perhaps, I thought, there was a basis for the haloes of saints. Years later, Russian scientists reported that they had successfully photographed this phenomenon.

Carrel set out with typical thoroughness to test her abilities. "I put her in a cabin," he told me, "a light-proof cabin. Then my assistants released various light waves normally invisible to the human eye—infrared, ultraviolet, and so on, up and down the scale. Each release had its own number of cycles. She would describe how each color appeared.

"We went through the spectrum in order, and then picked colors one after another at random, out of order. Every time, 100 percent of the time, she would come up with the correct color, with which she had previously identified that wavelength. There was no way that could be attributed to luck. She just has this extrasensory ability."

After that, one evening at dinner in the Century Club, I ventured to tell Carrel about my one experience with ESP. I had spent a weekend at a retreat a few years before in Stockbridge, Massachusetts. While there, I'd reluctantly decided to follow what I believed was God's will, rather than

134

pursue my own desires. An hour or two later, as I was looking across the Berkshire Hills, the mountain ridge seemed
to light up and become transparent and I felt I was looking
through it to the next range of hills. Later, when I turned
to my Bible and began to read, passages stood out in illu-
minated letters, giving them an entirely new meaning to my
mind.

When I told Carrel about this, I added a little apologeti-
cally, "I know it sounds far out, but that's how it was."

"Jim, your experience — the way you tell it to me — is as real
as this table. I can touch it, feel it. It's as real as that — or
more real.

Carrel went on to tell about the physical effect of mystical
contemplation. "Prayer," he said, "is not only worship, it is
the most powerful form of energy that one can generate.
The influence of prayer on the human body and mind is as
demonstrable as that of secreting glands. Its results can be
measured in terms of physical buoyancy, greater intellectual
vigor, moral stamina, and deeper understanding of the
realities underlying human relationships."

I was fascinated. I'd regarded clergymen as the experts
on prayer. But here was a distinguished scientist who seemed
to be crediting prayer with medical benefits and a great deal
more.

In an article for *Reader's Digest* he wrote that prayer was
a force as real as terrestrial gravity. As a physician, he'd
seen a man, after all other therapy had failed, lifted out of
disease by the serene effects of prayer. In fact, it was the
only power in the world that seemed to overcome the so-
called "laws of nature." When it does that, we call the event
"a miracle." But a stream of quieter miracles takes place in
men and women who have discovered that prayer supplies
them with a steady, sustaining power in their lives.

I asked Carrel if he believed in miracles.

He described his first encounter with a miracle, when he

accompanied a group of pilgrims to Lourdes in 1903. Among them was a young woman, Marie Bailly, whom he examined along with the others on the way, carefully recording her case history and her symptoms of rapidly approaching death from what they thought was tuberculous peritonitis. She was so ill that some were hesitant to carry her to the sacred spring on a stretcher. Carrel said he went to the spring and watched as water was sprinkled on her—she was too weak to be lifted into the pool. To his amazement, the woman's condition changed before his eyes.

"I saw the blanket subside, her distended belly contract. I immediately examined her again and found a process of healing that was taking place in minutes. The process should have taken years, if it happened at all."

What interested him almost as much as the recovery was to find that this young woman hadn't been praying for herself! She'd been praying for three atheist relatives. But he did find some people who accompanied her who were praying for her at that moment at the spring. The experience taught him never to dismiss evidence beyond his understanding. And also to know that there was a power in the universe beyond man's intellectual grasp.

The tense situation in Europe was an ever-present backdrop to our conversations. Civil war had broken out in Spain. Germany was using that war to test its weapons. The Republican government was rallying recruits from all over Europe to reinforce Spain's Marxist troops. It looked as though it was just a matter of time before the fighting erupted across the continent.

Carrel, with his stake in France, felt the danger intensely. He was concerned not only for his native country, but for all the democracies. His mind grappled with the problem of their weakness in the face of the totalitarian powers—Germany, Italy, the Soviets. They had a faith, he said. He had no love for Nazism, Fascism, or Communism, but he knew that their ideologies gave those nations an ever-flowing source of energy. By contrast, the democracies seemed to have discarded faith, and there lay the cause of their weakness and inefficiency.

I agreed and asked him what he thought could be done about it. It was a quiet Sunday, and we were sitting in the living room of his small apartment on 89th Street.

"Well, it's going to take more than churches to instill faith," he said. "More and more people don't go to church any more, and many of the millions who do don't seem to have sufficient faith to apply it in business, government, and daily life. Education should play an important role. Schools should train people for self-government, which requires character, social sense, and knowledge."

"I could have done with a good deal more training along that line," I admitted. "As a matter of fact, I discovered faith through some experiments of my own."

Carrel was interested and asked what I meant.

"It was my luck to get to know people who had a strong faith in God. When I asked one of them how his faith had come about, he said, 'It's not a question of trying to persuade your intellect that God exists. Instead, try sitting quietly and just suppose God is there. Listen and see what thoughts come into your mind.'"

"In other words, let your intuition reveal truth to you."

"Then my friend took things a step further. He said the thoughts that came to me might not be so much about the Eternal, as about me. They might have to do with my plugging into a source of power for my life."

Carrel asked if I'd tried the experiment.

"Yes. And I found it worked. I saw what was preventing that power from reaching me. I had to clean off the clogged points in my spiritual battery, so to speak."

"Remarkable. The mystics down the ages have stressed the same truth—in different language, perhaps. But they declare that communion between man and God requires an openness of spirit and obedience to his moral laws."

*   *   *

I had not yet met Mme. Carrel, but that summer of 1937 I received an invitation to spend some time with the Carrels at their home on Saint-Gildas, a small island off the north coast of Brittany, in the English Channel. They had bought the island fifteen years earlier as a sanctuary, away from the demands of work and the bustle of New York. The two had spent most of their summers there in the one building, an ancient, vine-covered, two-story house, with a small chapel of equal age adjoining it.

I had been traveling with Charles Haines on our mission through Europe to contact senior men in large industries in the Netherlands, Germany, France, and Switzerland. Our objective was twofold, to inform them about significant developments in the business world and to listen to their convictions. Through the influence of the Oxford Group, a growing number of businessmen were transforming relations with their workers, their competitors, and their governments. We told about a British industrial oil manufacturer who had opened his books to his workers and created model teamwork with the unions; a Canadian wholesale baker who had brought his industry together nationwide, improving conditions and eliminating cutthroat competition. We described how a national campaign by the Oxford Group in Norway had led so many businessmen and professional men to pay their taxes honestly that the government had had to schedule a special meeting to decide how best to use the windfall. These, and other examples, were highly relevant to current conditions in Europe, where class war was on the upsurge.

When I reached Paris, I was handed the Carrels' invitation. It took me a while to locate Saint-Gildas and even longer to find out how to get there. Haines discovered that a train was leaving shortly from a station on the other side of the city. I grabbed a taxi and arrived just in time to buy a ticket for a couchette, one of four open berths in a carriage. I'd been told I had to change trains next morning at a place called Plouaret. I tried to ask the conductor what time we would get there, but my ten words of French didn't help.

So I got into my pajamas and went to sleep. I awoke with the dawn and went into the washroom. As I started to shave I looked out through a slit in the window and saw the sign, PLOUARET, just as the train started to move. I grabbed my razor, rushed down the aisles, jammed all my stuff into my suitcase, raced to the door and flung it open. European trains are higher off the ground than ours and the ground looked an awful long way down. I hugged my suitcase to my chest, jumped, and hit the ground in a roll. After the train zoomed by, I walked down the tracks, back to the station, still in my pajamas.

I passed a small signal tower with a man in it. He gave me a very queer look. As I entered by way of the tracks, I saw a small train waiting, ready to go. "Is this the train to Trequier?" I asked. *"Oui."* I climbed in, opened my suitcase again, took out my shaving gear, and went to the washroom. By the time I finished my shave, the train had stopped. A fellow passenger said to me, "Trequier *ici*." I threw everything back into my suitcase and, with everyone amused at me, I got out, still in my pajamas. My instructions said, "Take an auto to Port Blanc." I found the garage, asked if I could change my clothes, and hired a car to take me to the little fishing village. To my great relief, there was a boat at the dock with Dr. Carrel waving. I don't think he realized how glad I was to see him.

That visit was like stepping back into a primitive world.

The island scenery was rugged and elemental—great rocks, marshy meadows with tidal pools, groves of wind-bent, stunted trees. Sunrise and sunset lit up this canvas of grays and browns into a fantastic scene of vivid colors. When the wind blew, as it often did and strongly, great waves broke over the boulders in mountains of foam and rolled head-sized stones up and down the beach. At other times the only sounds were the gentle lapping of the surf and the lowing of the small herd of cows on the Carrels' little farm.

This was a place where time was measured by sun and tide, not by the clock. The tides ebbed and flowed as much as forty feet. At low tide you could walk over the sandy sea bottom, between weed-covered reefs, to the neighboring island called Illiec and to the mainland. You had to watch that flow of water very carefully. Carrel told me a mailman had lost his sense of direction in a fog, turned the wrong way, and been drowned in the fast-rising tide.

My host was a different man in this island setting, less of an American and more of a Frenchman. He had left his native country when he was still a young surgeon because he felt too confined by the conservatism of the medical profession in his native Lyons. He had kept his French citizenship, but often said to me, "I owe more to America than I can ever repay. Americans made it possible for me to undertake my life's work."

But still he loved France, especially the Breton countryside and its simple, rugged men and women. When I arrived, I found he had settled comfortably into the old, gray stone house where he and his wife Anne had spent their summers for the past fifteen years. They both gave me a warm welcome.

Mme. Anne-Marie Carrel, widow of the Marquis de la Mairie, was a nurse by profession, and she and Carrel had first met at Lourdes and come to know each other in their medical work. They married in 1913. She had a son from her first marriage. She was a woman of great charm and energy, as powerful a character as her husband, about the same height as he, large-framed and large-hearted. She had commanding features with piercing eyes and a mass of gray hair swept back over her forehead. She was as firm-willed as her husband and, at times, fiercely independent; but I never saw them quarrel. During the years I knew them they were often parted by their responsibilities on opposite sides of the Atlantic.

Mme. Carrel made me at home at once. When she heard about my absurd journey on the train, she insisted that I learn French. She would teach me. We started the lessons with her pointing at different parts of my body—ankle, ear, arm—and she would make me repeat the French words. After a few lessons and a lot of laughter, even as determined as she was, she admitted defeat.

"In some things, Jim, you are very clever, but the good Lord left something out of your brain!"

In the serene atmosphere of Saint-Gildas I began to understand Alexis Carrel a little better. Away from the pressures of work and the pace of New York, he stepped back from the demands of scientific research and let his mind range over the world, the universe, and mankind. Early in the morning he would go out into the garden in his beret, robe, and wooden clogs and walk slowly up and down the path, between his wife's flowers and vegetables. A high stone wall supporting trellises of fruit trees lined three sides of the garden, sheltering it from the winds. He looked like a monk in his cloisters, meditating as he walked. Then he would go into his study and write out his thoughts.

If I had felt that Henry Ford had the profile of a prophet, this man appeared ten times more so, standing astride those island rocks on a little hill above the house, staring out at the empty white-capped water. He kept returning to the themes I had heard in New York, especially to the contrast between the mastery of the material world that science had afforded man, and man's ignorance about his own nature. Modern society, he said, had been built at random, according to chance scientific discoveries and the fancy of current ideologies.

We sat sheltered by a boulder from the spray one morning, as a rising wind made it difficult to hear each other.

"No architect builds a house without calculating the force of gravity," he shouted. "It should be no different when we build our societies. The essential needs of the human being, the characteristics of his mind and organs, his relations with his environment—all these are easily subjected to scientific observation."

"Then why haven't we done it?" I shouted back.

"You ask good questions, Jim. Until now man has been preoccupied with availing himself of all the abundance of the planet and dazzled by the material results of his scientific advances. But now civilization has reached a point where it threatens to destroy mankind."

Carrel went on to describe the unprecedented dangers of warfare with modern weapons, the imbalance between riches and poverty that had given birth to Marxism and Communism, and the retreat from morality in public and private life in France and the United States—the two countries he knew best.

When the noise of wind and sea became too great, we moved into the house.

"We have put so much emphasis on intellect and so little on moral sense. As Henri Bergson used to say, 'One of the qualities of the intellect is its inability to understand life.' Moral sense is so much more important than intellect. When that disappears from a nation, everything else begins to crumble. You see it every day when you read the newspaper—in your country and mine."

I asked, "So what can we do about it? Isn't the important

thing to start people changing the world by changing themselves?"

His eyes sparkled. "That's what I like about you, Jim. It's
why I went to live in America. You don't accept the status
quo. You believe in change. And you are right. That change
in society has to begin in the motives of men. But how is it
to be done on a great enough scale to reverse the flow of
materialism in our civilization?"

"Well, the only way I know is for people to start with
themselves, instead of pointing the finger or waiting for
others to start."

"Yes, that's clear, Jim. But what I'm searching for is not
just to restore values in the lives of individuals—even masses
of them. I'm after a renaissance of values in the life of modern man."

Carrel explained that the men of the Renaissance—Gali-
leo, then Descartes, and all the rest, had done a tremendous
service for mankind, but they had also sent us off course by
dividing the body from the soul. Science had taken off after
the intellect, and for centuries the soul had been neglected.
The material was the only thing considered real, and the
spiritual was pushed aside. Now we needed a second renaissance to bring them back together. We needed the passion
of the first one, but now we must put body and soul
together.

"I'm not suggesting that we abandon the scientific method,"
he said. "It's been man's greatest gift to man. We just need
to apply it to all that we've neglected. And that will meet
with enormous resistance from some scientists. It will take a
revolution to liberate man from their materialistic creed."

So it went, day after day. It was an education for me, and
one I appreciated all the more when I learned I was only
the third visitor invited to share that island retreat during
the fifteen summers the Carrels had spent there.

"So it comes back to changing a few scientists here and

143

there, doesn't it?" I asked, kidding him a little. "I don't know many scientists, but my impression is that they get a little set in their ways."

My host laughed. "I can see why you were a good salesman, Jim. But seriously, you stick to your argument. The logic of world events will change the scientists. They will be forced to understand that man is not able to manage the world by the caprice of his intelligence. And science, for the first time in history, may have a chance to remake civilization by remaking the world according to the laws of life."

"I sure hope they get the point before it's too late."

We not only talked, we walked; and I helped my host with simple chores around his farm. One day his big, dangerous-looking bull broke loose. Carrel suggested this would be a good opportunity for me to practice my skills with a rope. (He had extracted from me the stories I had told Firestone about my cowboy adventures.) He handed me a rope and very cautiously, with a climbable fence behind me, I walked close enough to the bull to throw it over its horns, while Carrel stood by with a .45 automatic in his hand, just in case. Somehow, I managed to get the bull back to its corral.

Later, when I told Charles Lindbergh about the episode, his only comment was, "I get the picture, but I'd have been a lot more scared of Carrel with a loaded automatic than I'd have been of the bull."

I had looked forward to observing some of Mme. Carrel's psychic powers ever since her husband had told me about them. What had sounded "far out" in the bustle of New York took on new significance in the setting of Saint-Gildas. The island's ancient monuments, the rugged scenery and the tide, sun, wind, and water combined to give me an eerie feeling of presence or forces I had not experienced before. Our talk often turned to the mysterious. My first encounter with Mme. Carrel's unusual gifts came one day after I'd been on a six-mile walk through brush and over rocks by myself while the Carrels were on the mainland. On the way, I lost the cap to my fountain pen, which I always carried clipped inside my back pants pocket. On her return, Mme. Carrel said simply, "We must find it," and she produced thread with a small weight on the end. She unfolded a map of the area, asked where I had walked, then tied the thread to her middle finger and moved her hand slowly above the map. Presently, as she passed over a certain place, the weight at the end of the thread began rotating slowly. We marked the spot on the map and the next day the three of us walked to the place high on the rocks and searched the ground. In a crevice in a pile of rocks where I had sat, Dr. Carrel found the cap of my fountain pen. Neither she nor her husband seemed surprised.

One evening we undertook an experiment. Carrel's brother Pierre was visiting. Madame had the three of us sit down. Then she held the pendulum over the head of each of us in turn. It swung in a small circle over Carrel's head, in a crosswise motion over me, and in yet a different way over Pierre. She said the motion was caused by the subconscious vibrations in her body reacting to each of ours. She left the room and closed the door. We took off our shoes and threw them at random under the rug, each of the six shoes a distance apart. Then she came back and held the pendulum above each of the six mounds in the rug. I watched carefully to make sure there was no signal passed between the Carrels. He stood with his back to her. Each time, the weight made the distinctive sign of the shoe's owner.

Mme. Carrel told me that in order for such experiments to work, her mind had to be absolutely free of any preconceptions or any desire for a particular outcome.

I asked Carrel if she was right every time. He said he'd tabulated hundreds of cases and figured clairvoyants, in general, were right about 85 percent of the time.

One morning, as we walked past one of the great dol-

145

mens at the water's edge, Carrel said that one of his great concerns was the study of the intuition in primitive people.

For example, Carrel knew of an army general who had been stationed in Haiti in the days of the sailing vessels. The general told him that from time to time he would see the natives up in the mountains putting their wares on their heads and starting down the steep paths on a day-long journey to the harbor. He would ask them, "Why are you going down now?"

"A boat is coming."

"How do you know?" There was no shipping schedule for the little port, and even if there had been, no schooner could have kept to it.

"It will come."

When they got down to the harbor, the boat came!

Carrel explained, "Those poor peasants had no education. They had some fifth-dimensional quality beyond intelligence. *That* is what we must study."

I would accompany Mme. Carrel to Mass on Sundays. We would put on our big overboots, because the sea bed was messy with tidal pools and strewn with jagged rocks when the tide was out, and we'd walk across a mile or so to the mainland. We'd take them off, stow them under a hedge, and go in to Mass. (And make sure to get back to the island before the tide came in.)

The Carrels had many friends in the little towns and villages on the mainland and loved to stop and talk to the Breton farming people. I would accompany them on their visits. On a shopping trip to the nearby town of Trequier we stopped and talked to an elderly man, a country doctor. The doctor lamented that in the past half-century he'd observed a great difference in the way people died. "In the old days," he said, "they had faith; they died in peace. Today even the peasants on the farms are materialistic. It's important to have two or three wheelbarrows, when one used

146

to be enough. And they die with some uneasiness, some fear. The calm and quiet and expectancy have disappeared."

I wondered how he would feel about New Yorkers.

*   *   *

As we sat around the fireplace one evening, I said, "This sure is different from life in Manhattan!"

"Ah, Jim, America is a wonderful country, but life in New York is too fast, too noisy. And that's the way Americans like it. I don't just mean all the commotion on the streets, but they like their social life the same way, always in groups. Man needs time for solitude and silence to recharge his spirit."

The comment threw a certain light on my friendship with Carrel. During the first half of the 1930s, he had spent a good deal of time with a group of scholarly men—they were the ones who encouraged him to write *Man the Unknown*. But by the time I met him, in early 1937, his interests were turning from the purely scientific questions, and he was searching more deeply for the meaning of life. Father Clifford died, and most of the "philosophers," as he called the scholar friends at the Century Club, were not very interested in his spiritual concerns. At this time he seemed to appreciate someone with the ears to listen, a basic sympathy and interest in his probings, and an inborn bent for exploration and discovery.

Over the years he had developed a deep rapport with Dom Alexis Presse, who had settled not far from Saint-Gildas. One day Carrel took me with him to meet this man, who once had been the abbot of a flourishing Benedictine monastery. Disillusioned by what he felt was too much prosperity, he tried without success to make the institution more austere. He left and wandered the countryside until he came on a ruined fourteenth-century chapel at Boquen, in an isolated stretch of the Brittany coast.

Carrel told me that Dom Alexis had decided, like St.

147

Francis of Assisi, to rebuild the original church, stone by stone, starting with the chapel. When he arrived he had just enough food for two or three days. His conviction was that he would stop there and build, and if he starved, he starved. The natives were suspicious of the stranger and stayed away from him. He built a little lean-to in which he slept at night, and in the daytime he worked on the building. On about the fourth day, he awoke to find a sack of potatoes by the building site. That was the start of silent support by the peasants and the community. Every morning they left a little something there for him. Later on, a monk joined him, then another and another.

The Carrels and I went to the dedication of the chapel. The monks had restored the walls but not yet completed the roof. The service was in Latin and the conversation in French—neither of which I understood. But somehow I absorbed the spirit of the community and the man. Carrel told me how much he had been drawn to this man. He was attracted, he said, not so much by the monastic life as by the man's insights into the future and by his mission to draw men closer to God.

Dom Alexis invited me to join him for a couple of weeks, and I've always regretted that I was unable to accept his invitation. My visit with the Carrels was drawing to a close. I was expected at a conference in Europe, and it was time to get back to America.

DAILY MIRROR

2¢

WEATHER Showers, Warmer
Details on Page 4.

Member of The
Associated Press
(Copyright, 1939.)

3 Cents Outside City Limits

2¢

Vol. 15, No. 254   C   New York, Saturday, April 15, 1939   FINAL EDITION 6 A. M. ★★★★★

RUMANIA, POLAND IN DEFENSE PACT

Britain, France Seek Soviet Air Aid

Stories on Page 2

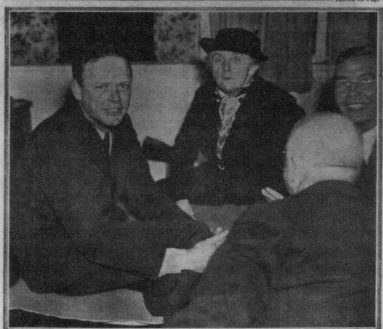

Lindy Comes Home Smiling

Colonel Charles A. Lindbergh, chatting amiably with three fellow-passengers, is pictured in his stateroom aboard Aquitania on his arrival here last night. Judging from his smile he's happy to be back.

Exclusive Photo by Dick Sarno, Mirror Staff Cameraman. Photo Copyrighted, 1939, by Daily Mirror, Inc.

Chapter

SIX

DURING THE AUTUMN OF 1937, I was in and out of New York and took every opportunity I could for visits with Dr. Carrel. As our friendship deepened, I became aware of two sides to his character. In public, and often in conversation, he gave the appearance of confidence, strongly assertive of his scientific knowledge and his opinions. But I found that behind this assured manner lay a self-questioning spirit.

Increasingly he questioned me about my own faith and was very interested in my stories about people applying moral and spiritual convictions to the problems of business, politics, and everyday life. He seemed to be seeking his own road.

Early in the new year of 1938, shortly after the death of Harvey Firestone, Carrel and I were having lunch together at the Rockefeller Institute when he suddenly said, "Charles Lindbergh is back for a short time in America. Before he goes back to England, I'd like to get you two to meet. Not just a social occasion, though I'm sure the two of you will get along fine." He paused and fixed me with his quizzical eyes. "I've known Lindbergh for about seven years now, and have the very highest regard for him. He is a genius: a brilliant technician, a wonderful aviator. But he's more than that. He has a truly remarkable spirit—and is a very great man."

I waited, somewhat mystified.

"I want you to tell him how God came into your life. He and I have talked about these things. He respects my beliefs, but I don't think he's found a satisfying faith himself yet. Possibly you can help him."

He suggested a date when he thought Lindbergh would be free and later phoned me to confirm dinner at a little French restaurant in Manhattan. I was more than a little nervous as I headed for that dinner a few evenings later. There I was, due to meet probably the most famous man in the world at that time, and the story my host wanted me to relate to him was a part of my personal history.

Charles Lindbergh could have stepped out of one of his well-published photographs—tall, slight, vivid blue eyes, unruly blond hair, a shy smile. Carrel was the genial host, putting us at ease, but as we worked our way through the hors d'oeuvres, I could see he was already moving toward the subject of my story. Carrel was never one to beat around the bush, charming though he could be; and before long, the moment came.

"Jim, tell us about that experience of yours on that skiing weekend."

It was about a dozen years ago. I was a young guy traveling for the luggage company in New England. One Friday evening, instead of heading back to Boston, I stopped off at a winter sports hotel in Winchendon, Massachusetts. The place was called Toy Town Tavern. This weekend it was full of young college students my own age or a little older. During dinner that evening the manager announced that there would be a dance across the way at eight o'clock. I hurried upstairs to my room to finish my reports for the company and came down to look for the dance. A desk clerk pointed me to a cottage down the path. I ran through the snow without a coat and looked into the place and there they were, all the young people, standing around. I thought, well, they're about to roll up the rugs and start the gramophone and get going.

Just as I walked in, a man standing by the fireplace started addressing everyone. "We don't all know one another; we're from different colleges; why don't we sit down and tell each other who we are, where we're from, and why we're here."

I had seen two or three girls in the dining room I wanted to dance with, and they were all there. When they introduced themselves I made a note of their names. I thought, now, there's a great hotel management for you, a great way to arrange a weekend. When it came around to the fourth or fifth person from me, a young man gave his name, where he was from, and then went on, "Frankly, I don't believe in this thing. I'm here to find out for myself." At that point I realized I was not at a dance. But it was too late, as it quickly came to my turn. I announced myself as Jim Newton from Boston, and frankly I'd come there to dance. That brought a big laugh. Someone said I'd missed the way. The dance was a hundred yards down the path. But if I wanted to stay, they were going to talk about some of the deeper things of life, and I was welcome. My reasoning at that point was that those girls were there, so why should I go to the dance? I stayed.

"The net of it," I told Lindbergh, "was that I was intrigued by a number of stories of lives that had changed. One young man across the room seemed to have something that I had always wanted—a sense of direction. When the time came to break up, the man leading the meeting said, 'Let's be quiet for a minute.' The only thought I had during the quiet was that the young man I was thinking about would cross the room and come over to me. He did just that. But I didn't have the nerve to talk to him, so I said, 'I'm going to the dance,' and went."

But during the weekend, while we were out skiing and tobogganing, I got to talking to him.

I asked him, "How did you find that sense of direction?"

He said he'd found it by experiment. He went on to tell me how he had used the Sermon on the Mount as a guide for his actions and motives. He had reduced it to four absolute standards—honesty, purity, unselfishness, and love. Then he went on to tell me where he'd not measured up to them.

Lindbergh seemed to be listening intently. I went on.

"I was feeling a little defensive by that time, so I went back at the young man, 'What do you mean by impure?' He said, 'Let's just put it this way—would you be willing to have your thoughts flashed on a screen before your friends, any time, day or night?' I said, 'Tell me no more. I understand.' He was the first person ever to have been honest with me, and, in fact, I realized that we were not unlike each other. I told him, 'I think you've been reading my mail, because I'm exactly like you.'

"At that point I ducked the issue. I said, 'I feel there's someone up there who hangs the stars out. I believe that. But suppose he's not that much interested in me, except perhaps when I do something wrong. Someone with a long beard who says, 'Don't do that.' "

Lindbergh smiled and said something like, "My theological upbringing was something like yours."

"Well, we went on talking and he refused to argue with me. Finally I said, 'Suppose I do as you suggest—turn over as much of my will as I understand to as much of God as I comprehend—suppose I do that—what will I have to do tomorrow morning?'

"I expected him to say all kinds of things—you have to do this, you have to do that. But instead he said, 'I don't know what you will need to do. But if tonight you make that decision, tomorrow morning *you* will know.' "

That seemed to rest the case, and so for the first time in my life I got on my knees with another guy and said simply, "I have my ideals, but I can't live up to them. I don't have what it takes. Okay, I've loused things up—If you're there and can call the shots, here's my will and my life. You run it, you fly it."

I expected bells to ring, but nothing happened. When I asked the guy what I should do in the morning, he said, "Maybe you'll get up five minutes earlier and just listen and see what thoughts come into your mind."

So I did, and when two thoughts came to my mind, I wrote them down on the back of an envelope. One was to go and give back the money I'd gotten "mixed up with mine" in a cash register where I worked as a high school kid on Saturdays. The other thought was that, as I went to my customers in New England, to tell them I hadn't been entirely honest. The trouble was, of course, I'd told my biggest lies to my biggest customers.

As I was leaving the hotel, I ran into that young man again and told him about my two thoughts. "What do you think?" I asked him.

He just looked at me and I looked at him, and finally I asked, "Is this direction, or guidance from God?"

He asked, "What do you think?"

I said, "I don't know, and I also don't know a better way to lose my job. But it's an experiment, and if it works, I think I've found the greatest thing in my life. If it doesn't, I guess I'm just right back in the mess I was always in." And I left.

"So, did it work?" Lindbergh asked.

"Yes, as a matter of fact it did. In the next several weeks

I noticed a new sureness and straightness, especially in my dealings with people. I started off each day by being quiet and giving God a chance to show me through my thoughts how he wanted me to live. That way, I began to experience a sense of direction I'd never had before. And that was just the beginning."

Carrel asked, "And did you go back to those men you hadn't been honest with?"

"Yes. I managed to get in touch with the fellow whose money I'd taken years before and gave it back. And as for my New England customers—were they surprised! Some seemed a little embarrassed. Most wished me luck."

When I told one merchant, one of the biggest, that I'd once cut a few corners with him but now I'd taken a new direction in life, he asked me why I'd told him this. Wasn't I afraid he'd report me to my boss and I'd lose my job? I said, no, I could find a new one. Then, wasn't I afraid he'd withdraw his account? I said no, but I wouldn't like that. Then what was I afraid of? I said I was really afraid that he would lose his respect for me. He said, "Young man, you've been honest with me, so I'll be honest with you. Till now I never did have any respect for you."

"Let's go back to your asking God to run your life," said Lindbergh; "people often make that sound like an emotional experience. For you it was obviously much more than that. Can you put the experience into words?"

"When I was a kid, I was asked to be a candidate for the school swimming squad. I couldn't swim, but my dad encouraged me to join anyway. I can vividly remember that first day when the swim coach tried to talk me into letting go of the edge of the pool.

" 'Just kick your legs and move your arms,' he said. 'You'll find the water holds you up.'

"I looked at my friends as they paddled around and I

believed I too would float, but I kept on clinging to the side. Finally I pushed away and found I *did* stay up. I had moved from *believing* to *knowing*. That's what happened to me when I made the experiment of asking God to direct my life."

Lindbergh nodded. Then he wanted to know who were these people I'd run into that weekend.

I told him that these young people, and others like them, who had found a quiet, realistic reorientation of their lives, called themselves—for want of a better name—the First Century Christian Fellowship. It had been started by an American, Frank Buchman, and it came to be known as the Oxford Group.

Carrel said that what he liked about my story was that my friends used the scientific, experimental approach. They didn't say I should believe this or that. They said, why not try this and see if it works.

"And another element that appeals to me," Carrel added, "is that they linked the spiritual with the moral and practical. I find that some religious people tend to separate theology from living. They focus on belief in the mind, as though it were not part of feeling and acting."

We sat on for a while. Lindbergh did not say much, but I could tell he was thinking. More than that, I felt we'd established a common bond. He didn't seem shocked or offended by my having talked so intimately at our first meeting. At one point he indicated that he'd never had any experience as specific as that. The closest he'd come to it, possibly, was on the Atlantic flight. When he had been really at the end of his strength, he had felt there was some unexpected force out there in control.

As we talked, I felt myself strongly drawn to this unassuming man. He was simple, direct, down-to-earth. That evening was the start of one of the great friendships of my life.

157

A week or so later, Lindbergh took a boat back to England, where he had left his family. His visit to America had been just long enough to attend to family business and to pass on to government authorities in Washington the information he had obtained about the growing military strength of Germany and the relative lack of it in Britain and France. Through his fame as an aviator and his training and experience, he was in a unique position to see conditions in those countries and to evaluate what he saw of their aviation industries and military production.

*   *   *

Before Carrel returned to Saint-Gildas, in the summer of 1938, he and I met a number of other times. Somebody once asked me why I thought Carrel enjoyed my company, since I was so much younger and had had little academic training. I suppose the answer is that I was myself, first, and that helped him to be himself. Before my Toy Town Tavern experience, for example, I had been defensive about not having been to college. If an easterner asked me what college I'd been to, I'd mention a western one. If a westerner asked me, I'd give the name of an eastern one. When I gave up pretending to be smarter or wiser or different, it was a great relief. I remember telling Carrel I'd never been to college; he simply said, "Well, you can be thankful for that. You don't have a lot of things to unlearn!"

One evening he launched into his plans for continuing his research on changing the physical condition of life. He said that he and his colleagues at the Institute had already established through their experiments on animals that the right diet led to remarkable changes in their life-spans and physiques. When they extended such studies among human beings, they would learn why in some areas of the world men and women are much more likely to live to be a hundred. Just as important was the field of the strains and stresses of modern conditions—the noise, atmospheric pollution, urban living—their effects on human life, and the changes that should be made.

"You see, Jim," he said, "it's within our power to remake man into what he is capable of becoming. In fact, it's our duty—the duty of responsible scientists." But it couldn't be done piecemeal. It needed the closest, most unselfish cooperation among physicists, chemists, geneticists, psychologists, and so on, to mold man into his best self.

I suggested, "You're saying we should work with God to improve the quality of the human race."

He agreed you could put it that way, though most of today's scientists would not be too happy with that language. But, yes, of course we were meant to use the intelligence and the intuition the Almighty gave us to fulfill his destiny for man.

As we walked downstairs after dinner one evening at the Century Club, we'd been talking about the Almighty. Carrel said to me, "Jim, you call him 'Christ,' don't you?" An elderly member, who was passing us on the stairs, overheard us and stumbled over a step as he stared at us in astonishment.

"Yes, I do think of him as Jesus. It's easier for me to picture him that way."

"I understand that. But I hear his name used in such petty ways, I no longer use it with most people."

He added, "When the Gospel is really lived, some of us will find it unrecognizable."

He surprised me another time when we were speaking of life and death: "Jim, when I get to the other side, I want to look up a whole list of people." He was absolutely serious.

"Such as?"

"Number one would be Aristotle." Why Aristotle, I asked him? Carrel said he was the first man who had really grasped the unity of a human being. In other words, the body shared in the spiritual, and the spiritual permeated the physical.

That was probably why Aristotle and his disciples always walked while they discussed philosophy and science.

I thought about Henry Ford and his walking and whittling.

Carrel sailed for France and Saint-Gildas late in June. I had already left for Europe and made plans to visit him and Mme. Carrel there. Mme. Carrel had arranged for the Lindbergh family to stay at an old house on the adjacent island of Illiec. At a press conference, he said that he looked forward to conferring with Colonel Lindbergh on the improvement of the glass perfusion pump and other joint projects, but he had made it clear to me that his main purpose was to escape from his Manhattan routine to the peace and quiet of Saint-Gildas. And while he and Lindbergh would no doubt talk about their work at the Institute, their discussions would range to far wider realms.

During the carefree weeks I enjoyed with the Carrels that summer, I came to know the Lindberghs and their children. Jon was a little boy, bursting with energy, and Land a baby of a few months. This was my first meeting with Anne Morrow Lindbergh. In most obvious ways the two were very different. She was small and dainty, with talents for writing and poetry. Her greatest interest was the care of her husband, children, and home. Her upbringing had been among the privileged; her father, Dwight Morrow, had been a lawyer, banker, and diplomat, a partner in J. P. Morgan and Company, a trustee of Amherst College, chief civilian aide to General Pershing. In 1927 he had been appointed ambassador to Mexico and in 1930 elected to the U.S. Senate from New Jersey. Anne's mother's greatest interest was in women's education: she was chairman of the board of trustees of Smith College. So Anne had grown up in a cosmopolitan and sophisticated atmosphere—very different from Charles's simple childhood among the farms and woods of Minnesota and his youth as a stunt pilot and a mail flyer—

160

although he had spent some winters in Washington, D.C. when his father was a congressman.

And yet there were qualities that Charles and Anne had in common. Both were shy, sensitive, and reserved, partly because of their own natures, partly no doubt because of the shattering experience of the kidnapping and death of their eldest son and partly because of the nonstop hounding of an insatiable press and public.

When I arrived on Saint-Gildas, the children were on the neighboring island of Illiec with two British women who took care of them. Charles and Anne Lindbergh were in Russia. The U.S. government had asked Charles to make a plane trip to Moscow to find out all he could about the strength of the Soviet air force and aircraft industry. Before that, earlier in the summer, Washington had asked him to make similar visits to Germany and France. The Lindberghs returned toward the end of my stay with the Carrels. We had about a week together and it was full of conversation.

I found that Charles and Anne were as broad in their interests as my French hosts. Some days it seemed as if the hours weren't long enough to say all that was on our minds. I remember several evenings after a visit to their home, Lindbergh and I would stand talking across the rapidly rising tide between Saint-Gildas and Illiec. As the waves crept up and water covered the rocks, each of us would back up. Our voices would get louder and louder as the distance between us grew, until we'd be forced to give a final shout, "Good-night, see you tomorrow!"

For the most part, we spent our days on the islands, alternately doing hard manual work, eating, walking, and talking. The Lindberghs were doing construction work on the outside of their house and its rock terraces. Two sturdy Breton men spent a good deal of their time at it, and we would pitch in. Then we'd walk—sometimes around Saint-Gildas, sometimes around Illiec, often joined by Carrel.

161

Late one afternoon, Charles and I were sitting on the crest of the jagged ridge of rocks that ran above his house. We looked across the island and over at Saint-Gildas, and I told him about a remark Carrel had made that morning: "The quality of life is more important than life itself."

"I know what he was talking about," said Charles, "the balance of body, mind, and spirit. One needs a healthy and disciplined body. One needs to exercise one's mind and reach into one's spirit—stay open to intuitions and follow one's convictions."

"I've learned I don't have the guts or wisdom to do that on my own," I said. "That's what giving my life to God is all about. He strengthens my spirit."

We sat in silence.

"Jim, when I'm flying, I'm a materialist—until I get off the ground." He went on to say that despite the best of preparation, when a flyer runs into something beyond the control of his own mind and body he realizes very quickly that he's in the hands of an unseen power.

"That happens to me plenty of times *on* the ground," I told him. "I don't mean that I face physical danger so much as that I face choices. Take smoking, for example. I used to smoke a pack and a half a day. I knew it wasn't good for my health, but I felt I needed it.

"I can remember the exact time and place I decided to give it up. It was after my experience at Toy Town Tavern, and I saw it as a basic question: what was governing my life, God or tobacco? I made some decisions on my knees, but I still went back to smoking when life got tough.

"One day I was traveling north from Florida on business with a friend from Philadelphia. We were sitting in the lounge of a Pullman car and I was smoking a Havana cigar—the best—which he'd given me. I'd smoked about a third, when it came as clear as crystal: this is it! I looked at the cigar and

162

said, 'Mr. Bond, that's my last smoke,' and I threw the cigar in the cuspidor. He looked first at the long butt and then at me. He didn't say a thing—I guess he could tell by something in my face that I meant what I said."

"And you never smoked again?" Lindbergh asked.

"No. I've been tempted. But something else gives me the strength to resist."

We were quiet a while and then Charles spoke. "What it comes down to is this, Jim: I've found that when you make a deep commitment, unforeseen forces come to your aid.

"Getting to the point of deciding is the hard part. Once you're there, it's simple. I call it 'reaching the core.' Carrel calls it 'experiencing spiritual rebirth.' You call it 'listening to the inner voice.' Whatever the words, I'm sure this reality is the force at the heart of the universe. That force becomes available to us in some measure, if our spirits are open to it."

I started to speak, then thought better of it.

Charles looked at me and said, "Isn't it strange that we talk least about the things we think about most!"

Despite the isolation of our retreat, the events of the world sometimes pressed in upon us, and of course we brought our concerns with us, and they colored our conversations. Carrel and Lindbergh took time to pursue their continuing research—the construction of an artificial kidney, for example, which would have advanced Carrel's work on organs outside the body. But the future of his research at the institute had become very uncertain. The Institute had just established a mandatory retirement age of sixty-five, and Carrel would be sixty-six before the next summer. I heard both men expressing their frustration that such a rule could stop such an important contribution to science. At the same time, I think they both well knew that Carrel had offended a number of his scientific colleagues by his outspoken views

163

and frank criticism of others, and that the Institute would hardly be expected to make an exception to the retirement rule in Carrel's case.

Carrel said one day, "I thought I was leaving professional jealousy and closed minds behind when I left France. The Institute was like heaven after Lyons. Flexner was so sensitive in allowing each of us to follow our own line of research. But with him gone and his successor so much of a bureaucrat, the atmosphere is becoming stifling."

Simon Flexner, the Institute's scientific director, had retired in 1935 and his successor, Herbert Gasser, proved to be no friend of Carrel. He made it clear that in holding to the new retirement age requirement, he would also be closing Carrel's laboratory. So Carrel was now beginning to look beyond the Institute to the establishment of his own center for study, which had been a distant dream for some years.

"What we need," he used to say, "is a complete renovation of our educational system." The heart of the trouble with our schools and colleges, he would say, is that they disregard the training of the individual in how to develop his own potential in conformity with the natural laws of the universe. For the first time in the history of humanity, according to Carrel, a crumbling civilization was capable of discerning the causes of its decay. For the first time it had at its disposal the enormous advantages of science. Scientific institutions used the analytic method—they considered man as a multiplicity and they studied his many parts. That was important and had to continue. But what we needed now was a synthesis of research on the nature of man. The individual should be considered in his structural and spiritual unity. And we should seek to learn something about the relations between the individual and his cosmic, social, and psychological surroundings.

He proposed to bring together carefully chosen scientists, each eminent in his own field yet flexible enough to work

164

together with others. This Institute of Man would pioneer the road to a great integrated body of knowledge on the nature of man. The place to start it was in the United States— "the only country in the world with the enthusiasm and resources to make it work."

Lindbergh and I encouraged him and promised to support him in any way we could.

*   *   *

But in the summer of 1938, peaceful as our island might seem, the continent around us was in increasing turmoil. It was the summer of Hitler's ambitions. He had already Austria without resistance; now he was threatening Czechoslovakia and Poland. We were hearing repeated rumors that Germany would declare war in August. Neither the French nor the British seemed prepared to take a firm stand.

My hosts had been so concerned about the likelihood of war that they decided to bury the family silver. On a day when their cook and gardener were off the island, the Carrels set about digging. I took a shovel, and together we dug a hole not far from the house and hid the silver. It was not until later, when I read more of the history of Europe, that I realized I had been taking part in a centuries-old custom only too common in these lands as the tides of war ebbed and flowed across the continent. Although war did not come to France as soon as many feared during that summer, the Germans eventually occupied Saint-Gildas, along with the whole of northern France.

Lindbergh talked about the urgency of the situation, telling us what he had gleaned at first hand during his travels. According to him, Germany had by far the most powerful air force. Russia had many planes, but they would be no match for the German ones. English and French air power, too, were inferior to Germany's. As far as ground forces were concerned, the German mechanized army was becoming very powerful. The only French counterweight on the ground seemed to be their elaborate Maginot Line. England, he said, had the most powerful navy, of course, but the great question was how superior aviation would prove over ground and sea forces. "I think the war in the air will be decisive," he said.

I asked him what he thought English and French policy should be. Certainly, it didn't look as if Hitler was going to back down without a fight.

He was pessimistic about England, having lived there several years now. He felt they had refused to believe, until the last few months, that there could be another war. Germany's annexing Austria and Franco's victory in Spain had shaken them a bit. But the real trouble, he said, was that there seemed to be a lack of spirit in the factories, in the Parliament, in business. There was no intelligent training or preparation for fighting.

"And France?" I asked.

Just about the same, he told me. They were too busy fighting each other. He thought they were making no united effort to do anything.

"Hitler has to attack somebody; I hope it's the East instead of the West," said Lindbergh. After all, Hitler's real enemy was the Soviet Union. National Socialism and Communism would never coexist peacefully. They were bound to clash sooner or later, if Hitler and Stalin stayed on their present courses. They were both totalitarian regimes, explained Lindbergh, and as far as he was concerned, he would rather see them knocking each other out than attacking the Western democracies. He had tried to suggest gently to people in France and England—as well as in the United States—that they shouldn't stir up the hornet's nest. "Keep quiet, and for God's sake look to your own armaments," he had told them.

Carrel chimed in, "I'm not in a position to judge the English. But I'm afraid you're right about my countrymen.

166

When war breaks out, we're brave enough. But by then it's too late." He was very worried about France. We were all worried, and our conversations seemed dominated by talk of war. And yet we would find ourselves turning to the metaphysical.

While the the Lindberghs had been in Russia, I had had another firsthand illustration of Mme. Carrel's psychic powers. The Carrels were concerned, because the Lindberghs were overdue. So Madame got out a map of Europe, along with the string and the metal weight. She started with Paris, Berlin, and Moscow and gradually moved around Russia. The pendulum did not respond until it was over the port of Odessa, on the Black Sea. Then it came to life, swinging back and forth. Its message seemed improbable: Odessa had not been on their itinerary. When they arrived, we learned that their plans changed in midvoyage—Odessa was exactly where they had been on that date.

One day, after dinner with Charles and Anne, we were in the living room. I remember it vividly: I was sitting on the couch with my back to the window and the view of the sea. Charles unexpectedly asked me to tell them about some of the things that had meant the most to me in life. "Anne would be interested, I know," he said, "in what you told me during that first dinner we had with Carrel."

I took a deep breath. Here we go again, I thought. So I told them about my skiing weekend, just about the way I'd told it to Charles. There was silence in the room for a while. Then Anne, sitting by the fireplace, said in her quiet way, "It must have been hard to talk about those personal things with someone else. Isn't it enough to be honest before God?"

Of course it had been. But, I told her, being honest with another person had done something very important for me. It externalized the things that had been going on in my mind and heart. It was a full disclosure of sorts.

"Was that necessary?" she asked.

"In a sense, voicing my inner self crucified my pride," I said, "If I had only prayed, I would have felt that I had only told someone who knew all this anyway. When I shared the truth with a person I trusted, though, I saw that I needed to change. And I also saw I needed to go on and make a commitment."

"What kind of commitment?"

"A commitment to relinquish as much of your will as you understand to your Creator—to the degree you know him or believe in him or recognize him or trust him—or whatever."

"Suppose you don't believe?" asked Charles. "Or suppose your beliefs aren't as certain."

"If you don't believe in God—and my own belief at that time was pretty vague—then you can make an experiment, just as I did at Toy Town Tavern. I asked God, if there was a God, to make clear to me what I should do. God did exactly that. He showed me the first steps I must take."

Anne asked whether what I'd heard wasn't just my conscience, something we were all born with.

"Possibly. I believe God made us all with a conscience," I answered. "What I experienced was something deeper, bigger. An inner voice that tells you not only what you may have done wrong, but an intuition about what you need to do, a direction in which to go, a feeling or illumination about some part of your life.

"What I'm trying to say is that there are times when it seems as if there aren't hours to do what needs to be done. The pressures are enormous. Well, what I found makes all the difference is to start each day with a short time when I consciously try to let God's presence soak in. It gives me a perspective on myself, on work, friends, life."

"Isn't that meditation?" Anne asked. "Don't all religions teach the importance of that—freeing oneself from daily demands and trying to find the deepest and clearest truth or voice?"

"Yes, but there's nothing vague about it. It's all in the New Testament. Be willing and obedient, and you will experience a new power and a new direction in your daily life."

"You make it all sound very specific," said Lindbergh. "I wish all human beings were capable of the things you say they are. But when you look around the world, human nature doesn't seem to be responding much to what you're talking about."

We went on about the state of the world, and I told them some stories of how changes in people had made a difference. We talked so long that when I stepped outside to walk back to Saint-Gildas, the tide had come in. I spent the night there.

I had to leave a few days later for an appointment in Geneva. Because the tide was in, I was taken to the mainland in the little boat. There was a small crowd at the Port Blanc dock that day, and a shout went up. I was a tall American, though not as tall as Charles, and was wearing the same kind of glasses he always wore when trying to avoid recognition. And I had blond hair. The crowd thought I was Lindbergh and greeted me with loud applause as I stepped onto the dock. People came pushing around and a couple of French girls were so enthusiastic, they kissed me. When I told Charles about it later, he accused me of fooling the crowd intentionally, so I would get those kisses! He would have been too reserved to let that happen.

The following day, September 15, 1938, Europe and much of the world held its breath. British Prime Minister Chamberlain was hurrying to meet with Hitler, along with French Premier Daladier. The German armed forces were poised on the border of Czechoslovakia, ready to swarm over that country just as they had done six months before with Austria. But now the question in everyone's mind was whether the action would precipitate a general war in Europe.

I traveled by train from Saint-Gildas to Geneva. In Paris the station had been blacked out for fear of air raids. A fellow passenger had come from London where, he told me, workmen were digging air-raid trenches in the parks and the government was issuing gas masks. In Geneva, I joined an international team of the Oxford Group that had been invited by Carl Hambro, president of the Norwegian Parliament, and other delegates to the League of Nations to address members of that body at a luncheon. The Oxford Group was now known as Moral Re-Armament (MRA) since Frank Buchman had emphasized the need for people and nations to rearm morally and spiritually, as well as militarily, in face of the threat posed by Hitler's totalitarian challenge.

The occasion could scarcely have been more timely. Among the speakers was J. A. E. Patijn, the Dutch foreign minister, who described how a basic change in his attitude had ended a controversy between the Netherlands and Belgium. Other speakers included people of opposing backgrounds—conservative and Socialist, black and white, management and labor. Just about the time Hitler and Chamberlain were meeting, these men and women were telling how they had resolved their conflicts. This demonstration of reconciliation was so dramatic that the *Journal de Genève,* one of Europe's most respected newspapers, issued a four-page supplement reporting the event and stories about these ambassadors of peace and understanding.

I sent a copy with a letter to Carrel. He replied:

We were very pleased to receive your letters, the newspaper clippings, the pictures and the two copies of the *Journal de Genève.* The fact that this journal has given so much space to the meeting is significant. The ideas expressed in Moral Re-Armament are obviously true. But they are not striking. The French especially have already heard it in several different forms. They would be skeptical. They might even go as far as to laugh at it. My feeling is that, on those spiritual foundations, something far more constructive should be erected, in order to give the project sufficient strength. Moral reconstruction is necessary, but insufficient.

Madame Carrel joins me in sending you our best wishes.

Yours affectionately,
Alexis Carrel

The next day he wrote me again:

We are leaving today for Paris. I intend to sail on October 1st. I have sent one of the *Journal de Genève* to Dom Alexis.

I read again those most interesting statements of Frank Buchman, Stanley Baldwin, Patijn, Hambro, etc. I have a tendency to believe that those men are not entirely on the right track. They have oversimplified the situation. . . . While I believe in the necessity of the spiritual development of the individual it does not seem to me that it is sufficient. One does not build a cathedral with religious principles.

It is probable that the Peace effort of the Oxford Group would be, at this time, considered in France as being as vain as the Peace Ship [of Henry Ford in World War I].

We went and saw Father Alexis two days ago and had a long conversation with him. He has very profound views on what should be done today.

I hope to see you in Paris.

During the next months, as the prospects of war became yet more serious, Carrel's attitude toward Moral Re-Armament was to become more appreciative.

171

Chamberlain returned to London from Munich with an agreement with Hitler which he said spelled "peace in our time." In fact, it only postponed the outbreak of war for a year, although that was a very crucial year for British rearmament.

I saw Carrel soon after he returned to New York from France in November and met with him often during the autumn and winter. He was unsettled in his spirit. He continued his research work at the Rockefeller Institute, but it seemed that his heart was not really in it. It was not just that he faced the deadline of retirement the next summer, but, more fundamentally, his mind was moving beyond the medical research to the wider field of speculation about the nature of man, which was for him of far greater interest.

Lindbergh and I, along with Ed Moore and Dr. Ralph Wyckoff, head of the Physics Department of the Rockefeller Institute until 1937, had all been encouraging Carrel to take practical steps toward getting his Institute of Man started, if he was really serious about it. Now he seemed to be ready, and he began contacting a number of scientists who were involved in research on nutrition, environmental protection, urban and industrial working and living conditions, and also his interests in mental telepathy, clairvoyance, and other ESP fields.

Ever since the publication of *Man the Unknown* in 1935, Carrel had become increasingly well known. Reviews of the book in newspapers and magazines had brought his name and his ideas before the public. In June 1938, he and Lindbergh had been featured on the cover of *Time* magazine because of their development of the perfusion pump. Unlike Lindbergh, Carrel seemed to enjoy publicity, and one evening in his apartment on 89th Street he said to me, "I think I should do more writing for the general reader. That kind of education of the public will bring support for the Institute of Man, as well as stir interest in our objectives."

I suggested that he meet my friend George Bye, a literary agent. He was a friend of DeWitt Wallace, founder of *Reader's Digest*. The *Digest's* condensation of *Man the Unknown* had given the book exposure. Carrel was delighted with the idea of writing for the *Digest* directly.

As it turned out, so were Bye and Wallace. We had lunch in the dining room of the Rockefeller Institute. Carrel and Wallace took to each other immediately. They discussed a range of subjects suitable for the magazine, and eventually decided on a first article, "Breast Feeding." If it was well received, the article would be the start of a series.

Carrel took the assignment as seriously as he would have taken any research project. He seemed cheered by the response of Wallace and Bye and went to work investigating the latest developments in the field of infant nutrition. The article was outstanding, so it was followed by a highly popular series—including "Health," "Married Love," "Work in the Laboratory of Your Private Life," and finally "Prayer Is Power." Carrel received offers from the *Saturday Evening Post* and other magazines and newspapers. It was interesting to me that Carrel made no concessions in these articles to the relaxing of moral standards, which many people seemed to feel was necessary to win popular approval. In fact, he stressed that the foundation for good health, happy married life, and raising children was an old-fashioned moral code—self-discipline, marital fidelity, hard work, and the serious pursuit of studies.

The last of his articles, "Prayer Is Power," which appeared two years after his first, went to the root of his conviction about man's spiritual nature. I saw him unfold the thoughts he had expressed many times in our private conversations: "Those who pray with sincerity will show in their faces and their bearing a tranquility and peace. . . . The habit of earnest prayer will profoundly alter your life. . . . Prayer kindles a depth of consciousness in a man so that he sees himself as he really is, recognizes his selfishness, pride, fears and greed—and sets out on a new road, a journey towards intellectual humility and moral growth."

But for Carrel, the spring of 1939 was a troublesome time. He was unhappy about his forced retirement from the Institute after thirty-three years of distinguished work there. But what made him angrier was that they were closing the Surgical Research Laboratory just when it was beginning to produce important results in tissue and organ culture and experimental oncology. They would disperse a group of scientists who worked well together, and would not name a successor.

But he was careful never to express these feelings publicly. "It's a family matter," he said about his relationship with Gasser, the new director of the Institute. "I don't want to harm the Institute. They've been wonderful to me." So, in his interviews with the newspapers, which gave wide publicity to his retirement, he maintained a positive attitude. And, as a matter of fact, the abandonment of his laboratory at his retirement was his decision. He was not prepared to continue under the conditions of limited funding and stricter controls that he knew Gasser would impose.

And as a Frenchman, the spring of 1939 weighed on him. The news from Europe became grimmer. In March German forces absorbed Czechoslovakia without opposition from Britain and France, and Hitler extended his influence over the Baltic and Hungary. Then, in April, France and Britain signed a treaty with Poland, promising to come to her aid if attacked. Italy invaded and occupied Albania. In May, Germany and Italy concluded a firm political and military alliance—the Berlin–Rome Axis. The Russians backed out of negotiations with England and France, which had been aimed at forming a front against further German aggression.

Anne-Marie Carrel had joined her husband in New York, but she soon became anxious to return to France. She was much more furious at the Rockefeller Institute than her husband. She wanted him to get away from New York, whose urban frenzy she had never liked, and she was cool toward his increasing involvement in writing popular articles and toward his plans for founding an Institute of Man in America. She felt their place was in their native France, especially in an hour of growing danger.

"Maybe Alexis and I can't do very much there," she said to me one day. "But he is a wonderful surgeon, and I am a nurse, and we know from the last war how much our experience will be needed. Alexis saved thousands of lives in the Great War by preventing gangrene. Nothing is being done now to prepare the hospitals and blood centers we will need. Now that his main work is finished here, that's where he should be."

*   *   *

Charles Lindbergh had arrived in America in April 1939. His decision to return with his family had not been an easy one. On Illiec he had told me that he and Anne missed their families and friends. And they longed for a place they could call home. Two things had kept them in Europe until then. One, everybody knew about: the intrusion of the press into their lives, a concern far less severe in Europe. What was less obvious was the unique service he had been rendering his country by securing information about the rearmament programs of Germany, Russia, and the Western democracies. But now, he returned to the United States hoping the press clamor would be less; and others would now be supplying the military information.

Charles left Anne and the children to follow on a later boat and came into New York on the *Aquitania* in mid-April. The Carrels and I received advance word of his coming and, as the Department of the Treasury is responsible for the customs service, I got permission from Henry Morgenthau, Jr., Secretary of the Treasury, for the Carrels and me to go out on the pilot boat with the Customs men to board the ship before it docked. When I saw Morgenthau in his office in Washington, he told me he had read Lindbergh's intelligence reports from Germany with great interest.

We sat talking in Charles's cabin, enjoying our reunion and waiting for the passengers to leave the ship, so that Charles could encounter less attention. Suddenly the door from the adjoining cabin flew open and a photographer lunged in, took a photo, and ran out. The photo appeared across the front page of the next day's *Daily Mirror*. We later learned that the photographer had bribed a steward to let him in. Two burly New York policemen came to the door and offered their services to help push through the waiting press crowd. They were afraid we might be injured. Charles thanked them, but declined the offer. I went out to scout the situation and found what seemed to be about a hundred reporters and photographers jostling around. We decided to fight our way through, Charles in the lead, then Anne Carrel, followed by Alexis. I took the rear. We pushed our way through a madhouse—yells, shoving, blinding flashbulbs. Carrel and I were separated for a while from the others. As fiercely protective of his privacy as ever, Charles wryly noted that it was a barbaric entry to a civilized country.

When Anne Lindbergh and the children arrived, the family settled for a few weeks into the Englewood, New Jersey home of her mother. Then they moved to a house they rented in Lloyd Neck on Long Island. Charles was called to Washington immediately on his arrival by General "Hap" Arnold, chief of the Army Air Corps, and put to work studying the performance of military planes and advising on means of speeding airplane production. Arnold also made him responsible for reorganizing the National Advisory Committee for Aeronautics (NACA), of which Charles was a member.

For the next five months he was busy with meetings in Washington and visits to aircraft plants and aeronautical research centers across the country.

A couple of weeks after his arrival in New York, Charles and Anne, the two Carrels, and I got together in Carrel's apartment and talked into the night. Charles said his priority for the moment must be anything he could do to improve the country's defense preparedness, especially plane production. He just hoped there would be a long enough breathing spell to strengthen America, England, and France before the fighting broke out.

If England and France concentrated on building their defenses and didn't provoke Hitler by threatening to attack if he moved eastward, he said, war would not be likely that year. But if they tried to protect Poland, as they had promised to do, war could come soon. The sad thing was, he believed, there was no way England or France could stop Germany's advance eastward. He felt they didn't seem to realize that their own security lay in allowing Hitler to clash with the Soviets.

This was the end of April 1939, and the Nazi–Soviet nonaggression pact wasn't signed until late August. Hitler was not to invade the Soviet Union for another two years.

Charles wanted to know about Carrel's plans for the Institute of Man. Alexis said he had approached several distinguished scientists in various fields, but so far none had been willing to join him.

"Perhaps the next step is to look into a possible location," I suggested. "And to think about getting financial support, so there is something tangible to put before people."

Charles thought it would be wise to start with a small nucleus of scientists to which others would be attracted.

Carrel responded to these suggestions, and we decided to start by making a date with Carrel's colleagues, Dr. Wyckoff

177

and Dr. Albert H. Ebeling,* and also with Ed Moore, who had introduced me to Carrel. When we got together for lunch, Charles offered to donate four hundred acres of a family property, High Fields, near Hopewell, New Jersey, where Charles and Anne had lived in the early 1930s. The next day was a Sunday and we all drove down to High Fields and decided it would be a good site for the institute. I undertook raising funds for the construction of a laboratory.

Carrel was greatly cheered by our practical support. However, at this point, he felt he had to leave for France to see at first hand what was happening there and to join his wife on Saint-Gildas.

* Dr. Albert H. Ebeling was a long-time colleague of Carrel, working with him especially on tissue culture. When Carrel retired from the Rockefeller Institute, Ebeling moved to the Lederle Laboratories, taking with him the famous "immortal chicken heart" tissues.

Chapter

SEVEN

ALEXIS CARREL had returned to France on the eve of the war he had anticipated. I received a letter from him, written on August 24, 1939, in reply to one from me. His last paragraph foreshadowed the outbreak of hostilities.

I was delighted to receive your letter and the articles about Moral Re-Armament. It is highly gratifying that your efforts have been rewarded with such success. In France, the best papers have reproduced on the front page the description of the meetings of New York and Hollywood. [These were meetings at Madison Square Garden, May 14, and the Hollywood Bowl, July 19, to launch MRA in the United States.] Moral Re-Armament has been extraordinarily well received. *L'Illustration,* which is the best weekly illustrated paper in the world, printed on August 5, on its front page the striking picture of the Hollywood Bowl and of the 30,000 people who were present at the meeting. Next page there is an excellent article on the same subject: "Dr. Frank Buchman, through his faith and the tenacity of his propaganda, has awakened the conscience of the world . . . in their struggle, the spirit has always in the final count conquered the material."

It is truly a magnificent success to have attracted the attention of so many people to the necessity of moral values.

We went several times to see Dom Alexis. We spoke often of you. Dom Alexis spent some time at Saint-Gildas. We were extremely sorry you were not with us. It was a meeting never to be forgotten. Dom Alexis is, I believe, a great man and a saint. He understands fully the necessity of both spiritual and moral growth. He is much better physically—his monastery grows daily. People are flocking to him. He is starting a great work. I hope you will see him again. Dr. Buchman also should know him.

I am very pleased that you saw DeWitt Wallace and gave him my two short articles.

Unfortunately, the march of events in Europe is menacing all our plans. Tonight, perhaps, the sinister ringing of the tocsin from the charming little church which you can see above our hill could announce general mobilization. And the destruction of Europe will begin. Already, forty men have left our small village of Bugueles for the Navy. Again, war—like in 1914. I will write soon—Madame Carrel joins me in sending you our most affectionate wishes.

A few days later that tocsin sounded. The Carrels were still on the island when Hitler sent his forces into Poland on September 1, 1939. I remember the day well. Charles Lindbergh and I were due to have breakfast together at the Engineers Club in New York. He was coming in on a night train from Washington and I had arranged to meet him at Penn Station. While I was waiting for his train I went by the newsstand and there, on the front page of each paper, were huge headlines—GERMANS INVADE POLAND.

I was watching at one exit and Charles came out through another. We missed each other, but later met up at the Engineers Club. He was as stunned as I was by the news.

We spoke again of England and France. Of how they would ever be able to undertake their promise to come to Poland's aid. Of what America's policy would be and how Russia would react.

"I wish we could have prevented Alexis and Anne from leaving," I said. We pictured them on Saint-Gildas as the war news reached them.

Charles suggested, "Let's phone Wyckoff and Ebeling and see if they can come over and we can figure out what we might do for the Carrels."

While we were waiting for them, we went out and walked around Fifth Avenue and 40th Street. As usual, Charles put on his glasses and pulled his hat low over his brow. We spoke of Hitler and Roosevelt and the building campaign to get us involved in the war.

"If only our press was not so inflammatory!" said Charles. He felt it was all too easy to whip up emotions at a time like this.

He said he didn't trust the press to report him accurately, so he'd stayed away from any public statements. At the same time, he felt he had a duty to speak out, because he knew the strength of Germany better than anybody and what we'd be getting into if we went to war.

It was, I knew, more than an academic decision for him. He hated publicity, and more that that, he feared that renewed public interest in him could make life difficult for Anne and the children—even endanger their lives. I sensed that the memory of his son's death was never far from his mind.

"I may just have to come out publicly against our getting into war," Charles said. He was well aware that if he did he probably would have to resign his commission and reconcile

183

himself to the fact that his services to the aviation industry would no longer be welcome.

When Wyckoff and Ebeling showed up, as well as Carrel's Russian friend Bakhmeteff, we talked about what we could do to help the Carrels. We agreed that we'd have to postpone any further work on the Institute of Man. Wyckoff said he felt sure that Carrel would offer his services again to the French government, as he'd done in World War I to help organize emergency medical facilities. We decided to send a cable offering to help finance a research hospital, or whatever would be of greatest assistance to him.

"I wish he were on this side of the water," said Charles. "Carrel could accomplish far better long-term work for his country over here."

"But you know very well," said Wyckoff, "that they'll both stay if they find they can help."

When I began receiving letters from Carrel, they reflected the growing confusion, as well as his own uncertainties, as France was plunged into war.

September 18, 1939

Dear Jim,

I had the great pleasure to receive yesterday your letters of August 19th and 29th and the newspaper clippings. It is most gratifying that you had such a success in California. This awakening is, I hope, of real significance. Will the people of America understand that civilization is at stake? Do they realize the profound meaning of this war? It is certain that a return to the faith of the first Christians would immensely help the renovation of our world. But it is certain, also, that Christian civilization is in greater danger today than when Attila invaded Gaul and Italy in 451.

We are still in Saint-Gildas because, during the first days of the war, it wasn't possible to guess what would be the new aspects of the fight. Of course, I must try to help, even in an extremely small way, and at the same time to further our general plan, which is far more important than anything I can do from a surgical or medical point of view. I did not, therefore, reenlist in the army. Tomorrow we will motor to Paris. I will see some of my medical friends, also some of the men in the Army Medical Corps, and ascertain whether they would be interested in the development of new and better techniques, for instance, for the treatment of hemorrhage and shock, of asphyxia by gases, or of any other subjects. I do not believe that much has been done in France except about transfusion of preserved blood. But I doubt that they will know what will be the most pressing needs. It is a cruel deception for me to have to give up, at least temporarily, the High Fields plan [for his institute]. I will write soon from Paris. . . .

> Yours affectionately,
> Alexis Carrel

October 13, 1939

Dear Jim,

We went back to Saint-Gildas for three days and we had the great pleasure to find your letters. . . .

By the fire in the library, we spoke often of you and the Colonel. Cigale [the dog] was sleeping as peacefully as she did last year during our conversations. We paid a short visit to Dom Alexis on our way back to Paris. He is in complete peace, undisturbed by events, and continuing his work of prayer and thought. He has still eight monks with him. He believes that in spite of the war, our plans should develop.

If I write other articles for *Reader's Digest,* I will be delighted to send them to your little committee. It is a most important thing. . . .

I have realized very clearly that I must help as much as I can those who are victims of this terrible calamity. The amount of suffering is going to be gigantic. I am officially connected with the Ministry of Public Health. But there is no means of action in this administration. No money and very few men. Therefore I am starting elsewhere to work on the very concrete problem of improving the technique for conservation and transportation of blood for transfusion—also for the treatment of shock and of infected wounds. I am going to be associated with Dr. Gosset, Professor of Surgery at the University of Paris, in this work. If Paris is not bombarded and if sufficient laboratory facilities are obtained immediately, we can progress, I hope, quite rapidly. But facilities for work are extremely poor.

You are right. Christian civilization is at stake. Do people in America begin to realize the extreme danger of the situation?

Madame Carrel joins me in sending you our best wishes.

Affectionately yours,
Alexis Carrel

November 20, 1939

My dear friend,

I had the great pleasure of receiving your letter of November 6. It is probable that I shall soon go to New York. That would be useful from several points of view. In particular, concerning transfusion and conservation of blood, and of the use of oxygen. Here we have been backward, sometimes 20 years behind the United States. It is the same thing as in 1914. On the other hand, the material organization is a great deal better. But the intelligence less so. There is much to be done. But the war has a much different appearance than the last one. The principal danger is perhaps from inside. I have seen many things that are profoundly interesting. The real significance of events is not understood even here. Since my arrival in Paris, I have seen many people but they do not have the same spirit as they had in 1914. What a strange war. There are the most contradictory rumors. But it seems as well that the Germany of today is not as united as the Germany of 1914.

Anne is beginning to organize a very useful work which she will carry out at the front. She has joined forces with former companions of Edith Cavell and Louise de Bettignies, condemned as they were, either to death or to forced labor. She leaves tomorrow to join one of the armies. She is perfectly delighted, naturally.

At the moment I am busy pushing the organization of a center for study of techniques essential to be perfected. It is therefore possible that I may leave for New York shortly. . . .

Very affectionately yours,
Alexis Carrel

November 27, 1939

Dear Jim,

I have had to become interested again in shock, hemorrhage, blood transfusion, wound infection, chemotherapy, gas therapy. I am attempting to do what I can to help the men who are going to be wounded. It is incredibly difficult to accomplish anything. Everybody hates everybody else. There would be an immense material progress in this country if there was a spiritual change. It is quite surprising to witness the effect of antagonism, fear, jealousy, selfishness on the results of the work of those entrusted with the defense of the nation. No "moral re-armament" here.

I have met many people and made important discoveries.

Some young men are realizing clearly the meaning of the European situation. Mostly young officers. They are scattered and come from widely different quarters. Their main interest is not political, not economic, but mystical. Very much like your friends—still more like Dom Alexis. They are telling me that this spirit is spreading among young people in the universities, the factories, the farms, the army. The left wing of these young people, who are as profoundly Christian as the Christians of the first centuries, is not far from the right wing of the young Communists. I spoke to them about the Oxford Group in America. They told me that the Oxford Group in France had some influence. There is no doubt that both movements come from the same deep impulse. They also believe that a material embodiment should be given to this growing mystical soul.

My own feeling is that no time should be lost in constructing the doctrine which must be substituted for Marxism. There is an immense and ubiquitous propaganda by Russia. Russian propaganda cannot be opposed only by force. The political, economic, social, and spiritual structure of our civilization has to be renovated. . . .

It seems to me that a profound change is taking place silently within the minds of the French youth. This change expresses itself in two ways: Christian mysticism and Communism. If this war does not destroy everything in Europe, there is, I believe, a real possibility for the renovation of our civilization. The disastrous results of materialism and hatred have become obvious within the nation. Many people want a moral and intellectual renovation.

I would like very much to go back to New York and work for a while in Wyckoff's laboratory. Nevertheless, I have to consider very carefully the situation which results from the needs of the war, the psychological attitude of the people, the relative value of what I can do in this country and in New York.

Madame Carrel is extremely happy because she is going to work at the front. She sends you her heartiest wishes.

Yours affectionately,
Alexis Carrel

Carrel's proposed journey to New York was delayed until May because he had continued negotiations with the government for the establishment of a field laboratory and perhaps a field hospital. He was also reluctant to leave Anne behind, but she was determined to push ahead with her nursing crusade. Convinced at last that he was getting nowhere, he booked passage on a ship sailing from Genoa on May 18, 1940. The timing was ironic. The authorities suddenly approved the construction of his field hospital as he was leaving. Its building was quickly completed, but no equipment or personnel were provided. And while he was sailing the Atlantic, Hitler at last invaded France.

It was a very unhappy Carrel whom I met when the *Champlain* docked on May 28. "Jim, I made a big mistake to come to America now. But I was so frustrated by those bureaucrats. Even with the war upon us, they were still only concerned with their reputations and their rivalries. I was even more powerless than in 1914. Then, at least, I had the Rockefeller Institute behind me, and I could get some cooperation from the army."

He plunged into work immediately with the director of the American Volunteer Ambulance Corps, who had returned from France with him and had promised to build him a one-hundred-bed mobile hospital. Working with an architect, they designed it and began construction. Then, on June 22, France surrendered to Germany. To Carrel's dismay, the hospital was offered to England, which had evacuated its troops from Dunkirk but was still at war.

Alexis became desperate for news from his wife. His efforts to obtain information about her from the State Department brought no results. When he talked to me about it, I called Charles Edison, who was at the time Secretary of the Navy, to see if he could do something. He contacted Sumner Welles, Undersecretary of State, and Welles instructed our embassy in France to make inquiries. Very soon, the embassy sent Carrel a cable saying that Anne was safe at Saint-Gildas. He learned that she had enough food for the moment but was short of coal to heat the house and to cook. The Germans had seized their two cars and boat, and had occupied Illiec, but they had left Saint-Gildas alone.

"I can never thank you enough, Jim," he said to me. But I was more concerned about Alexis than about Anne. He seemed close to a breakdown. Some of his friends and I persuaded him to go for a rest to Nantucket Island. It proved to be just the right place, and when I saw him again in New York in October, he was in command of himself again.

"Nantucket was like a big Saint-Gildas. Those fishermen reminded me of my Breton friends. And the sky and the wind and the waves were like home to me."

But he was far from tranquil in his spirit: "I don't understand America any more. The people remind me of my countrymen before Hitler attacked us. They don't think war will ever reach them. And most of them don't want to get involved with the struggle in Europe. That I can understand, though I think they are shortsighted. But I am worried about how divided the country seems to be—the majority who want to stay neutral, and those who want to get into the fight. Not only are they divided in their opinions, they get so *angry* with each other."

The war and what to do about it were the main topics of conversation when Carrel, Lindbergh and I, sometimes with Bakhmeteff and others, had meals together. Carrel might start the discussion, for example, by asking Charles why he was urging America's neutrality in the war.

Charles would respond in his typical logical manner by reviewing the steps that had led him to his position. He said that during his visits to Germany in 1936, 1937, and 1938, it had become absolutely clear to him that Germany's military strength in the air was outstripping the combined capabilities of the democracies in Europe. So the crucial question was—what were Hitler's intentions?

"It looked as if Hitler was expanding economically and politically through Central Europe," Charles said. "But if France and England tried to oppose him, he would use his armed might. And, of course, that's just what has happened."

Carrel objected. "But, Charles, how could France and England stand aside when Poland was invaded?"

Lindbergh repeated his opinion that France and England should never have entered into a treaty with Poland. Hitler knew theirs was an empty threat. The real tragedy in all this, Charles maintained, was that Hitler was pushed into a fight with the countries of Western Europe, which he hadn't wanted or planned on.

"Perhaps if America had stepped in at that time," objected Carrel, "Hitler would have pulled back."

"There's no way of knowing for sure," replied Lindbergh. "But I don't believe that the American people would have stood for that. Even if Roosevelt had dared to intercede, we were in the same position as France and England. We were not prepared for effective military action. We're not prepared today."

Carrel came back with the argument that the American people should face the situation that Germany and Italy were now in the process of taking over Western Europe, and now that Moscow and Berlin had signed a nonaggression treaty, Hitler was free to overrun Central Europe as well, and maybe North Africa. With Mussolini, he could dominate the Mediterranean.

"Can America afford to allow the totalitarians to achieve that?" he asked. "Doesn't your country have to step in before it's too late?"

Charles countered that he believed that Germany and Russia were inevitable enemies, despite the strange pact they had signed before Hitler invaded Poland. Sooner or later, they would be at each other's throats. Yes, he agreed that America should act, but Washington's influence should be directed toward resolving the conflict between Britain and Germany. Hitler well might welcome the opportunity to make peace with England, withdraw from France, and concentrate his energies eastward. "Far better to let Germany and Russia use their guns against each other," he said.

Carrel, too, had no use for either Nazism or Communism; but he wondered whether Hitler would really agree to peace with England without America using military force.

Maybe not, Charles said, but it was worth trying. Certainly far better than going to war with Germany. That would only open the door to Russia to step in and take over a devastated Western Europe.

In the meantime, he added, we should build our military strength in this country just as fast as we could.

So it went around and around each time we met, and certain convictions deepened in both Carrel and Lindbergh. Carrel wanted America to come to the aid of his people by whatever means—negotiations, medical aid, food and clothes, and if necessary military intervention. Charles insisted that America must not make the same mistake as France and England—jump into war unprepared. It was not our war. It was one more round in the conflict that had plagued Europe over the centuries and from which people like his grandparents had escaped to the New World.

Carrel's presence among us made our debates more than an intellectual argument. He said one evening, in reply to

192

Lindbergh: "Logically, Colonel, you may be right. But as conditions get worse in my country and the others that Hitler has seized, can Americans really stand by and watch the suffering without doing anything?"

Despite his sympathy for his friends in France and England, Lindbergh felt we shouldn't let feelings—pity, fear, or anger—rule national policy. We must take the long view, he said, and see what would best end the suffering. He felt that Roosevelt was using all kinds of pretexts to get us more and more involved, until war became inevitable.

Lindbergh's distrust of President Roosevelt, and Roosevelt's antagonism to him, went back at least half a dozen years. He had told me how, in 1934, Roosevelt had abruptly canceled domestic-airline air mail contracts and turned air mail delivery over to the Army Air Corps. Without giving the companies an opportunity to defend themselves, Roosevelt had accepted the findings of a special Senate committee, which accused the Post Office of inequities in awarding the contracts. He had shut down the service without any investigation.

Charles said that he had sent Roosevelt a telegram that was released to the press, charging unfairness to the airlines. It said Roosevelt was making a mistake in ordering the Army Air Corps to fly the mail. There would be severe consequences, he believed, as the corps was not equipped to handle the operation. As it happened, there were crashes, and a dozen pilots were killed. The president had to back down and allow the private airlines to fly the mail again. "He's never forgiven me for that," Charles said to me.

When Charles returned to America in 1939, he at once began active duty as a colonel in the Air Corps. Roosevelt had sent for him to come to the White House—their first meeting. Charles had told me that Roosevelt had been charming. One couldn't help liking him. But he felt the president was just too smooth, too much of a politician—he didn't trust him. But he was our president, and Charles was set to cooperate.

Their cooperation did not last long. Following the outbreak of war in Europe, Lindbergh began to make speeches urging America to remain neutral. He and Roosevelt were on a collision course.

*　　　*　　　*

During those difficult months of 1940, it seemed as though Alexis Carrel's life was being frustrated at every turn. He was separated from his wife, his country was at war, the Rockefeller Institute was closed to him, and his hopes for his Institute of Man were dimming.

As we sat at dinner in the Century Club or in his apartment, I could sense the battle that was being fought in his heart and mind. At times he talked, as he had so often, about the dynamic role that science must play in revealing man's true nature, and the relations between man and the universe. At other times he spoke wistfully of the men, like his friend Dom Alexis, who had devoted themselves to the mystic's search for reality through oneness with God.

"Jim," he said once, "I want to be like smoke in the wind at God's disposal."

And later, "God's love is the great reality. It is the mortar that holds the bricks of civilization together."

He was too shy, perhaps too proud, to tell me of the spiritual despair that was later revealed in his diaries. But I felt that he was frustrated by that very balance between intellect and spirit which he prized so highly. He was too disciplined a scientist to abandon himself to the way of the mystic, and yet enough of a spiritual pilgrim to be dissatisfied with purely scientific pursuits.

Harvey Firestone's often repeated words came to me: "The way of the pioneer is always rough." Carrel had devoted his life to blazing a trail, through the narrow-mindedness of some fellow scientists and church dignitaries alike. He was a champion of free and thorough inquiry into the human potential. But the further he searched, the more he found depths of the human spirit that seemed to defy the intellect.

As the weeks went by and 1940 came to an end, Carrel became increasingly ill at ease in America. One evening with Charles and me, he said, "It's becoming more and more difficult for me to sit in New York and know that my country is sliding into hunger and disease. I feel I must go back. There must be more that I can do in France than here. I need to get a clear picture of conditions over there. Then I can be in touch with you and maybe you'll be able to rally some help."

Charles and I felt it would be much better for Carrel to stay on in America, rather than return to an occupied country. But he was determined to go. He was to be accompanied by James Wood Johnson, a philanthropist who had bought a large supply of vitamins, which they hoped to smuggle into occupied France for distribution to the undernourished children.

"I'll be back in a couple of months," he said to us. "I must see Anne and see for myself just what the conditions are. Then Johnson and I will have specific information to give to the American government and our friends."

Anne had answered a letter from him, in which he had written that he was coming home. She urged him not to come, saying he would be a virtual prisoner. But he left before her letter arrived.

In our last conversation in his apartment, he said to me, "I don't know what I'll find over there, Jim. I've made my plans to come back, as you know, because I may be a lifeline between America and France for my people. But I know how ruthless those Nazis are. Will you do something for me, if they hold me? Will you approach Charles Edison again, ask him to use his influence?"

195

I promised to do so. As we looked at each other, I'm sure he realized as much as I how perilous a voyage he was taking.

On February 1, 1941 Charles and I went down to see him off on the American freighter *Siboney,* sailing for Lisbon. We stood on the dock and waved as Alexis leaned over the rail, waving back. It was our last sight of him. He never returned.

We tried to keep in touch with each other through letters, but it became impossible once America was at war. Carrel and Johnson got into Spain and were horrified by the starvation and lack of medical care. They were not allowed to take the vitamins into occupied France and left them to be distributed in Spain. As they traveled through France, Carrel received a note from Anne on Saint-Gildas and was able to join her. Then they went back to Vichy, where Marshal Pétain headed the government of "free" France. Pétain received him warmly, and when Carrel talked of his dreams for an "Institute of Man," Pétain offered to subsidize it. Carrel accepted and went to work, despite the obstructions placed in his way by the medical profession. Carrel's decision to pursue his humanitarian work in association with Pétain's Vichy government later earned him bitter criticism from the resistance forces backing de Gaulle.

Long after the war, when I met again with Anne Carrel, she told me about her husband's determination to focus his research on finding answers to the problems of children. Later, his Institute of Man in Paris was to reach into the more controversial fields of Carrel's interests—hypnosis, mental telepathy, and ESP. Anne worked with him in these studies.

The Carrels refused to accept any special government favors, such as extra food or heating fuels. She stood in line on cold, early mornings. Their privations—he was now seventy—undermined his health. In the summer of 1943 they got away for a rest on Saint-Gildas, and there he suffered a heart attack. He was rushed to Paris and recovered. But a year later, he suffered a much more severe attack, just after Paris was liberated by the American forces. While he lay ill, he was viciously and unjustly attacked by the liberation government for allegedly collaborating with the Germans. This was one blow too many, and in November 1944, he died.

At this point I was in the Army, and bits and pieces of all this news reached me as I was moved around. Once, when it appeared he might have died, I did enlist the help of Charles Edison. He was able to discover that Carrel was then still alive and at work. News of his death reached me when I was stationed at Fort Lee, Virginia. My wife Ellie and I had rented a little apartment over a garage in Petersburg. I sat there and quietly cried as I read the news. I felt the pain of those years of separation, years I believed might have been more fulfilling for him if we'd been able to persuade him to stay in America.

After the war in Europe came to an end, Anne Carrel came to the United States. I heard of her arrival in New York from Anne Lindbergh and was able to reach her on the phone just before I sailed to the Philippines with the Army. Although she was ill, after all she had been through, her voice rang out with delight when she heard me on the phone. Anne Lindbergh welcomed her warmly and did everything to restore her health and peace of mind until she was able to sail with her nephew to Argentina, where she went to live.

I had a letter from Anne Lindbergh soon after I arrived in the Philippines in June 1945:

I have seen Madame Carrel three times now. Once just after she landed, once a few days ago, and the following day. . . . The first time we talked all afternoon—from two till six. It is true she is very, very sad, not so much at his death itself, which she has accepted, but because he died *complètement désespéré*—in complete despair. The privations they had to go through were also unbelievable, and she felt they also killed him. She feels also that had she been able to reach him while he was in America (which she tried to do—she sent him a letter telling him not to come back to France, which he never got) she might have saved him all this.

I told her, however, that I believe he would have suffered just as much—perhaps even more—from feeling he should be there, that it was his duty, etc. She said, yes, perhaps that was so—for apparently he said during the worst time, we have done what is right—what we should have done (by coming here).

This is one of her comforts. Another is the devotion of the young doctors of the Institute in Paris, who were "like sons" and in whom she feels the seeds of what he taught and believed are being carried on. This is a great hope and a great justification and comfort. They were around him until the end, one of them always sleeping there at night, unknown to Dr. C., in case he had need of them.

Also it was a great joy and comfort to her that Dom Alexis managed to get there—only a day—before the Dr. died. She had sent for him weeks, perhaps months, before. He just managed to get up by some freight train. Dr. C. was quite conscious and put his arms out to him, saying, "Ah— Father—you have come. Now you will not leave me." Of course he did not, till the end, and it was a great joy and comfort to him.

Mme. Carrel looks worn and thinner, but still *amazingly* the same. She still gives the impression of enormous strength, and even vitality. It is true she was *very* ill, suddenly, a short time after his death. She had been poisoned, I gather, by taking too much saccharin. But she has completely recovered from that.

She is warmed now by the love of his friends and lives for that and for what she can give to the world, through them, of her husband's memory and thoughts. I talked to her about how this was what she must do, since she was so close to him and so many younger men and women could still draw from him through her. She lives for this. There are also, I believe, short articles which she wishes published. . . .

She is not broken, she is not bitter, she is full of belief and even a kind of peace at having done all she could, and at the thought that he is happier now. She is even the same as to her intense interest in life—in you—in us—in all the children. She laughed about them, looked at all their pictures and analyzed them on sight. I took Jon in to see her before he left for Camp. He remembered her and wanted to see her. She was gay—even though lying on her couch with lumbago—and showed all her real interest in Jon's mason jar of guppy fish!

She had your letter on the table beside her bed and told me to read it. It warmed her and meant everything to her. She is sad not to see you. She lifts her hands with that gesture ("But what can I do!") so familiar, but she understands.

Yes, she is even gay. She laughs. She tells with relish stories of the occupation—what she said to the Germans, how she fooled them, etc., etc. All this amazed and heartened me. What a woman she is!

She is going to have her back x-rayed for lumbago and after that I hope will come out here. I hope and expect C. home soon. This has been a long, strange, sad spring. I seem to have seen only people steeped in tragedy or sadness . . . I wanted you to know that Mme. C. is still the same and that your love and prayers have reached and helped her. That you are close to her, even though so cruelly separated now.

199

My love and thoughts to you and Ellie. The children loved your cards—How good of you!

Anne

It was not until the early 1960s that Ellie and I heard the full story of Carrel's last years from Anne Carrel herself. We were in Buenos Aires and called on the Marquis de la Mairie, Anne's son by her first marriage. On the spur of the moment, he and his wife offered to drive us up into the Sierra de Córdoba, some five hundred miles to the northwest, to the village of Cumbrecita, where his mother was living.

Anne was working with an eye surgeon and was at the hospital when we arrived at her apartment. Her son told us to hide in the apartment and went over to bring her back, without telling her that he had brought us. When she came in, I stepped out from behind a door. She exploded with surprise and excitement. She seemed to have lost none of her vitality. She was actually assisting in operations—delicate ones on the cornea, with surgical instruments she had devised.

We talked for hours about her husband and years past. I told her how we had tried to communicate with them during the war, but apparently our letters did not get through.

"That was the hardest thing of all for Alexis," Anne said. "We didn't know correspondence was being held up. He began to feel his American friends had deserted him—even you and the colonel."

Then she went on to tell me what had happened during his last months and years. Trouble began when he ran into the opposition of some medical men and bureaucrats who were jealous of his institute or resented his employment of certain scientists. Valéry Radot, who was appointed minister of health after the liberation, finally stopped Carrel's work at the institute on the grounds there were suspicions of his being a Nazi collaborator.

I told her I'd heard that, and Charles Lindbergh told me he had investigated the charges when he went through Paris at the war's end and had tried unsuccessfully to reach her. He went into it thoroughly, as Charles always went into anything, and found the charges were absolutely unfounded.

"Of course! You know what had happened?" She explained how she and Carrel had gone to the German embassy one day on a business matter—to get help in feeding starving French children. They were surprised to find themselves in the middle of a party there, and left as soon as they could.

"Then rumors went around that the Germans had entertained us at a party at their embassy! You know how Alexis felt about the Nazis when he was in New York. He felt much more strongly, living in occupied France. Why, many of our staff at the institute were members of the Resistance, and we protected them."

They had refused all the gifts and special treatment the Germans had offered, although they had no heat in their apartment. He had to go everywhere on his bicycle and she had to stand in line before dawn to buy food. When the newspapers took up the charges against Carrel, who was in poor health, the persecution was too much for him. He suffered a second heart attack and died.

"Truly, Jim," she said, "I see now how dear Alexis brought some of these blows on his own head. You know he was never one to keep his ideas to himself. He was so mad at some of those doctors who tried to stop his work. He spoke out and hurt their feelings and they turned on him when they got the chance."

I thought of how Thomas Edison, too, was often his own

201

worst enemy by his outspokenness. But Carrel lacked Edison's tact. His sweeping statements on matters outside his expertise often made needless enemies.

She put us up for the night and we spent part of the next day with her. When we asked her about her work, her face lit up. "I like to think Alexis would approve of what I'm doing. His last years were devoted to children. It's the children up here especially that I'm trying to help. They are so poor and they have such poor medical help. At this hospital we can really make a difference."

Ellie and I agreed that Alexis would be very proud of her.

We kept in touch with Mme. Carrel in Argentina and received her letters with special delight. She would address us as "Little Oyster" and "Pretty Butterfly." She called me "Oyster," she said, because I had a way of surrounding the disagreeable things that came my way with a cheerful acceptance. Ellie was "Butterfly" because she flitted lightly with a loving touch from person to person.

One example:

Jim, my very dear "Little Oyster" and you Pretty Butterfly,

I often think of you both, and am so sorry to be so far from you.

I realy was very sick, and if the surgeon was not such a wonderfull man, it is very probably that we would not have seen each other again on earth. But the truth is that now, I am entirely in good health and have recovered my activity. I am working each morning at the hospital, from 8 to 1 o'clock, without being tired. I think in thoses conditions your prayers are very effectifs and the best is that you continued, to pray for me. . . .

The worst is to stay such along time without a line from you. And also I realy don't know if my letter will reach you at the adress you put on your letter, because Butterfly and yourself are always going from a new point? . . .

I am very happy to heare, that you feel so much better, but my dear boy, I am not entirely persuaded, that you have taken enough time to recover entirely / let me tell you that you are an *old fool* if you feel something wrong, and dont pay great care of you. that's mother oyster advise, and Alexis would be very angry with you, if you don't pay attention to my advise. What have you to answer at that, stupid fool?

I am working very hard on Alexis notes, it's terrible, because his wrighting with pencil is half gone, and I don't find any one to healp me in this work.

Edward is gone to France? Sorry not to be there to recived him at Saint-Gildas I immediatly wroth a letter to Dr. Crépin who will take care of him, but I dont know how they will anderstand each others because Edward speak English and very little Fremch and Crépin, speak only French, but perhaps the Holy Gost will give them the understanding who is necessary beetwen them.

Don't speak to me to be good, since Alexis left me, I am only a made dog without master, no home, . . . that God will, it's enough.

My two children I send you my best love

23rd June 1962
Mother Oyster

*   *   *

Ten years later, on June 28, 1973 the centenary of Carrel's birth was celebrated at Georgetown University, in Washington, D.C. Lindbergh was invited to speak, but he was scheduled to be in Europe that day. Georgetown wanted to postpone the celebration or move the date up, but Lindbergh responded, "You can't move Dr. Carrel's birthday around. I'll be there."

I went with him and listened to his brilliant tribute to the life and work of his friend. Typically, Charles's speech was a well-balanced evaluation of Carrel's many-sided genius. He began by describing his meeting with Carrel and their work together on the artificial heart, and then he continued:

I soon found Carrel himself even more fascinating than the laboratory projects I pursued in his Department of Experimental Surgery. There seemed to be no limit to the breadth and penetration of his thought. One day he might discuss the future of organ perfusion, for which I was building an apparatus. On another, he would be talking to a professional animal trainer about the relative intelligence of dogs and monkeys, and the difficulty of teaching a camel to walk backward. I once looked up from my work to see him step into the room with Albert Einstein, discussing extra-sensory perception. Not long afterwards, at an Institute lunch table, he was worrying about the environmental effect of white bread on French peasants, and the effect of civilization in general on our human species. "No one realizes," he said, "how many genetic defects modern man contains."

Lindbergh spoke of Carrel's startling contradictions:

According to his mood, Carrel could work with a precision that caused the admiration of the scientific world, or he could speak with an abandon that brought criticism heaping on his shoulders. He might straighten his back and assert that "all surgeons are butchers," and assert that "all people are fools," or sit at his desk and write that "on the scale of magnitudes man is placed midway between the atom and the star." He had a character that attracted the love of those who knew him well, and a blunt tactlessness that created many enemies.

Lindbergh told of Carrel's dream of the Institute of Man and continued:

> In eulogizing Carrel, one might emphasize his skill as a surgeon, his pioneering work in fields of tissue culture, his treatment of wounded in World War I, his suturing of blood vessels which brought him the Nobel Prize, his perception and his depth of vision. Personally, I can say that he had the most stimulating mind I have ever met. But to me his greatness lay primarily in his comprehension of man and life as a whole, of the infinite elements and qualities that through epochs have emerged in human form, the miracle of their existence, the mystery of their origin and destiny.
>
> Alexis Carrel realized how closely, on this earth, the qualities of body, mind, and spirit interweave and that—looking toward the future—the advance of one is essentially dependent on the others.*

I was astonished when Charles agreed to hold a press conference afterward: he had avoided the press so much of his life. The journalists had not been allowed to be present at the centennial ceremonies. As I watched and listened, he answered question after question about Carrel. Then he would be asked a question about his wife, or what he usually ate for breakfast, or his views on women's rights.

"We're here for the centenary of Dr. Carrel, and I'll an-

* From the monograph, *Papers of the Centennial Conference at Georgetown University,* June 28, 1973; pp. 29–32.

swer any reasonable questions about him, if I can. Anything else—forget it!" And he smiled. Throughout the interview he was relaxed and courteous, but firm.

At the end of his life, Carrel, like Lindbergh, had suffered at the hands of the press. I'm sure he would have appreciated Charles's handling of them that day.

Chapter

EIGHT

DURING THE CONFUSING MONTHS of the "phony war," between Germany's invasion of Poland in September 1939 and the breakthrough into the Low Countries and France in May 1940, I saw a good deal of the Lindberghs. For the first couple of months they were living in a rented house in Lloyd Neck, on the north shore of Long Island. I went out there on a Sunday, September 3, the day England and France declared war with Germany. I drove up to their door with a sixty-pound turtle, which I had bought from a guy who was going to use it for soup. It looked in poor shape after its journey from Florida. I knew the Lindbergh's seven-year-old son Jon was crazy about turtles and thought he might enjoy restoring it to health.

"We'd better put it in Land's wading pool for the moment," said Charles. Land was their vigorous two-year-old toddler. Charles and Anne and I then went swimming, and afterward we walked the beach and talked about what he would do now that Europe was at war.

He felt the simplest thing would be to go on doing what he was doing before—working with the Air Corps, NACA, the aviation companies, research companies, and research centers. God knows, America needed all the help it could get in looking to its air defenses. But he wasn't sure that would satisfy his conscience. It was important to prepare for war, he said, but even more important was to prevent America from getting into one. Surely he was as well equipped as anyone to wake our people up to the realities.

The trouble was that if he spoke out against getting into Europe's war, the administration would probably force him out of his work in aviation. He wanted to take the initiative and go on inactive status rather than let them do that.

Charles said the choice would be easier if it weren't for the family. As soon as he spoke out, he'd be the target of the news media once again. That meant their harassment at home. The fanatics would be drawn like shavings to a magnet. That could endanger Anne and the children when they were alone.

"What does Anne say?" I asked him.

"You know Anne. When she knows where I think my duty lies, she'll back me 100 percent."

Charles phoned me the next day. He had made up his mind. He would go ahead and publicize his stand in articles and on the radio. He was sure Fulton Lewis, Jr. (a popular radio commentator) would get him on the air, if asked, and he wondered if I thought DeWitt Wallace would be interested in an article on the subject for the *Reader's Digest.*

When Charles made up his mind, he went to work with determination. Within a week, he was writing an article for Wallace and showing me the draft of his radio statement on Fulton Lewis, Jr.'s show. His talk was a clear and moving call to Americans to hold to George Washington's warning not to become entangled in European alliances. He stressed the point that this war was one more of the age-old squabbles among European powers, and Americans should not let sentiment cloud their judgments. If we allowed ourselves to be drawn into the fighting, we would become involved in a disastrous life-and-death struggle. Our frontiers did not lie in Europe, despite the propaganda of the media.

"What do you think, Jim?" he asked, when I returned it to him.

"I think it's good. The question I have is the part where you attack the administration as well as the press. I wonder if it wouldn't be better to lay off Roosevelt for the moment and see which way he jumps. He may feel the pressure of public opinion is too great, and slow down. After all, the polls make it clear that the big majority of people want to stay out of war. If you attack him, it's sure to hurt his pride, and that may make him only push harder."

Charles grinned at Anne, across the room. It seemed that she had told him just about the same thing.

Charles removed the passage.

After supper I drove him into New York to catch a night train to Washington. There he was going to tell his boss, General Henry H. "Hap" Arnold, about his radio talk. He thought it probable that Arnold or his chief, Secretary of War Harry Woodring, would ask for his resignation from active status in the Air Corps.

That was exactly what happened, he told me, when I joined him in Washington later that day. Arnold had apparently been understanding and said he didn't want to see Charles go, but appreciated his position. He saw nothing unethical in the statement—Charles had showed him the text—and asked if he could show it to Woodring. Charles had said he'd rather Arnold didn't. Later, Arnold said he'd already told Woodring about the radio talk, and Woodring had been very annoyed. The president would certainly get on his back about it.

Charles included me in a lunch in Washington with Anne

and Fulton Lewis in the Lindberghs' apartment at the Anchorage. While we were eating, Colonel Truman Smith arrived. As U.S. military attaché, Smith had invited Lindbergh to Berlin in 1936 to investigate the strength and quality of the German Air Force. During that and subsequent visits, the Smiths and Lindberghs had become close friends. The two went into the bedroom to talk privately. Later, Charles told me that Smith had been asked by Arnold, who had been asked by Woodring, who had been asked by Roosevelt, to offer Lindbergh the specially created cabinet post of Secretary of Air if he would cancel his radio talk and refrain from pushing for neutrality.

Charles said, "I asked Smith if Arnold thought I would accept the bribe. He only laughed and said, 'Of course not. But it was a message we had to deliver.' "

It was not until that moment that I realized just how worried Roosevelt had to be about Lindbergh. The president understood how powerful Charles's influence would be on the public mind at this critical time. The date was September 15, 1939, just two weeks after the outbreak of the European war.

I went on ahead to the Carlton Hotel, from which Lindbergh was going to broadcast. He had asked me to make sure everything was set up right. CBS and NBC had received permission from Mutual to carry the talk—so it would have full national coverage over the three national networks. Six microphones, two for each of the broadcasting systems, stood ready in a small room in a red and gold suite on the third floor. I checked with the engineers on the location of the mikes and made sure that the plainclothes policeman at the door would admit no unauthorized persons.

All went well at the broadcast. The text of the talk was carried in the *New York Times* and the *Herald-Tribune* and was well received by the public, judging by the correspondence that poured into the networks.

DeWitt Wallace phoned to tell Charles that he liked his article and had accepted it for publication. The *Digest,* as was its custom, arranged with *Atlantic Monthly* to have it published there first. In the article Charles took his argument a step further than the broadcast. He wrote about the war as a conflict "within our own family of nations, a war which will reduce our strength and destroy our treasures."

Charles's position may seem strange to those who did not live through those difficult years, 1940–41. Even those of us who did, tend to forget that Lindbergh expressed the views of the great majority of Americans. While they were strongly against Hitler's Germany and wanted an Allied victory, public opinion polls showed that up to 80 percent of voters were opposed to our entering the war. Non-involvement in foreign wars was still, as Charles pointed out in his speeches and articles, a traditional element of American foreign policy. This belief was reinforced for him by his family and Midwestern upbringing. The sturdy, self-reliant spirit of the Scandinavian immigrant settlers strengthened both his tendency towards isolationism and his distrust of Roosevelt's engineering of involvement, which he felt was an infringement on representative government.

In the autumn of 1939, I was in and out of the Lloyd Neck house, often staying with them for days at a time. As Charles began to travel, making speeches across the country and continuing his work with NACA, he handed me the keys to his car and his New York parking pass, so I could use them on my trips to and from the city. In November the family moved to the old Morrow home in Englewood, New Jersey, where they had lived earlier, because the Lloyd Neck house was not heated for winter living. But they rented a more substantial house on Lloyd Neck for the next couple of years.

Once Charles had made up his mind to speak out to his countrymen, it seemed to me he had become freer in his spirit. Although he was increasingly concerned about the course of the war and America's danger of involvement, he now seemed able to shed his anxieties and relax as we swam, walked on the beach, and played with his sons. The whole family became involved in our horseplay and practical jokes. Anne called us a couple of overgrown boys. More than once I sank into bed after a dinner and an evening full of conversation only to find my bed had been short-sheeted by the two young women, Soeur Lisi, the children's Swiss nurse, and Christine Gawne, the secretary. One evening I picked up the glass tumbler from its shelf in my bathroom and took my usual drink of water. Water dribbled down my chin. The same thing happened a second time, before I found tiny holes in the filigree work near the top of the glass.

The most spectacular prank came after a dinner at which I had performed one of my parlor tricks—putting a lighted candle in my mouth and keeping it there for half a minute. During this hilarious meal I got some candle wax on my trousers.

"Give me your pants, Jim," said Charles, after dinner. "I'll get Soeur Lisi to get the wax off." He led me to the clothes closet under the stairs and I foolishly went along with him, took my pants off, and handed them to him. Then I stood there in the dark. Nothing happened. Before long I realized I'd been had. I felt around in the dark, found a raincoat, and wrapped it around me. Then the door opened a crack and I saw what I recognized as the barrel of a tear-gas gun pointed toward the floor. Charles had brought it back from his visit to China. It had been part of the emergency equipment given to him and Anne to keep crowds from damaging their plane as they brought vaccine to the disastrously flooded areas. They had never used it.

There was a terrific bang. I'd closed my eyes and was holding my breath. I punched the door open, almost knocking Charles down, and groped my way into the kitchen, where

Soeur Lisi was pressing my pants. I seized them and ran out into the fresh air. Our horseplay took his mind off the grim world, and it was part of our growing friendship.

On another occasion, during a visit to their Englewood home, Charles said to me, "I've learned through yoga how to stop my heartbeat. Take my wrist and feel my pulse while I concentrate." He leaned back and looked up at the ceiling. After a minute or so I felt his pulse grow weaker and weaker until it stopped. Then it gradually came back. It was impressive, but I was sure it was a trick. He then showed me that he had balled up a handkerchief under his armpit, and as he pressed his arm to his side, he gradually cut off the flow of blood.

I used that trick some years later in a field hospital in the Philippines during the war. A very brassy blond nurse came around as usual in the early morning to take my vital signs. When I stopped my pulse with a balled-up handkerchief the brazen expression on her face was replaced by one of consternation. Then she saw my big grin, threw down my arm, and flounced off, her composure shattered.

*   *   *

One evening in October 1939, after he had been meeting with former President Hoover and others in New York, Charles invited me to bring two of my friends from Moral Re-Armament, John Roots and Ken Twitchell, to dinner at the Engineers Club. His mind was full of the war, Lend-Lease legislation, and so on. Twitchell and Roots made the point that, whatever happened in the war, mankind had to find a new way of living, between men and between nations. Human wisdom had failed, and statesmen, backed by people in all walks of life, had to seek and find God's answer to the hurts and hates of the past. Lindbergh agreed with them but asked how practical people could be persuaded to do that. They outlined Frank Buchman's current campaign to get 100 million men and women listening—prepared to face personal, national, and international issues in the light of God's will. Well-known figures were being asked to speak in the United States and in Europe over radio networks on this theme.

After they'd left and we talked about the evening, Charles said to me, "Moral Re-Armament attracts a fine type of person. And it fires them with a great enthusiasm. You are all dedicated to important goals. But as for me, you know I am no joiner. I have the feeling your friends are trying to get me into a movement. I feel what is needed is the other way around—get movement into people but leave them free to move in their own way."

I didn't argue with him. Of course, that's what MRA was all about—to get movement into people.

Lindbergh kept up the pressure of his speaking and writing. He gave a second radio talk over the Mutual System in October, covering some of the same ground as in the first program but going into more detail on the reason America should keep out of the war.

Anne decided she would use her pen to fight in her own way the same battle that Charles was waging to maintain the peace. She finished an article she called "Prayer for Peace" on November 26, a follow-up to Charles's arguments. He was impressed with its message and felt that ideally it should appear in the *Reader's Digest* at Christmastime. Unfortunately, in order for the January issue to appear on the newsstands around December 20, it had to be printed in late November. Charles telephoned me that evening, November 26, and I promised to call the *Digest* first thing the next morning.

I did so and found that most of the January issue had already gone to the printers. Kenneth Payne, the editor, said he'd try his best, but they must have the manuscript that day! Anne's secretary, Christine, typed it in time for the *Digest* messenger to pick it up. Payne called her back to say that he liked it and would take out two other articles to make room for it. The messenger would call the next morning for the final corrected copy. In order to have it ready, after everyone had gone to bed, Charles got up and spent half the night retyping it for Anne.

I arranged two more meals for Charles with friends. The first was a dinner shortly before Christmas of 1939 to which he brought Anne to meet Ken and Marian Twitchell and Frank Buchman. It was Lindbergh's first meeting with Buchman. When Charles asked how successful their "100 million listening" had been, Buchman characteristically asked Twitchell to tell him. The radio broadcasts had had a big response in Britain and America and had been rebroadcast in many parts of the world.

Buchman said to Charles, "The arts of reconciliation have not kept pace with the arts of war. Our job is to demonstrate God's power to heal divisions." He told Charles about the work MRA was doing to mediate between management and labor in the aviation industry. Communists had been stirring up serious conflicts in the unions, and our military strength was in jeopardy. The mayor of Seattle had asked Buchman to bring some people of MRA into Seattle to find an answer not only to Boeing, but to other plants throughout the city.

Afterward, Charles said to me that he had liked Buchman. He commented on his magnetism and openness. "There's no doubt the movement is doing good work, though I don't pretend to understand what generates all their enthusiasm," he said.

Early in the new year, 1940, Lindbergh hosted a lunch at the Engineers Club for two of my friends—John Roots, a journalist, and a British unemployed workers' leader, who had left the Communist Party because of MRA. Charles had never met anyone quite like him and was interested in his story of why he had become a Communist and why he had decided to abandon it. His infant son had died of starvation when he was unemployed, and in his bitterness, he had set out to smash the social and economic system; it was at that vulnerable time that he had been enlisted by the Communists. "I cannot blame a man for turning to anything that opposes the existing order under such circumstances," Charles said. The man had left the party when he was challenged "to take part in the greater revolution in human nature" offered by MRA.

In late December, Charles told me that he and Anne and young Jon were going to visit his mother in Detroit. I asked if they would like to see the Fords and offered to try to arrange it. When I phoned Henry Ford, he responded warmly and invited us for lunch in his home.

The five of us had a leisurely meal, at which Ford introduced the Lindberghs to one of his health foods, carrot juice. Charles drew out his host on some of his favorite topics— the insanity of war, of wars in general and of this one in particular; the impact of wartime on the auto industry; Ford's dreams of seeing industry decentralized. Then the Fords took us on a tour of the house, their birdwatching porch, the library—plus swimming pool, bowling alley, billiard room, game room, these last all built to hold their son Edsel's interest in the home.

On the way back in the car, Charles said, "That man is fascinating, bursting with ideas. Some of them are far out, but they're always stimulating." He liked Ford's concern about building small factories out in the countryside, with each employee having a plot of land, so workers could be in touch with nature and augment their diet during times of depression. Nevertheless, Charles thought Ford's River Rouge assembly plant was much more likely to be the way of the future.

*   *   *

Early in January 1941, when I was with them in their New Jersey home, Anne said at supper one evening that she wished she and Charles could get away for a few days. Charles was bone tired.

I suggested a boat trip down the Florida gulf coast, past the Everglades. I knew a hundred-mile stretch below Everglade City that was virtually uninhabited.

The idea captured their imaginations, and a couple of weeks later they were on a train south. I had gone down and borrowed a thirty-foot cabin cruiser and hired a guide, a twenty-five-year-old fellow I knew, Charlie Greene, who had been an Audubon game warden in the Everglades. Charles and Anne bought their tickets to Tampa, but got off the train at Haines City to avoid the press. I met them there and drove them to a cottage I'd rented on Captiva Island. My mother had stocked it with provisions for the trip. Everything was perfect, except for the weather. It was the coldest January I'd known in Florida.

"Stop apologizing, Jim," said Charles, with a twinkle in his eyes, "just accept that God knows what he's doing and enjoy it." He and Anne seemed to, and I relaxed. We stayed on Captiva for five days, planning the boat trip, walking on the white sand, swimming in the breakers, sailing in my center-board sailboat. We played a crazy game in the moonlight, with a strong wind kicking up high breakers: we would see who could plant a stick furthest out in the sand before the next wave rushed in. Anne was right in there with us, despite her diminutive size. Of course we all got soaking wet.

When we finally set off down the coast, the water was rough. Charles and Anne had a lively time keeping a pot on the stove as they cooked the first meal. We stopped at Marco, "the end of civilization" for that stretch of land in those days, to fill the water and gas tanks, and from there on we were running down the wild mangrove coast. Each evening we anchored in the lee of an island—the first night, it was Indian Key. Next day we turned into Shark River and made our way up through the mangrove swamps. Birds were everywhere. Anne kept exclaiming at the cloudlike formations of ducks, ibis, pelicans, and egrets. The river kept forking, running through smaller and smaller bayous until the tree branches closed over us. We climbed into the dinghy and Charles, Charlie, and I had to hack our way through in places. We were in a primitive world, the silence broken only by the cry of a bird and the occasional splash of a fish.

"What a sense of humility this place gives you!" Anne said. "It's an unspoiled world in which man seems to have no part."

At one point Charlie Green wanted to shoot some ducks. Anne dissuaded him. "Let's just manage with fish and the food we have."

As we sat and watched the stars brighten above the trees that night, we talked again about this peaceful, uninhabited territory.

"Wilderness," said Charles. "People need it and miss it. It's frightening to think that in a few years our children and their children may not be able to experience it. It feeds the soul." And then he added that he'd had a part in making that wilderness disappear.

When I expressed surprise at his statement, he explained. He had given his life to aviation because he had a dream of how it could unify the world. He had hoped it would bring people together, give different civilizations the opportunity to enrich one another. But look at what was happening. People were being brought into contact and man was penetrating remote places, yes, but who would argue that all that was benefiting the world or helping the world to live peacefully?

"Charles, no one will argue with you that your flight to Paris made the world air-conscious. But the way the world uses the airplane is something beyond your powers to decide. Anyway, I think air travel will prove more of a blessing than a problem."

Charles said he hoped I was right about that. What concerned him even more at the moment was how the airplane would be used if all-out war broke out in Europe. Hitler was building a gigantic air force capable of destroying millions of lives, and along with them, cities and the treasures of Western civilization.

Anne said quietly, "I was with you and I saw what you saw and felt what you felt. But you can't hold yourself responsible for German rearmament."

We went off to bed, Charlie and I in the stern cabin and Charles and Anne in the forward one. Usually I was asleep in no time, but that evening I was awake for a while, with Charles's convictions about aviation as a destructive force going through my mind. Next day I brought the subject up again. We had cruised out of Shark River and down the coast to Middle Cape. We anchored the boat and walked inland along a strip of hard sand, fringed with coconut palms.

"You've told me a little about those visits to Germany, Charles. I'd like to hear more."

They were an eye-opener, he told me. He had felt a big responsibility as he was the only American in those years, 1936 and 1937, to have the opportunity to see what giant strides Hitler was making in building his air force. Goering and his staff had let him see their planes, factories, and research centers, and had even allowed him to fly those planes. Washington knew very little about them, as did London and Paris. Because of his training and experience in aviation he was able to interpret what he was allowed to see and weigh its significance. He had passed all this on to Truman Smith, the U.S. military attaché in Berlin, and Smith had sent it on to Washington.

I interrupted, "Why did Goering let you see all that?"

Charles thought Hitler might have wanted America to realize that Germany was becoming a power to be reckoned with—not so much as an enemy, but as a proud nation determined to restore its prestige in Europe and the world.

Charles added that, of course, there were other projects that Goering only hinted at, but he was not allowed to see. He felt Goering might have underestimated how accurate a picture Lindbergh could draw from the amount he was shown. It was clear to Charles that their air force was being built as an instrument against Europe, not as a long-range weapon against the United States. There was a great emphasis on fighters and medium-range bombers, but almost none on heavy, long-range bombers.

He had alerted Washington about Hitler's air strength, but, ironically, he didn't know just how little that information had sunk in with the president and his top advisers.

Relaying the same information to Britain had been frustrating. The British ambassador in Berlin had actually had a pretty good idea of German air power and had begged Charles to talk to people in his government about what he'd seen. Apparently, they hadn't believed the ambassador. Charles did his best but was met with English calm and indifference. By the time Chamberlain confronted Hitler at Munich, some of the English had been awakened. They started to step up their aircraft production. But, of course, by then it was too late—they were far behind German production.

The French, according to Charles, were more realistic, but the trouble was that France was permeated by the Left—by cynicism and hopelessness. They lacked the spirit and energy to get the country on the move. Soviet Russia was probably most realistic about Hitler's Germany, but he thought their repressive system had prevented them from developing their aviation adequately. They were relying on American technology. They seemed to have large numbers of aircraft, but he didn't know how good the maintenance and quality of their work was.

I said it was strange that after all he'd done to give America, Britain and France such essential information about the buildup of German air power, some had begun to call him a Nazi sympathizer.

"If you don't want to face facts," Charles remarked, "it's sometimes comforting to call the bearer of those facts bad names!"

Anne stopped the conversation saying there would be plenty of time to talk about these things back home. She seemed determined not to let what people said get under their skin.

From the Middle Cape we sailed south to Marathon, midway down the Florida keys. We had reached civilization again, and took on fuel and ice. There was even a telephone, and I called home. I was told there was a telegram for Anne from *Reader's Digest,* saying that the British Information Service had requested permission to reprint her "Prayer for Peace." Anne thought I was joking when I told her. She thought perhaps they hadn't understood the article, or, then again, maybe they had begun to realize what they were up against in the war. She telegraphed permission, provided they reprint the article in full.

I made the mistake of buying a couple of newspapers; they only brought the war nearer. Hitler had made a fiery speech suggesting that total war was just around the corner. He attacked both Churchill and Chamberlain and made any hope of peace look very distant.

One morning as Charles and Anne and I sat in the bow of the cruiser while Charlie threaded it through the channels of the Everglades, Charles began talking about his old airmail and barnstorming days. Some of his most amusing experiences had taken place when he was doing the mail run from St. Louis to Chicago in 1926. It was one of the first routes in the country, and extremely primitive. Before taking off from St. Louis he'd call the Chicago airport on a pay phone. "How does the weather look?" "Not too bad. Clouds up at maybe five hundred feet. Not raining at the moment." So he'd take off—at night, of course.

Once, flying the mail, Charles was caught in a fog with no place to land. He flew above the clouds until he used up his gas so that the plane wouldn't burn when it crashed. Then he took to his parachute.

The fog was down to ground level and he landed on a barbed-wire fence, with a cow a few feet away, quiet as a mouse. The barbed wire tore the leather flying suit he'd borrowed from Phil Love, a fellow cadet at Kelly Field and a good friend who had joined him on the airmail route.

When Phil saw his suit, he hit the roof, or pretended to. "You've torn my pants, Slim. You'll have to get me a new suit."

"Not on your life," answered Charles.

"At least, get it fixed."

"No, sir."

"But when I loaned it to you, it was with the understanding that you'd return it in the same condition."

"Yes, but Phil, the one thing you didn't take into consideration was an Act of God. That's what this was. If you don't believe me, ask the cow."

That suit was to become the source of friendly jibing for as long as the two were alive.

Occasionally the engine would give out, or sometimes the clouds came down so low he'd have to find a field to land. One day, when barnstorming, there just wasn't a flat field. Too many trees and hills. The only place he could land was a little village with a main street running through the middle of it. He got down on the road all right, but when the weather cleared, taking off was more difficult. He had to run up between the buildings, and in the process a wing scraped the front of a hardware store, and all the store's pots and pans came clattering down. The store owner just stood there. Then he stepped forward and welcomed Lindbergh. The ensuing publicity resulted in sales that more than compensated for the damage! A couple of days later, when the plane was repaired, he ran it down the street a second time, but not before taking meticulous measurements of the width of the street. All went well.

It was clear to me as he told these stories that Charles had begun to relax.

Now the days were hot and the water smooth. In the evenings Charles, Charlie, and I went out in the small boat spearing crayfish off a sandbar, where we anchored for the night. When we got back Anne was studying prints on the smooth sand.

"Charlie, what are these marks?"

"These little ones, neat and close together, are the footprints of 'coons. See, they come out of those bushes to pick fish thrown up on the beach. Those big ones over there are the marks of a crane. And, see that deeper mark—made by claws digging in where a bird took off. Those smudges— that's where his flapping wings brushed the sand. That line running up the beach—where a 'coon dragged his fish."

She was fascinated that he could read the beach like that. It was as if he knew a secret language, she said.

We spent a couple of days sailing around in the keys. Then back northward, cruising into Whitewater Bay and anchoring near an enormous bird rookery on an island, pelicans roosting in the upper branches of the trees and cormorants below them.

We made our way up through the Ten Thousand Islands. People thought this was an exaggerated name until they were photographed later in an air survey during the war, and they found there were fourteen thousand of them.

Charlie did some fine navigating through the shallows. When he came to an isolated small island, Rabbit Key, we anchored and all went ashore to look for crabs. We found none, but picked up handfuls of conch shells to take back to Jon. Anne fell in love with the island.

We went on up to Cape Romano and into Little Marco Pass and were now near the end of our trip. Charles and Anne cooked a final breakfast. I watched them, Charles frying eggs and Anne making pancakes, handing our one skillet back and forth. They were laughing and kidding, and I thought, I must get them away more often. But what was it about this boating vacation that had relieved the tension?

Anne answered my question later that day as we cruised into Estero Bay. "Jim, what terrific days these have been for both of us—even the difficult things—getting stuck on shoals, cutting our way through the mangroves, the cooking, the pitching bunks. The humor that's built on those things. It toughens friendship. It encourages understanding. And I think all that's just as important as the strange and beautiful world you introduced us to."

*   *   *

As soon as they got back north to Englewood in early February 1940, the Lindberghs moved to the new house they had rented at Lloyd Neck. I was visiting them there one day. Charles, Anne, and I had just said good-night to young Jon and Land, and the three of us were standing at the head of the stairs. Charles said quietly, "Jim, if anything should happen to Anne and me—" he stopped. "The boys. Would you keep an eye on them?" "You know I would, Charles." No more was said. What greater measure of trust could I have? I thought.

Charles resumed his writing and his consultant work for the Air Corps in a civilian capacity. He also talked with Pan-American Airways about using land planes on possible transatlantic air routes. In April the stalemate in the European war was broken abruptly by Germany's invasion of Norway and Denmark, followed by the thrusts against the Netherlands and Belgium. By the middle of May the Nazi war machine had breached the Maginot Line. I was at Lloyd Neck when it happened.

Lindbergh was surprised by how quickly the Maginot Line had failed. To him the German air and ground attacks were a deadly combination. The old static trench warfare and defense operations of World War I seemed gone forever, and he felt the big question now was how navies would stand up to air power. He worried that the British Navy's ability to keep the sea lanes open and prevent an invasion were a thing of the past. The Navy certainly hadn't prevented Hitler's taking Norway.

In June 1940, following the conference with Ford about the Rolls-Royce aero engine, Charles and I had returned to New York on the night train. As usual when traveling together, I booked a Pullman compartment for the two of us in my name. If anyone learned that Lindbergh was around, there would be a commotion of introductions, hand-shaking, and autographs.

There was an upper and a lower berth in the Pullman compartment. We flipped a coin and I won the lower. Before we went to bed that night, we sat and talked for a while and Charles surprised me by pulling a garter snake out of his suitcase. His uncle, who was living with Charles's mother in Detroit, had given it to him as a present for his young son, Jon. We played with it, letting it climb up our arms.

As I was about to doze off that evening, I opened my eyes and saw a long, slender object slowly descending above my head. Then it dropped on my covers. The snake was loose on the train! Alarmed, I jumped out of the berth and heard Charles chuckle above me. When I turned on the light, I saw that he had been dangling a moistened, tightly rolled Pullman towel.

We went on a number of railroad trips together, and I learned a good deal about traveling from him. His early flying days had made him extremely conscious of conserving weight in his luggage. He showed me, for example, how he wrapped his razor, toothbrush, and comb into an old sock. He taught me a useful trick when traveling in an overnight Pullman. I used to slip my wallet inside my pillow and turn the open end away from the aisle, so no one could snatch it. Unfortunately, I would occasionally forget it in the pillow and leave my wallet on the train. Charles first slipped his wallet into one of the socks he was going to wear the next morning before putting the wallet under the pillow. Then he'd be sure to retrieve it when he dressed.

Charles arranged with CBS to go on the air again, and he began meeting with senators, American Legion leaders, and other prominent men who were increasingly concerned about the propaganda efforts to get America into the war.

In his broadcast, Lindbergh advanced a new argument against participation in the conflict. He said that while Germany's air power was proving a powerful weapon in Europe, America had nothing to fear from it on this continent. The Nazi war machine was geared to attacking over short distances, and the Atlantic ocean gave America an immense advantage in the defense of its own borders. We were in no danger from Germany or anyone else, provided we looked to our own air defenses. There was no justification in terms of military security for our becoming involved in the war. Since Lindbergh was regarded by his countrymen as the foremost authority on aviation matters, his words carried weight. The polls continued to show a majority of the people on his side. But the speech marked the start of public attacks on Lindbergh by some politicians and members of the administration. From that time on, he became the central figure in the pro- and antiwar furor that divided America until Pearl Harbor.

Charles was well aware of the strange role he had assumed. Just before I left the East to spend some time in California, he spoke wistfully about being attacked as a traitor for trying to keep America out of a war he didn't believe in, when he would gladly fight for his country in a war he did believe in.

He went on to tell me that he had accepted an invitation to speak at a mass antiwar rally at Soldiers Field in Chicago. It was held on August 4 and was his first appearance before a major live audience. Nearly forty thousand people attended on a hot summer afternoon.

My activities that summer were of a different kind. I joined Mina Edison, Thomas Edison's widow, on the West Coast, where she had gone to take part in public meetings of Moral Re-Armament in Los Angeles and at San Francisco's World Fair and in a world broadcast with Frank Buchman. She also addressed the San Francisco city council and was guest of honor at a dinner given by Louis B. Mayer for Hollywood celebrities. She spoke about her husband's bringing light into homes around the world, and the need to flood people's hearts and minds with God's illumination at a time of confusion and despair.

After completing a week of meetings in San Francisco and the Bay Area cities, Frank Buchman invited a hundred or so associates to a quiet haven on the shores of Lake Tahoe in the Sierra Nevada. He felt a heightened dedication and personal effectiveness were needed in the face of the world crisis. He believed that America and the democracies needed moral as well as military strength. He also believed that national will and effort in time of war depended on spiritual insight, personal sacrifice, and discipline.

Out of the daily informal meetings, conversations, and meditation there was born a unity of commitment. This also led to some unexpected forms of creativity. An informal evening of entertainment resulted in the production of a colorful stage revue, *You Can Defend America,* which was performed in scores of cities across the country in the coming months, usually sponsored by local and state defense councils. Along with it, a handbook of national defense by the same name was written. General Pershing, hero of World War I, broke the rule of a lifetime when he wrote a foreword for it.

I was in the middle of these activities, responsible especially for the publication and distribution of the handbook, while Lindbergh was touring the country, speaking at large meetings and rallies. Our paths did not cross until October, when we met in Washington and had a chance to catch up on each other's news. Despite our totally different activities—his public speaking and writing against involvement in war and my efforts to build civilian morale in the face of war—I felt at one with him. Charles had recently become active with the America First Committee, headed by General Robert Wood, chairman of the board of Sears, Roebuck. I kidded him about "joining a movement."

"No, Jim, it's not a movement. It's just a joint effort by all kinds of people of different viewpoints to keep America on the right course."

"Sounds just like what I've been doing this summer!" I said.

"Maybe it doesn't have quite the moral and spiritual bite," he said with a laugh. He was hardly about to relinquish his independence to any group. America First and other groups provided him with a means to arrange meetings and publicity. As long as they remained sincere about keeping the country out of war, he felt he could work with them, even the pacifists and the leftists. But he never let anyone tell him what to say, and he never told them.

Charles was increasingly active with America First, and he was certainly its most popular speaker. Pressure was put on him to become its national chairman. He declined. The last thing he wanted to do was to become involved with organizing, he told me. He would have found a desk job deadening. And apart from all that, he felt he was too controversial. Eventually, he settled for becoming a member of their national committee, which involved no executive duties.

There was no doubt about Lindbergh's popularity among those who opposed America's entry into the war. He spoke at a dozen meetings, with huge rallies in New York, Los Angeles, and San Francisco, as well as in St. Louis, Minneapolis, and Philadelphia. His last speech before the Japanese attacked Pearl Harbor was at Madison Square Garden in New York. He had to decline many more requests than he could accept, partly because he took great care in writing each address, making each one different, relating each to the current tenor of public thought. I sometimes watched him prepare his speeches. He would write out a draft, change it, rewrite it, and change it again. Thousands would be listening, he said. They were entitled to the best he could give.

He welcomed suggestions from Anne and from me, when I was there, and weighed them carefully. My main concern was that he not antagonize his opponents needlessly. As the weeks went by, the outcry against Lindbergh became more and more violent. His reputation and his arguments seemed to infuriate a growing alliance of interventionists as he became increasingly outspoken. Charles was never one to pull punches, and he felt he had to be explicit about the groups he felt were misleading the public. He charged them with flooding Congress and the press with propaganda, and with pursuing personal gain, or the interests of foreign governments.

There was increasing pressure on him to name individuals and organizations. He and I agreed at the start that putting labels on his opponents would only lead to bitterness and division. Sometimes he would write a first draft that expressed his blunt opinions about people and their motivations, then he would hand the draft to me and laugh when I started to object.

"I know what you're going to say, Jim, but that's the truth, and some day it's going to have to come out in the open."

Charles remained remarkably cool in the midst of dirtier and dirtier attacks on him—as a Nazi sympathizer, a traitor, and a dupe. Finally, at a press conference in April 1941, Roosevelt likened him to a "copperhead," a historical reference to northerners with southern sympathies who criticized Abraham Lincoln during the Civil War.

This was too much for Charles. What angered him most was that the president had made the charge in reply to a question as to why Lindbergh had not been called into active military service. Charles felt his loyalty and patriotism were challenged.

Charles was told of the attack that afternoon. He took the night train to Washington, and the next day met with Truman Smith and Senator Clark of Missouri, men whose judgment he respected. Then he boarded the evening train back to New York and phoned me early the next morning at the Gramercy Hotel, where I was staying. He wanted to see me, he said.

Charles sat quietly in the hotel room, voicing his feelings, laying out his options. "It boils down to three possible courses of action. One—do nothing. Two—launch a public attack on the president, defending myself and calling his bluff. Three—write privately to Roosevelt, resigning my commission since as commander in chief he has publicly questioned my fitness to serve as an officer. Do you see any other alternative, Jim?"

I said I didn't. Which did he really feel was the appropriate course?

Reluctantly, he said he felt it must be the third. His commission meant a great deal to him; but this was a point of honor.

I asked if he would be making a public statement. He thought about that and shook his head. If others wanted to come to his defense, that was their responsibility. Any debate in the press would just make matters worse.

"No, Jim. To be called a traitor and not resign my commission would run against my conscience. That's all that matters. I must remain free to speak out for what I feel is right and to condemn what I feel is wrong."

In his mind it was settled. The following Monday, after talking with Anne, he mailed his letters of resignation to Secretary of War Henry Stimson and to the president.

During the spring and summer of 1941, events in Europe had heightened the pressures to become involved in the war. In mid-April German forces advanced through the Balkans and into Greece; in May the Luftwaffe launched its heaviest raids on British cities to date; in June Hitler invaded Soviet Russia; in July Roosevelt quietly sent American forces to Iceland; in August the German troops swept through Russia; and in September Roosevelt ordered the Navy to shoot on sight at any German or Italian warships entering areas "necessary for American defense."

At the beginning of May, after a visit with the Lindberghs, I had seen Charles off to speak in St. Louis, Minneapolis, and Chicago. "I'm getting tired of these speeches, Jim, and even fed up with the endless hand-shaking, committee meetings, conferences, and small talk. I know people mean well, but it wastes so much time and energy." But he continued with the heavy schedule during the next months. I did not see him for most of the summer, as he was in the West and Midwest, while I was helping conduct civilian-defense morale training centers in Maine and elsewhere in New England at the invitation of governors and mayors.

One morning in Concord, New Hampshire, a friend handed me a newspaper with an article quoting from a speech Lindbergh had just made on September 18, in Des Moines,

233

Iowa: "The three most important groups who have been pressing this country toward war are the British, the Jewish, and the Roosevelt Administration. Behind these groups, but of lesser importance, are a number of capitalists, anglophiles and intellectuals, who believe that their future, and the future of mankind, depend upon the domination of the British Empire. Add to these the Communist groups . . ." The headline announced that Lindbergh had made a frontal attack on the Jews, accusing them of pushing America toward war. The charge was echoed in newspapers around the country.

My first reaction was to wish I had been with Charles. Anne and I had advised him against making statements like these. When we next met he told me what had happened.

He had always said that if he felt we were on the edge of being pushed into war he would pull out all the stops and name names. He'd felt we'd reached that point. There was no longer anything to be lost by telling people the facts, he said. And it might help. The press had jumped on the Jewish reference and blown it all out of proportion. In fact, he had spoken of Jews with restraint and sympathy for their persecution. He had said: "It's not difficult to understand why Jewish people desire the overthrow of Nazi Germany. The persecution they suffered in Germany would be sufficient to make bitter enemies of any race. No person with a sense of the dignity of mankind can condone the persecution of the Jewish race in Germany."

He went on to tell me he knew there would be an outcry, but characteristically, he refused to retract his statement. I admired his courage, but I added what I had said earlier, that any naming of the Jews, however tactful, would only make it harder for him. In fact, Anne had urged him to change the remark, as he would surely be tagged as anti-Semitic. One result was that the public protests divided the ranks of America First and the other antiwar groups, which seemed to strengthen the hand of the interventionists.

In a few weeks all this furor was swept aside when the Japanese planes struck Pearl Harbor on December 7, 1941.

Chapter

NINE

IN MARCH 1941, before Lindbergh had set out on his speaking engagements, I persuaded him and Anne to get away for a break, as we had done the year before. Again, we sailed—this time in a slightly larger boat, the *Aldebaran*, a thirty-two-foot yawl equipped with an auxiliary engine and small dory. We took no guide, but followed much the same course down the coast and into the Everglades, and from there we ventured out to the Tortugas.

We set off from Fort Myers Beach on March 7 heading southward, entered Big Hickory Pass, and anchored for the night. There was a strong wind blowing the next morning, and as we went into the gulf through the narrow, unmarked pass on an outgoing tide, we ran aground. We had no success in pulling the boat off the shoal, so I went in search of help. While I was gone Charles and Anne, concerned with the pounding the boat was getting, transferred cameras, books, and papers to shore. I returned with a fisherman and his big motorboat. We hitched a line from the boat to the *Aldebaran,* and, waist-deep in breakers, we put our shoulders to her stern and heaved until at last she swung clear. The fisherman towed us into the lee of the island, where we anchored for the night. Charles and I spent most of the evening plugging a leak in the stern.

So began a strenuous, invigorating voyage. Our muscles ached; our clothes were often soaked with seawater; we were short of sleep and food. But our minds were free, our spirits refreshed, and the bonds of friendship drew closer.

Only one discordant moment clouded our journey, and that came early on. We had anchored behind an isolated island and were sitting on a log in a clump of trees. A small fishing boat appeared, and as it glided past, an older woman saw us. She pointed our way and we heard her say to another woman, "There he is!" Then they went on and didn't return.

Charles had stiffened and gone white. Even here, Lindbergh had been discovered. I realized what the years of hounding by the press had done to him.

There were happier moments. Anne walked along the water one day, enchanted by the many shells—pink, mauve, white, yellow—almost as many as on the beach at Captiva. "Look," she said, holding up a shell, "a gift from the sea!" *Gift from the Sea* later became the title of one of her most successful books.

We continued south and probed our way into the Everglades jungle. Anne kept a diary and later gave me a copy of her notes. Here is her entry for March 15, which captures the fascination of the wild world through which we floated:

Start up Shark River after breakfast. It is cold and bright. Again that strange river opening up before us with its long armed mangrove roots reaching down into the water—gray dead branches and queer animal-like stumps and roots. And birds fluttering up before us as we enter a new bend. Smooth, still, silent and endless, opening up for miles and miles a maze of different streams and rivers. The sense that this is not man's world but an endless eternal world of jungle and jungle life. We are intruders, but not so much as last year in the motor boat. Cold lunch as we run. After lunch, as the river narrows, we take one fork after another and run off the map. We put up the jib and jigger and sail before the wind, silently, with hardly a ripple, and startle birds. Blue heron, great white heron, ibis, water turkey, swallow-tail kites (above us circling, unafraid) and little brown ducks fluttering away under the bushes.

We get stuck once on mud, pull off, go up another river. And at sunset we seem to be at the end. We are pushing through bushes with the sails down. It is still quite deep—6 feet or so—but the mangrove branches meet about our heads and their roots scrape at the keel. C. and Jim get out the axe and hack at branches that catch in the stays and push us back ("just as if we were really going somewhere!" I say.) The deck becomes strewn with branches and leaves—stiff slippery green leaves and red-stained branches and those gray nut-like buds.

It is like a dream where the vehicle you are riding becomes something else and you go straight on over land and water. A car becomes a train, a train becomes a boat. . . . This boat, pushing its way through the jungle, has surely become another creature—a land creature—it is sprouting leaves!

We stop in a wider pool—overlooking the savannah—the lop-sided moon and a stray palm. After a hot supper the boys swing the compass by the stars as I wash dishes. I have a "new boy" feeling *always* in this world of practical action. I can learn of course by rote

239

(and what security it gives one) to know how to steer, to trim the sails, to tack, to put up a tent, to take it down, how to tie a rope—*right.*

That evening Anne commented, "There are so many twists and turns of the stream, and so many forks, it must be easy to lose all sense of direction."

I told her what I'd learned from an old hunting partner: make a mark with your knife on a tree root at water level. Then wait for a while and watch whether the water rises above the mark or falls below it. All these rivers are tidal. If it rises, you know the flow of the stream is away from the gulf. If you go against the flow, you're bound to get to the mouth of the river. If the level has fallen, you go with the current. However much the stream twists and turns, you'll get there in the end.

She was glad to hear that. "Dearly as I love it here, Jim, I want to get back to the children sometime!"

As Anne was making sandwiches the next day, she said in frustration, "Why are they making harder and harder butter these days to spread on softer and softer bread?"

Somehow that led to a discussion of the different characteristics of males and females. Anne said initiative was a basic masculine quality and a basic feminine one was intuition, and they rarely were found in one person. Charles said he thought activity and contemplation were fundamental traits of both men and women. No one was 100 percent male or female, he said, we were all a mixture.

Then we got into a lively discussion of what God had intended human qualities to be—what the ideal man would be. Anne had the final word in saying that a true man of God must be partly adaptable to human wills, but totally adaptable to the divine will.

The next day we penetrated even deeper into the Everglades, hacking our way through the branches until we broke

Nobel laureate Carrel was a scientist above all, but at Saint-Gildas pursued his interest in mysticism and psychological phenomena.

Left: At the Rockefeller Institute for Medical Research in New York Dr. Alexis Carrel found unmatched opportunities and freedom for his investigative endeavors.

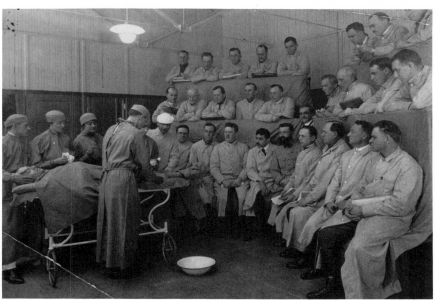

During World War I, Carrel (in white cap) demonstrates his highly successful techniques for the treatment of war wounds.

Anne and Alexis Carrel on Saint-Gildas.

The Carrels and me on a dig in the tidal sea bed.

Anne Carrel stands between Saint-Gildas and Illiec, where a forty-foot tide runs.

The Carrels were my hosts on Saint-Gildas for two memorable summers.

Carrel, lost in thought, between the islands at high tide.

TIME

The Weekly Newsmagazine

Painted for TIME by S. J. Woolf

LINDBERGH, CARREL & PUMP
They are looking for the fountain of age.
(See MEDICINE)

Cover of *Time*, June 13, 1938, featuring Lindbergh, Carrel, and the perfusion pump. This was also the day their co-authored book, *Culture of Organs*, was published.

Below: The Lindberghs' house on Illiec.
Right, top: Lindbergh, the Carrels, and me in Lindbergh's stateroom on the *Aquitania*, when the photographer burst in and surprised us.
Right, center: The Lindberghs fly over Saint-Gildas on their return from Russia.

DAILY MIRROR

2¢   WEATHER   Member of The Associated Press   2 Cents Outside City Limits   2¢

Vol. 15. No. 254   C   New York, Saturday, April 15, 1939   FINAL EDITION ★ A. M. ★★★★

RUMANIA, POLAND IN DEFENSE PACT

Britain, France Seek Soviet Air Aid

Stories on Page 2

Lindy Comes Home Smiling   Colonel Charles A. Lindbergh, chatting amiably with three fellow-passengers, is pictured in his stateroom aboard Aquitania on his arrival here last night. Judging from his smile he's happy to be back.

Charles Lindbergh on Saint-Gildas, with Illiec in the background. Some evenings we ended our conversations shouting to each other as the tide separated our islands.

Charles was best man at Ellie's and my wedding. She stands beside her sister, Roberta Whittemore.

Above: Anne and Charles Lindbergh setting out on an afternoon sail at Captiva Island. Left: Anne, deep in thought, in the wilderness of Shark River.

Anne and Charles on Lost Man's River. Our three trips to the Everglades wilderness were a total relaxation for the Lindberghs.

Anne, muffled against the cold at the start of our first Florida trip.

Charles and Anne on the beach at Cape Romano on our way to the Everglades.

On the Gulf of Mexico each day was a joy for Anne.

How will Jon Lindbergh get down the mast his father has painted with molasses? This happened on our third trip.

Collecting coconuts on Cape Sable, on our way to the Florida Keys.

Sailing at a clip on the Gulf enroute to the Tortugas Islands.

Hacking our way through the mangroves at the headwaters of Shark River.

Charles Lindbergh in 1973. (Richard Brown photos)

Charles and Anne, 1973. (Richard Brown photo)

Lindbergh's grave on Maui. "If I take the wings of the morning . . ."

out into a big fork in the river and eventually emerged into the eastern end of Tarpon Bay, having come almost full circle. Then we decided to launch out into the gulf and head direct for the Dry Tortugas, a group of small islands more than a hundred miles southwest, beyond Key West. It took us a little more than twenty-four hours. We each stood four-hour watches, steering by compass and the stars. Again, Anne in her diary described the experience vividly:

> I am alone with the stars. I steer by Regulus—dim under the clouds—and then Spica. The moon, a mangy half-eaten one, is behind the mainsail. But sparkles on the waves. It is easy, a light breeze, sailing before the wind, but after two hours my limbs go on just as well as before, but my mind no longer swings free over the world. It, too, is tied to the sea, the sail, the rudder. I say poems—but can only remember the most familiar. "Let me not to the marriage of true minds—admit impediments. . . . It is the star to every wandering bark, whose worth's unknown although its height be taken." "White in the moon the long road lies." Then I turn around and find the shame-faced gray of the morning has replaced the silver of moonlight on the waves behind my back. The gray clouds faintly, dirtily pink on the eastern horizon. And the stars are paling ahead of me—so that is it—that is why I am so tired, suddenly flattened out, and the glory and magic has gone from the world. It is dawn.
>
> The sun rises at 6:40. The moon still rides high in some wispy pink clouds. With the sun, a wind came up and the sea. I was pulling with all my might against sea and wind to keep her on 260 degrees . . . arms, legs, bracing on the floor, sometimes standing up. . . . Down the wave and then climbing up it, and pulling her over the crest again. It reminded me, oddly enough, of

241

labor pains, climbing up that hill, always the same, straining against it, in the power of something stronger than you. Then the easing up for a moment—down the trough of 240 degrees—a little breathing spell— then pulling her up again and then in the power of the wind—holding your own against it—pulling her back.

I wondered often if I could last out until 8 o'clock. My hand was cramped stiff and my arm and chest sore. When Jim came out at 8, I was trembly with fatigue and could not hold on to the bucket and lost it over- board, getting water. It was very rough. I made Jim some coffee, rigging up a contraption with a strainer and elastic to keep the pot steady on the stove. And then go down to rest—not to sleep, but not to move, to relax, in deep peace.

After supper one evening in the Tortugas I got Charles and Anne reminiscing about their survey flights. Then I turned to Charles: "What do you look back to," I asked, "as the most decisive moment of your life so far?"

"Let me think," Charles began.

"I don't have to think," said Anne. "It was when I decided to marry Charles." There she had been, she said, quietly enjoying life either at college or with her family in Mexico. Her parents had been supportive, encouraging her inter- ests—study, books, music. She was twenty-two and had a general idea of what she wanted in life—a year abroad, maybe a career, and in due course a husband with the same interests.

She told how, out of the blue a tall, good-looking world hero had walked into her life. He was from another world— that of adventure, the limelight, aviation, mechanics. In contrast, she was rather shy and stay-at-home, not at all ad- venturous. They had really only one thing in common: they thought the world of each other.

242

"From the moment Charles took me up in his plane, life became an adventure." She described how on one of their first flights a wheel fell off in midair and Charles had to crash-land—but not until he had packed her into the cockpit with seat cushions. She said if she had known all they would go through in the next twelve years—moving from house to house and from country to country—she might not have had the courage to say yes.

Charles hadn't had a watershed experience. Marriage was certainly a big event, he said, though perhaps not quite as traumatic for him as for Anne. He smiled at her. "At least, it didn't change my life-style all that much!" He stood up, leaned back against the rail beside her, and looked up at the stars.

In his life, he said when he did begin to speak, each significant experience seemed to grow out of whatever went before. But perhaps one event preceded everything else—it had happened in the Utah desert in 1928, thirteen years earlier.

He described how, a year after the transatlantic flight, he'd made appearances all across the country, and then through Central and South America, in the cause of aviation. All was well: he was at the heart of his chosen field, aviation, working on establishing a transcontinental airline.

Flying into the sunset on his way across the country, he decided on the spur of the moment to land on the desert and sleep by the plane, instead of going on to his hotel, where the press always seemed to find him. He walked around for a while in the dusk and then lay on the ground and stared up at the stars, brilliant in the desert air. He listened to the silence and felt at one with the stillness and simplicity of sand and space. Looking up at the silver, ghostly silhouette of his plane, he felt a deep kinship with that complicated machine. Simplicity and complication. Nature and technology. He was part of both. But how to achieve a balance between them? He didn't want to live like a hermit in the desert, nor did he want to be swallowed up by the pressing demands of his daily concerns.

He needed time to contemplate and to think, Charles said. He needed the inner awareness necessary to screen out the unimportant and lead him toward a clear objective. As the night wore on, he sensed that he needed to shed the unessential concerns and retain only the possessions and activities that were compatible with his intuition and awareness. His "busyness" was upsetting the balance of body, mind, and spirit.

Then he went on to say it was not really a question of giving up things he loved. Fame had become a burden, with all the publicity it brought. Wealth was no temptation. Anne and he had all that they physically required. Ambition was no problem; he was succeeding in his profession.

Perhaps the decision he made was not so different from mine, he said. He did not then and did not now think in terms of a personal God directing him. But then and there he let go of his physical, mental, and spiritual appetites in a search for balance, for the core of his being that could discern the true values of life.

"So it changed your life," I said.

Charles laughed. He said the strange thing was he'd been no less busy since that night—in fact, he was busier—with consulting work in aviation, military duties, international survey flights, research with Carrel. And yet, much of the pressure and distraction was lifted from his life. He'd given away the mass of gifts people had showered on him after the Paris flight. The Missouri Historical Society took most of it. *The Spirit of St. Louis* went to the Smithsonian. He'd cut out the "ceremonials"—all those social occasions, public and private, at which people wanted to fete him. He did nothing just for money. And he had given up trying to answer the piles of correspondence that poured in—except for essential matters.

That last remark made me smile. Anne had told me the procedure he'd developed for dealing with the mail that stacked up on his desk. When he came home in the evening or back from a trip, he'd take a handful of envelopes in his right hand, flip through them with his left, looking at their return addresses on the upper lefthand corner. If he saw a name he knew or something that interested him, he'd pull it out. The rest of the mail slid into any handy container, where it would remain unopened for later transfer with other papers in a wicker basket to the Yale University library. That was why Charles had insisted that I write my name large and clear in the upper lefthand corner of my envelopes. Anne used to say wistfully, "I wish I could do with my letters what Charles does with them—just toss them into a barrel."

I told Charles I could identify with his desert experience. It was akin to my decision to take a leave of absence from Firestone. One day in Los Angeles I'd just stopped in my tracks. Something inside had asked me a question I couldn't answer and couldn't dismiss. "Do you really want to live this way for the rest of your life—however interesting the work, however high up you go, however much money you make?"

I'd tried to slow down, but I couldn't. It was my nature to go, go, go. When I took a look at my life, I knew I had to take *time*. I had to stop and *breathe*. I had to ask Mr. Firestone to let me take a leave of absence.

I knew I had to *let go* and trust I would find the next goal for my life.

We spent four days in and around the Tortugas. One day, when the skies were clear and the seas calm, we took turns using our one diving helmet in a dozen feet of crystal-clear water off Hospital Key. It was Anne's first diving experience and she quickly adjusted to the strange, underwater motion. She called it "wading through invisible molasses" and shot up triumphantly with a piece of coral in her hand. It's a new and beautiful world, she reported, and told us of the purple sea fans, luminous blue, yellow, black, and white fish gliding in and out of the ferns and waving coral branches.

On another day she had a less pleasant experience. We were sailing in a high wind as we arrived at Tortugas, without the engine. I was at the tiller. We jibed and the heavy boom swung across the deck, and as it came toward Anne she grabbed it, trying to keep it from going past her—but found herself being swept overboard. I couldn't let go of the tiller, so as Anne swept by I leaned as far forward as I could and was just able to grab her by the belt and jeans. She let go the boom and fell back into the boat. Charles came back from the bow with a wry grin. "Thank you, Jim, for saving my wife by the seat of her pants."

We talked a good deal about the war and the struggle for the hearts and minds of Americans. It was March 1941, and before the fighting in Europe stepped up. I was reminded of a stinging attack by a writer trying to make the point that Lindbergh was a Nazi lover. He told the story of Charles receiving a medal from the hand of Goering, second only to Hitler.

As we sat in the shade of a palm tree watching waves break on an island beach, I said, "Charles, I'd like to hear exactly what happened at that dinner when Goering pinned his medal on you."

He hadn't pinned it on, Charles said. Goering had a small red box in his hand, and came up to Charles as he arrived at the dinner. Before Charles understood what was happening, Goering had put it into his hand. Truman Smith, the American military attaché, came up and he and a German interpreter translated what Goering was saying. Only then was it clear that Goering was bestowing a high-level medal in honor, he said, of Charles's transatlantic flight and his contributions to aviation. "It was all a big surprise to me and to Ambassador Wilson, who was our host that evening."

"But you didn't hand the medal right back."

He was very intent on explaining the event to me thoroughly. The dinner, he said, took place in October 1938, while he was on one of his visits to find out the strength of the German air force. There were other reasons for the visit: before going to Germany he had been in Paris for private discussions with Premier Daladier and other top officials. Charles had suggested to them that the French try to purchase airplane engines from Germany. This was immediately after Daladier had met with Chamberlain and Hitler, and tensions had been eased between their countries for the moment. Germany was the only country capable of providing the engines, and France urgently needed them. After Daladier and the others recovered from shock at his suggestion, they began to consider it. Charles offered to sound out the Germans secretly during his visit to Berlin.

That apparently wasn't all. He was given another secret mission. Charles found that Ambassador Wilson had planned the dinner in the hope that Wilson might have the opportunity to persuade Goering to use his influence with Hitler to alleviate pressure on the Jews—specifically that the Jews whom they allowed to emigrate would also be allowed to take at least a part of their financial assets with them.

To have handed back the medal would have sabotaged all that. And it would have slammed the door on obtaining the air force intelligence data. Later that evening, Goering drew Charles aside and told him about the specifications of the JU-88, a new light bomber that we didn't even know existed. Altogether, it would have been an unthinkable diplomatic blunder to hand the medal back. It would have been an insult, too, to his host, the American ambassador.

247

And the medal had seemed no big thing at the time, he said. He had received medals from most air-minded countries. The German one would join the rest in the *St. Louis* collection.

The moment he had returned to Truman Smith's residence, where they were staying, and showed Anne the medal, she had said, "Albatross." She was prophetic.

I asked Charles if either of his diplomatic projects had worked out. He said they had not. The French and German governments did work on an engine deal, but Hitler's attack on Czechoslovakia had finished it off. Whether Goering could have helped the Jews even if he'd wanted to was a question that was never answered. The following month, November, there were terrible anti-Jewish riots, the *Kristallnacht,* when the Nazi thugs broke Jewish shopwindows and sacked their stores. That was the start of the real persecution.

Charles added that they had still been on Illiec that autumn and had even contemplated renting a house in Berlin. Charles wanted to learn all he could about Germany; but when they heard of that anti-Semitic violence, they knew they could not live in a country that treated people in such a way.

From the Tortugas we headed back across the gulf into a nor'wester. The sea was rough, the wind cold, and the rain came down in torrents. Water found its way in down the mast and through the portholes, so everything was wet. The wind was so strong that when we sighted the Florida coast off Cape Romano the drift had taken us miles southeast of our course. Finally, as we went in to dock at Marco in the darkness, when we turned on the engine, it cut out. But none of this lowered our spirits, except that the precise Charles was shocked by our straying so far off course.

It had been Anne's turn to cook supper that evening, before we reached Marco. Charles and I could hear her singing to herself. Being an economical soul, she had cooked a vegetable soup and thrown in all of the leftovers. She just about cleaned out the galley. The concoction tasted terrible, and Anne and I left most of ours.

"I'm sorry," said Anne. "It's a disaster."

"Absolutely delicious," said Charles, and proceeded to eat all of his. It was typical of his humor and gallantry.

Another memorable meal was a breakfast for which Charles decided to cook pancakes. Our pancake flour was used up, but he used regular flour, and finished up all that was left. He kept on cooking until there was a huge stack of pancakes, each giant-sized.

"They look like manhole covers," I said as we sat down to eat. We ate and ate. Anne gave up early on. I kept going until I was absolutely full, and there were still a dozen or so left. We started to clean up the table, and Charles began wrapping the pancakes in wax paper.

"What are you going to do with those?" I asked.

"Put them in the refrigerator."

"Oh, just throw them out. The fish'll enjoy them."

"No, no. I'm saving them."

"You'll never eat those, Charles."

"I can eat them right now."

"You know you couldn't."

"Jim, if you'll eat half, I'll eat half. Right now."

We sat down again and poured syrup over them. I managed to get through two or three and had to stop.

"Are you through? What's the matter?"

"No more room."

He shook his head and went on eating. He worked his way through every last one, though I knew he had to be totally stuffed. Then he carefully folded the wax paper and put it away.

The next day our trip was over. They went back to Lloyd

Neck, and a couple of days later I had a letter from Anne, in which she wrote:

As for what the trip gave us and how different the world looks after it, I can hardly begin to say—I should like instead to quote some lines from Saint–Exupéry (badly translated):

"But there exists an altitude of relations where gratitude, like pity, loses all meaning. It is there that one can breathe like a prisoner set free."

Safely home this afternoon to find all the family, including Soeur Lisi and Christine well. The shells are a great success.

* * *

Charles left shortly afterward on his America First campaign. I saw them from time to time on Long Island. In mid-August 1941, the family moved to Martha's Vineyard and stayed there through the summer and autumn and on into December. The place gave them more privacy from the mounting publicity and the more and more strident attacks on Charles.

I was struck by Lindbergh's calm in the midst of the uproar. "I feel I'm fighting a losing battle," he said one day, when I was with them on Martha's Vineyard. According to him, Roosevelt had engineered things so that just a small incident could draw us into a declaration of war. Charles's audiences seemed as enthusiastic about his campaign to have the United States build military strength and, at the same time, use its influence to bring about a negotiated peace in Europe. But he could sense that in the country at large more and more people were beginning to feel that we should intervene.

We talked about these things as we walked the rocky beach on Martha's Vineyard. It was late November and a cold wind was blowing. Suddenly Charles said, "Let's swim."

"Are you crazy? In this weather?"

He knew my weakness, hating, like him, to turn down a challenge. So we both took off our clothes—the beach was deserted—and he dived in. I went in more carefully, wading in up to my shoulders. I didn't want to get my hair wet and have it freeze in the wind. Charles swam for a minute or two and claimed he was enjoying it. We dried ourselves off as well as we could with our handkerchiefs, dressed, and went on walking.

Next morning we were out there walking again. He dared me once more to swim, and this time I dived in, hair and all, and found I felt much more comfortable and my hair didn't freeze. It taught me a lesson for life—if you're going to do something, do it all the way. Halfway, you'll only be uncomfortable and ineffective.

On December 7, Pearl Harbor Sunday, I was in Philadelphia, where the revue *You Can Defend America* was being performed at the Academy of Music. Soon after we heard the news of the attack I phoned the Lindberghs and they invited me to join them.

"It's almost a relief to have the waiting over," Charles said. "But I feel a weight in my stomach when I think that the best of our young men are heading out in a hail of bullets and grenades."

"What will you do now, Charles?"

What he wanted to do most was to have his commission reinstated and serve in the Air Corps. There was plenty to be done in aviation by a nation at war, and he felt he could be of help. He knew that there might be a great temptation at a moment like this to race ahead producing planes quickly without understanding just what kinds of planes were needed. The first priority was to establish a clear program.

But some people in high places really had convinced themselves he was a traitor, he added. He wasn't sure how they would receive him.

I said I wondered if he would be going on with his America First work.

"Of course not. I've always made it clear that if we get into war, however shortsighted our policies may have been, I will support the war effort 100 percent." As far as he was concerned, America First was finished.

I suggested he might think of making a statement for the press, so there would be no doubt in anyone's mind about his intentions. Before the day was over, Charles had produced one and tried it out on me. The statement ended with: "We must now turn every effort to building the greatest and most efficient Army, Navy and Air Force in the world. When American soldiers go to war, it must be with the best equipment that modern skill can design and that modern industry can build."

He issued it through America First and refused to make any further public comments. His one concern now was to think out how he could best serve in very practical ways. A few days later, he was in Washington offering his services to General Arnold. Rebuffed by Roosevelt in his attempt to serve in the Air Corps, then turned away by Pan-American and the aviation company United Aircraft at the administration's insistence, he was welcomed by Henry Ford. Charles began his work as a consultant at Ford's massive plant at Willow Run, designed for bomber-plane production.

In early January 1942 I received a letter from Anne:

I wish you could have seen us the night you telephoned—I, half way up the stairs with a bottle of milk for the baby, saying in surprise, "why, it's Jim!" to the ring, before C. had answered it. . . . I don't think my brief words of thanks were enough over the telephone of your thoughtfulness of all the children. How you got exactly the right gift for each one I don't know—and exactly the right card, too! They were all very pleased. Land sleeps with his football—at least

252

it is by his bed. Anne looks a picture in her pink Kate Greenaway wrapper. The baby (named Scott Morrow at last!) really needs and will use that beautiful sleeping bag in this Michigan weather. And Jon has your woodstains kit with his treasures in his desk. I suggested he write you himself and he said shyly, "Yes—but most of all I'd like to see him—he's a nice man."

C. said thoughtfully, "Jim took a lot of trouble over those gifts—he puts people and relationships first. I didn't use to—but I think he's right."

C. is off to Hartford for the moment, where he is working part time with United (Pratt & Whitney)—a sort of extra job. He says they are fine people there. And they seem to need him badly. . . .

There is much in your letter we would like to talk to you about. Your ability to find a core of silence in the middle of all the clamor of the day—and take it in and be enriched by the clamor too. But all this must be postponed for a talk some time.

All our thanks and thoughts for the New Year.

Anne

While Charles was on Martha's Vineyard, I consulted him about something that was very much on my mind. During thirty-six years of eventful living I had remained single, not because I didn't find girls attractive, but largely because the demands on my life had made me wary of taking on the responsibilities of marriage, and also because I hadn't been sure that any of the women I had met was really the one for me.

Now I was becoming convinced that the right one had appeared. This was no love at first sight. I had known and worked with Eleanor Forde since 1927. Ellie, who was a Canadian by birth, was a woman of great capacities and had

253

taken an important role in the early years of the Oxford Group. She had written one of its most prominent pieces of literature, "The Guidance of God." She was an inspiring speaker and also one of the most effective in helping individuals to find a faith and experience a change in their lives. In fact, Frank Buchman counted her among his most responsible colleagues. He had put her in charge of preparing a national campaign in Canada, whose effect Prime Minister Bennett summed up in a message to Buchman, "You have made the task of government easier. Your influence has been felt in every village and city, even in the remotest outposts of the Dominion."

Quite apart from all that, Ellie was a very attractive woman, with a good sense of humor (which counted for a lot with me), a straightforward friendliness, and a warm heart. Sometimes I thought she felt about me the same way I was getting to feel about her. It was clear that I had better watch my step with her unless and until I was absolutely sure.

As we strode along the beach, I told all this to Charles, finishing up, "I'm as sure as I think I ever will be about her. What do you think?"

"Jim, that's the most dangerous ground anyone could tread on! I appreciate the trust you put in me. I know you pretty well now. I don't know her. Even if I did, how can a third person enter into the chemistry of the most important relationship there is between two people?"

"Well, tell me this. How did you decide about asking Anne to marry you?"

He said she was the finest girl he'd ever met. He had come to the conclusion a while before he met her that he ought to look around for a suitable mate. He was twenty-six, able to take care of a wife and family, and marriage seemed a good thing. So he'd been looking carefully at the girls he met—this was after the Atlantic flight, and he was meeting plenty of them. He'd go over in his mind what he liked about different ones, and what he didn't like. Then he met Anne with her family in Mexico. He wasn't aware of anything electric at the time. One thing he liked was that she never strained to make small talk with him the way other girls did. Anne was willing to be quiet. Later he just couldn't get her out of his mind.

"Charles, I feel that way about Ellie a good deal of the time. But you were twenty-six. I'm thirty-six. I'm well set in my ways. And Ellie probably is, too. There must be an awful lot of give and take in marriage. Do you think I'm that flexible?"

"As I've told you, Jim, when you care for someone, you're terrific. You put out as much as anyone I know. Just do what you recommend to me from time to time. Be quiet and listen to your inner voice."

He was right, of course. And my inner voice had been murmuring that Ellie was the one. So I plucked up my courage as 1941 came to an end and proposed to Ellie. I found that she was ready to share the pains and perils, and maybe the joys, of being the wife of a maverick like Jim Newton. Not that life was uninterruptedly rapturous from then on, chiefly because I had been used to being my own boss, going my own way, for quite a while.

*   *   *

In February 1942, I received a remarkable letter from Anne Lindbergh, which Ellie and I treasure. It was written from Martha's Vineyard, where she was spending some time with her children, while Charles was working in Detroit and traveling. I quote from it at length because it is not only revealing of her views on matrimony, but of the quality of her own marriage:

Charles has told me a little—though really not very much of his conversation with you—that you are thinking of getting married but that there are some difficulties—and he's told me I should write you. I protested that maybe you wouldn't be so eager for my general ideas on marriage as he was—that anyway it seemed presumptuous to write you when I hadn't talked to you—except generally—on the subject and when I didn't know any of the particular factors of your particular case. But he says, no—it's all right—write anyway—I think it might help him and I know he won't mind. So I go ahead, still somewhat uncertain.

I told him I was the worst possible person, in one sense, to write you on this subject, because for one thing, I am highly prejudiced in general *for* marriage and also highly prejudiced in particular in favor of *your* marrying. I think you would make any girl a wonderful husband and I think you would be a wonderful father. In fact, it seems a crime to me that you should *not* be married. I mention these two items bang-off first in my letter because, chiefly, I want to try to wash them off the slate. They are prejudicial to the case. And there couldn't be two worse reasons for getting married (i.e. 1. marriage is the perfect state, 2. marriage is the perfect state for me!). The only thing that I can do is quite simply to put before you some of my feelings about marriage and to let you measure up your own against them, which may or may not be helpful, remembering always how different my case (when I got married) is from yours—a girl of 22 and a man of 36.

I went through such agony of indecision before I married Charles that I sometimes think I learned everything there was to learn in those months. I've been re-learning it ever since, of course, but basically most of the big lessons of life were in those months. The biggest thing I learned, and with the biggest shock, was how little sheer logic and pure rationalism counted. (That's why I don't pay so much attention to "difficulties" or objections to marriage which arise from purely rational standpoints—such as differences in age, occupations, backgrounds, experience or type of education.)

I had my life pretty well planned out in a hazy way—what I wanted to do—my work, my interests, friends. I even knew the man I wanted to marry—or at least the kind of man. I believed in marrying for love but I also believed that you married a man who had the same interests as you, the same general outlook on life, a man who was close to you in mind, in spirit, in understanding—a man with whom you felt at ease, at home, free, able to work, your best self liberated, a man who gave you confidence and security. Mutual interests, outlook and understanding were the things I prized most.

Charles satisfied none of my conditions—apparently not, at least. I said about him, when I first met him, that he was a man with whom I had nothing in common but youth! He came from a world of action and I from books. Our interests, experience, educations, and outlooks could not have been further apart. Every rational argument in me told me not to marry him.

I did not think of a home and children very rationally or concretely—I should have, I suppose, but even then, when I did think of it, it was impossible to imagine Colonel Lindbergh "settled down!" In a *home*! With a family! There would be no time—we would always be flying around in the clouds. I felt sure we would be unhappy.

And yet I married him. I married him because of one overwhelming certainty in my mind. That I had never in my *life* come across any individual so fine, so clear, so true, so utterly good, so real. And though we have been married a long time and I have met a great many people and admired and loved many of them dearly, that feeling has never changed. Of course, I disagree with him often and feel sometimes deeply grieved when the crystal clarity, the burning purity, the sheer goodness doesn't shine through to other people. But that doesn't change the feeling or belief in what he is.

257

I put this certainty in the balance and against it I weighed everything else, everything I had hitherto loved in my life, writing and understanding, peace and security, a career, independence that I wanted (a year abroad, a year earning my own living) and people—all the people who were close to me, who understood me, with whom I had that flash of wonderful divine understanding—people who made me want to write, people who made me feel my world and my work was important, and happiness, too. I put them in the balance, for I did not think we would be happy. I put it all in the scale—and on the other side, just that one certainty of belief in him. But it outweighed all the rest.

I got back everything I put in the balance as lost—every single thing and heaped up and overflowing with things I never dreamed of, as well, most of it in Charles or through Charles or my life with him. But it all comes back in one way or another, and happiness too.

I don't know what the moral of this little tale is, except that you've got to have an overwhelming feeling to outweigh the rational objections and then they don't matter—or rather, something else matters more.

The second thing I learned was that "happiness" didn't matter as overwhelmingly as I thought. I found out that the pull to life was much stronger than the pull to "happiness." Charles *was* life, real life, like pure sunshine or pure fire. There was no sham about him. There were no words between what he said and what he was. And it was true all the way through, right down to the bottom of him. The conflict for me was one between life and happiness. And I chose life—I think you've got always to choose life. I can remember my mother saying to me, in the middle of the decision, "But what is the feeling uppermost in you?" I had answered in weariness and anger, almost, "I wish the man had never crossed my horizon!" She said, very wisely, "That is only because you are tired of the conflict." I was not only tired of it, I was afraid of it and afraid of life.

My rational arguments had all told me the truth. They said happiness and safety and security and comfort all lay the other way. They lay in a planned and regular life, they lay in companionship with someone who understood me, someone who could talk the same language, love the same things. They were right, of course. But marriage should, I think, always be a little hard and new and strange. It should be breaking your shell and going into another world and a bigger one. That is why, when I get a letter from a friend who is engaged and who lists all the things she and her fiancé have in common ("And he likes France, too, and he likes books,"!), I always think a little mournfully, "Oh, yes, she'll be happy, or, but she'll never grow up now, she'll never change, she'll always be the same. She'll be caught there in that nice comfortable box." And when I hear of two people getting married under some unconventional circumstances, or against difficulties, or from different worlds, then I think, "There—that may not be a happy marriage—but, still, they must have felt strongly to overcome that difficulty, and that's a good omen—and anyway they'll grow, they'll learn about life."

But to say one shouldn't marry for happiness is not to say one should marry for unselfish reasons. What a trap that is! An old schoolteacher of mine used to warn me "Never marry a man to reform him!" I'm sure she was thinking of drunkards and adulterers—being sternly puritan and she evidently thought I had an "uplift" nature. But there is a real truth in that. I feel like saying sometimes, "Only marry for selfish reasons." But the word "selfish" is not right. It would be better to use the words "self-integrity". Only marry for reasons of self-integrity. The old schoolteacher was a little right about me. I wouldn't have married a man to reform him, maybe, but I might have married one in order to be reformed, or from a sense of duty, or because it was a "good" thing to do, or to "help" someone else, which is just as bad.

This is really what the guru in *The Pool of Vishnu* is talking about—in his insistence on equal relationships, where there is no sense of superiority or inferiority, moral or other—no sense of duty or self-sacrifice—no sense of other people's standards. You know how he keeps saying that duty is often made an excuse for following the letter and not the spirit of the law.

He keeps talking, too, of the difference between "internal surrender, which is humility," as opposed to "external self-sacrifice, which is pride."

I think, too, of that beautiful sentence that you often quoted to me about the date tree giving forth dates, not in order to do good to the world, but simply because it was its nature to give forth dates. It is not a question of "good" or "bad," but only of "true." How to be true to the real "nature" of "self" in one. But it takes so much patience and insight and burning honesty to find out.

This is really all I know. You, Jim, know so much more than I knew at the time I got married that I cannot but feel you will make the right decision if you have time and quiet to think about it. You know things instinctively and intuitively, too, not just in the mind. Charles says to me, "But you can't just *abandon* rational thinking!" Of course not, but one must never forget, as I think you have said, that it is just an instrument. On the whole, in the past era certainly, people were apt to let it become the master and not the servant. There is such a beautiful line in the first installment of Saint-Exupéry's new book in the January *Atlantic*. He says, "I know as much about temptation as any Church Father. To be tempted is to be tempted, when the spirit is asleep, to give in to the reasons of the mind."

You know all that. What we are apt to forget, I think, or

at least what *I* am, is to narrow my conception of spirit, to confine it too much to mental processes, to mind, heart, consciousness or, even expression. I need to be told what I was the other day by Mrs. Loines. I have been in bed for six weeks or so, rather miserable much of the time, and one day I protested to her, in an effort to find some spiritual exit out of my discomfort. "It seems to me that in sorrow or even in pain the spirit is sharpened, it is closer to reality—it flowers. But in sickness like this, it just dies. I become just body—just sodden clay."

And she said, "You have too narrow a conception of spirit. You think of it as mind, as consciousness, as flowering or fruit, as awareness. You forget that the body is also an instrument of the spirit, and perhaps equally important. Perhaps you have been neglecting it. Perhaps you are meant now just to think 'How good and flat this bed is' and 'How good it is to breathe—like taking a drink of water.' "

I hand this on to you as the most acute piece of wisdom that has come to me for some time.

Do not let my letter worry you or, I hope, feel it is an imposition. It is rare to be able to help another person *directly* (exactly when or how one wants). Rilke says "a whole constellation of things must be right in order to succeed a single time." I think, myself, Charles had his own ulterior motives for wanting this all down in writing!

If I *had* married a man "to reform him," I would have had a job on my hands, wouldn't I! Don't, of course, answer this. It isn't the kind of letter one answers. Take that time to yourself to think.

> Our best wishes and thoughts to you always,
> Anne

Chapter

TEN

I N FEBRUARY 1942, I had lunch with the Lindberghs on Long Island, and afterward Charles took me to the Long Island Aviation Club and gave me a flying lesson. I had taken lessons back in Akron in the 1930s, and this was not the first with Charles, but it was the most memorable. We went up in a small dual-controlled Stinson. Charles limbered up by doing a few minutes of acrobatics—which proved he had a stronger stomach than I. Then I did a few takeoffs, maneuvers, and landings. As we taxied to the end of the runway for a final takeoff, he said, "Pull over here."

"Now," he said, "take off over the runway and across the field."

I looked across the field; it seemed a very short distance. "Can we do that?"

"Well, try it."

"But there are power lines over there."

"Well, try it!"

I gave it the gun and we roared across the grass. Then I pulled back on the stick. We lifted off, but the power lines were too close. I pulled back harder on the stick. No, we weren't going to make it. I looked back at Charles in the seat behind me; his eyes were on the instrument panel. Then he looked up at me.

"I can't do it."

"Are you through?"

"Yes."

He pulled on the stick and we nosed up sharply over the power lines, with a few feet to spare.

As I thought about it later, I realized that there had been plenty of room to go under the lines if necessary. I realized, too, that he was not being foolhardy; he was teaching me the most important lesson: you could often do more than you thought you could, and a plane could often do more than you thought it could.

Shortly afterward, I was inducted into the Army and sent to Camp Blanding near Jacksonville, Florida for basic training. I received a letter from Charles in May 1942, as I was completing that training:

I thought you would be given a classification that would permit the full use of your talents and experience along the lines you have been following in years past, and in which you have exceptional ability. However, it may be that your entering the army will turn out to be best in the long run— for some reason which I can't explain, I am inclined to think it will be.

But I miss seeing you and talking to you about current trends and war developments. Letters are all right *in between* visits, but even when there is time to write them they do not make up for the give and take of conversations. Some things may be said better in a letter, but certainly not as many things—and then there is getting to be less and less that one can put down in writing these days. Too much of life is becoming a "military secret."

I am finding my work with the Ford Co. of great interest and I enjoy the chance to be with my mother in Detroit during most weekends. Anne and the children (there will be another one this fall!) are still at Martha's Vineyard. I hope to bring them through to Detroit soon, but we have not been able to locate a satisfactory place to live as yet.

Jim, I should think you could be of greatest value to the war effort by being assigned to the Firestone Co. to carry on the work there in which you have had so much experience in the past. Have you considered that possibility?

I can send no news that you don't read about in the papers. Naturally, we are all greatly concerned about the continued heavy shipping losses, and about the outcome of the campaign on the eastern European front, which will probably get fully underway in the next few days or weeks with the coming of hard ground and summer weather.

Anne and I missed our yearly trip to Florida and the Everglades and Keys more than I can tell you. (Even the December and January swims at Martha's Vineyard didn't make up for it.)

I know how difficult it is to write when days are long and full of hard physical work—and especially when one's mind is full of other things. Don't lose sleep answering this—letters are welcome, but never essential where friendship is deep—but if and when you have the time to write, Anne and I are always glad to hear from you, and wanting to know what you are doing and how you are getting along.

Best as always,
Charles

After basic training I went through officer candidate school in the Quartermaster Corps at Camp Lee, Virginia, and after earning my commission I was given leave and went up to Mackinac Island, Michigan, where Ellie and some of my friends were just finishing a conference. Afterward, at Henry Ford's invitation, I went down to Dearborn and met Charles, who had just returned from an intensive research course in high-altitude flying at the Mayo Foundation in Rochester, Minnesota. I went with him to the Bloomfield Hills home, north of Detroit, which he had rented, where Anne and the children had joined him during the summer.

We had a lively dinner together. There was much to talk about, as we had not met for eight months. Charles had spent almost all his time at Ford's Willow Run, where B-24 Liberation four-engine bombers were beginning to come off the giant assembly lines.

He told me that the government, the military, and the company had all insisted on jumping into production with minimum preparation. They had pushed for unrealistic deadlines, and Charlie Sorensen and Ford himself went along with them without planning properly for trained workers, of whom they had very few, or raw materials, which were in short supply.

Ford was a genius with automobiles, he said to me, but when it came to airplanes he was out of his depth. Building a plane demanded higher standards and different techniques. The workmanship on the first B-24s was so poor that Charles recommended that they be rejected. Sorensen thought Charles was attacking him personally.

"Have things improved?" I asked him.

"A great deal. But I've been only too glad to escape into a cockpit whenever I can. Testing this new P-47 Thunderbolt restores my sanity."

When Charles described a few of his experiences with the new P-47—a piece of the engine cowling coming off in flight, the engine cutting out at forty thousand feet, the landing gear jamming—I told him my idea of restoring one's sanity was somewhat different from his.

Charles said he would not have stayed on at Ford long if it hadn't been for Ford himself. His simplicity of life, his philosophy, made him a great man in Lindbergh's eyes.

Many years later I ran across a copy of one of his letters, which illustrated that regard and esteem:

Willow Run
July 30, 1942

Dear Mr. Ford:

I want to add my congratulations to the many you are receiving today, and to tell you how much interest and pleasure I find in taking part in the organization you have built.

My friendship with you is one of the things I value most highly in life. You combine the characteristics that I admire most in men—success with humility, firmness with tolerance, science with religion—I shall not attempt to make a longer list. Possibly the thing I admire most about you is that you have built one of the world's greatest industries without letting it change your own outlook and character.

It must be of tremendous satisfaction to you to see the results of what you set out to do so many years ago. It is certainly an inspiration to other men, and will continue to be long after this present period of war is over.

With my best wishes,
Charles A. Lindbergh

It was on this visit that Charles told me he'd been wrong about Germany invading Britain. The British fighter planes and their Navy seemed to have stopped Hitler across the Channel. He had been right about the fearful slaughter that would take place if Hitler attacked Russia. But Hitler had made the same mistake Napoleon had; and think how much could have been saved in Western Europe if he'd been allowed to attack eastward at the start. If our government had not been distracted by the European war he doubted whether Pearl Harbor would have happened. He didn't have any doubt we would eventually force the Japanese back, but what it was costing now to regain our footholds all across the Pacific, from Hong Kong and the Philippines, all the way to New Guinea!

"You know where I'd really like to be?" Charles turned and asked me at one point.

"I can guess."

"In a combat unit, where the real testing is done—of men as well as machines."

I looked across at Anne. She was sewing a button on one of the children's clothes. I knew how she felt about the war, and that she would never try to hold her husband back from where he felt his duty lay. But she must have been grateful that he was working for Ford in Dearborn for the moment, and not in New Guinea.

"We've talked a lot about me, Jim. How about you? How is it going in the Army? How have your values held? Have you started smoking or drinking or running after women?"

"No." We grinned at one another and I decided to tell him a bit about my Army life. So I launched into a story about my friend, the first sergeant. The first night in OCS we had been packed into a barracks with bunks against the walls and cots down the middle—hardly enough room to walk between—naturally, I got one of those cots in the middle! As I went to bed, I said to myself, am I going to kneel down to say my prayers as usual—or will I just slip into bed and say them there? Well, I got on my knees and while I was there, a big guy came by in the dark and tripped over my legs and nearly fell.

Next morning he came up to me during a ten-minute field break and said in a ringing voice, "What the hell were you doing down there last night? You tripped me up and I could've broken my neck."

"I was praying."

"Praying!" he yelled.

At that moment, a friend of mine came by. He was a small, tough character from the New Bedford textile mills, where he had been a union leader. In the Army Reserve he had risen to be first sergeant before becoming an OCS candidate. He stepped between me and the big guy, stared up at him, and said, "You heard him. Can't a guy pray if he wants to?"

The big guy backed off, muttering, "Okay, okay."

The first sergeant and I got to know each other over KP— 4:30 A.M. to 7:00 P.M. When he asked me why I was having such a good time washing pots and pans, I told him I had decided when I joined the Army that I was going to enjoy life no matter what came my way.

Before long, he was asking me a lot of questions about what I believed—he was an atheist. Our decisive conversation took place a month later when we were both on guard duty. We paced off our separate beats, but each time we returned to our post we continued our conversation. "By the end of it," I concluded, "he decided to try a new way of life. He had gone through the same thing I had at Toy Town Tavern." Charles was listening intently.

"Although he used much more colorful language about himself when he addressed the Almighty!" I added. He smiled.

*   *   *

I soon received orders to report to Fort Benning, Georgia for an infantry officer's training course, and from there was assigned to Camp Lee, Virginia to run training courses in a variety of weapons. I understood that if I did the job right

I could expect to remain there for some time. So I felt that this was the time to embark on marriage with Ellie. She agreed. When I had the opportunity to get a short leave, I went up to Detroit and asked Charles if he would be my best man at the wedding.

"Jim, I'm honored. But I'm not much of a man for ceremonies. To tell you the truth, I've been to one wedding in my life, and that was my own. If it were for anyone but you, I'd turn it down flat. Let me think about it. What would I have to do?"

"Just stand there and give me support and hand me the ring at the right moment."

He asked me about the press.

"I've thought of that. It'll be a small private ceremony at the home of friends in Washington."

He asked about the minister and the sort of fuss he would make.

"We have the ideal man, a bishop—the least episcopal bishop you'll ever meet, Charles. George West was an artillery man in World War I. He's bishop of Burma—loved by Buddhists and warring tribesmen as much as by his Christians. A big-hearted, unconventional Englishman."

In the end, Charles accepted. In early March he and I met in Washington in his room at the Mayflower Hotel. We talked most of a morning and when lunchtime came, ordered food to be sent up to the room, so Charles would not have to be seen in the dining room.

Shortly, there was a knock at the door, and I started to get up to answer it. I did so automatically, thinking, as I always did, that the press might have tracked him down. Charles pushed me back into my chair, saying seriously, "No, Jim, you're in uniform; I'll answer it."

There I was, in my second lieutenant's uniform—"the lowest form of life known to man," as they had called it in the service—but to Lindbergh the uniform of the United

States military overrode our informal comradeship and his fear of the press. For me it was a new insight into his deeply felt patriotism. (As it turned out, it was the waiter at the door.)

My friends, Van Dusen and Margaret Rickert, opened their home in the quiet Cleveland Park section of Washington, and Ellie and I were married there, with some of our close friends on hand.

Ellie quickly entered into the friendship with the Lindberghs. They warmly welcomed her open nature and staunch individuality. Certainly, Ellie was no fading flower. She had gone to the housing center at Camp Lee, and when she was told there was nothing immediately available (meaning: nothing for anyone as lowly as a second lieutenant and his wife), announced that she would remain in the office until something was found. When closing time came, she continued to sit. The staff saw that they had met their match and came up with a small garage apartment—our home for the next two years.

Our opportunities to see the Lindberghs were limited, but we carried on a correspondence that ranged from the practical to the mystical. A letter written by Anne within a month after our marriage is typical:

What a time for a Virginia ham!

The meat rationing, the empty counters in Detroit—and there was your ham. I have been away for two weeks, but Charles and the children have had the ham all to themselves and it has been a household "staple." Did you know that it was one of Charles' favorite foods? He has always loved them. So you sent us a real present, appreciated by everyone. Mother and sister came with me for a few days and we could still feast on ham. "That ham certainly helped," said the cook. Thank you a hundred times.

I have just had a few days with Charles and now he has

271

gone off again for two weeks. During that time we got your nice letter. How could you write, with all that you are doing? We both appreciate it and have spoken so much of you. I wish more than anything that we could all meet.

This has been a chopped up winter, and it seems to me I have not yet digested what is happening in the world and to us. The things that are not yet digested in one's own mind and heart are hard to share. The period of getting married is like that, too—and you must be feeling that, although you both had learned so much more before you got married— you had a head start.

I have not yet learned quite how to deal with those periods when one is learning and living too fast to digest. There was a wonderful story once told by André Gide of a trip he took through the jungle, very fast, with African guides. One morning the native guides sat around in a circle and refused to move. When Gide urged them on, saying he was in a hurry to get somewhere, they looked up at him seriously, reproachfully, but with complete rock-like firmness, and said, "Don't hurry us—we are waiting for our souls to catch up with us."

I should think you and Jim must feel like that in the army life you have been shot through. I shall send you a tiny book, the Bhagavad-Gita, or The Lord's Song. It is a very old approach to the eternal problems. It is the story of a man who was torn by indecision as to what part he should take in a civil war. He felt he could *not* take part in it—all his instincts, training and teaching and inspiration seemed to be against it. The Bhagavad-Gita is the answer that God gave him. In the words of the preface, that answer is: "That the spiritual man need not be a recluse, that union with the divine Life may be achieved and maintained in the midst of worldly affairs, that the obstacles to that union are not outside us, but within us. . . ."

Tonight this must get off—and I must go and give Scott, eight months old today, with a first tooth, his evening bottle—to send you our thanks for the Ham and your letter, and many thoughts of love to you both always,

Anne

With three-day leaves we managed occasional meetings— in Bloomfield Hills, Washington, and New York. One of the most memorable was in New York, in December 1944, when I had travel orders to New York for an appointment to get special eyeglass lenses. Ellie and I took the opportunity to have dinner there with the Lindberghs. Charles had recently returned from five months in the South Pacific. He and I had been surrounded for months by the weapons of war. Ellie and I had received a letter from Anne in which she wrote that she had heard from a friend that Charles had been attacked by a Japanese plane and had shot it down. I asked Charles to tell about it.

It had happened fast. He was flying a P-38 Lightning in a squadron, and as they came up over Amahai, west of New Guinea, he saw enemy planes below. He dived down in line until a Japanese fighter appeared directly ahead. They raced toward each other at five hundred miles an hour. Charles could see his tracer bullets spurting at him as he held the enemy plane in the ring sight of his guns. Charles raised the nose of his plane slightly to avoid a head-on collision. The Japanese pilot did the same. He looked to be aiming for a crash. At the last moment Charles hauled back on his stick with all his strength and felt a big jolt of air as they missed each other by a few feet. As he banked, he saw the Japanese plane twisting below, out of control. Finally, it splashed into the ocean.

"Thank God for your marksmanship, Charles." I thought

of our pistol practice at the cottage on Captiva, and his remarkable accuracy.

I knew he had flown fifty missions, although as a civilian he wasn't supposed to be doing it. But combat wasn't the most important thing, as far as he was concerned. It was significant only insofar as it involved realistic testing of the planes. As it turned out, his most helpful contribution down there had been something a lot less spectacular. He had found that the American pilots had been given no proper training in how to handle fuel consumption. The effective range of P-38s was less than six hundred miles. He had taught them to increase that range to more than seven hundred miles by reducing cruising speed and adjusting the controls.

Even more important than saving fuel, the increased bombing range had allowed them to catch the Japanese unprepared when our planes attacked bases they thought were safe. Charles had also shown our men how to double the bomb load of their F4U Corsairs.

But combat, he conceded, was a terrible enterprise. The worst part for him, he said, was to experience war's dehumanizing effects. Air warfare was especially difficult. It was either like the combat he'd just described—like knights in modern armor—or it was death and destruction at a great distance. He would drop a bomb load and look back to see a flash and a puff of smoke far below him. He would sometimes visualize the broken bodies and shattered buildings. But it was more often far removed, impersonal.

When he had been on the ground at Biak, he had seen the slaughter of Japanese soldiers, holed up in their caves against our bombs and firepower. Almost no prisoners had been taken by either side. We hear a good deal about Japanese atrocities, he said, but we don't hear about our own ferocity.

We were soon talking about what we needed to learn from

the war. What could man retrieve from the disaster that would prepare him for a better way of living?

Ellie said, "Don't we have to learn the lesson that human wisdom has failed? That we need to listen to the Lord to find His ways of working together, instead of grabbing what we want, as individuals and nations?"

"Of course you're right, Ellie," Charles responded.

And then he told us that although he had trimmed down his luggage to the bare minimum for years, he had learned to add a copy of the New Testament. "It was more than worth its weight," he said.

In the entry for April 3, 1944 in his *Wartime Journals,* he later wrote: "Purchased a small New Testament at Brentano's. Since I can carry only one book—and a very small one—that is my choice. It would not have been a decade ago; but the more I learn and the more I read, the less competition it has."

"I don't have quite the confidence you do, Ellie," Charles continued, "but I do know that man can no longer put all his faith in science and hope to survive."

He went on to say that mankind had been worshiping science and had gained power at the expense of the quality of life. Now modern man must allow the material power science had given him to be directed by moral and spiritual truths.

I looked across the table at Charles as he leaned forward, talking so seriously to my wife. I thought of the similar thoughts that Alexis Carrel had expressed, and I also thought of my first dinner with Lindbergh, hosted by Carrel, half a dozen years before. Charles had moved a long way in his thinking.

Ellie and I had sent some Christmas gifts to the Lindbergh children, and received a letter from Anne that was more than one of thanks. It let us into the heart of the family in the vivid way that only she could do:

I feel very lax not to have written you earlier about all the lovely things you sent the children for Christmas & especially because—from the way they were appreciated—I know such thoughtfulness went into them. I must say first of all that Land's (raccoon) tail *made* his Christmas—He made me pin it to the back of his overalls and he pranced around in it all day—completely transformed! (I know that was not its intended use, but it doesn't matter.) He then put it on his pajamas and slept with it. When I asked him what he liked best for Christmas—he smiled his wide "Thumper" smile and said "my tail"! The baseball will come in useful later but the tail is still supreme. Jon was equally pleased—if not so demonstrative—about his checker board. And Anne was entranced by the beautiful Blue Satin Apron marked *Army*—I try to keep it for special occasions but whenever I am not watching, she climbs up & puts it on—over overalls, nightgown—no matter what! ("Uncle Jim's apron," she calls it! And it's Aunt Ellie's "book of songs.") I had not seen the book of Carols and it is a very lovely one—Stories & Carols & all the ones I love best (The Holly & the Ivy—etc.). Anne loves me to sing songs to her before she goes to sleep. And that is now one of her favorite books. Last night I sat on her bed & sang out of it—and Land came in the door & joined us.

Scott's wonderful large-size Elf—looking somehow very much like Scott ("Son of Santa Claus" as Marta always used to call him!) has been appropriated by Anne—though Scott sometimes gets a swat at him. He reposes in the old cradle in the sitting room—in between times and is always a welcome surprise when found.

You are much in the hearts & thoughts of all the children & "the box from Uncle Jim & Aunt Ellie" was a real part of our Christmas.

Charles is away just now, gone to the West Coast on a

short trip. He is pretty disturbed by world events & just as restless as ever. I wish there were something he could bite into that he felt was leading somewhere. In the meantime the children are well & happy & adjusting well to school— and still raising the roof at home.

I leaped out of bed yesterday thinking that someone was hurling pots & pans down the backstairs. It turned out to be a Goldberg contraption that Jon had rigged up in the attic with the motor of his Erector Set—a wheel—& an old tin pan suspended from a small crane—several rat traps etc.— & a few tin cans. When it goes off you really think all the plumbing has exploded.

Jon does it to wake Land in the morning & to retaliate for Land's singing "Silent Night" in the early hours of the morning in his sleep!

I'm glad you liked the Peguy (book). He was certainly a voice crying in the wilderness—But they are reading him now.

I wish we could see you again. No more eye appointments?

I must go in to Scott who—from the sound of it—is being a little Samson with the bureau drawers!

One lives from day to day—but this waiting period is hard. Harder on men than on women who are more accustomed to waiting and for whom it is easier to live from day to day—

We think of you often—

Our Love
Anne

In May 1945, shortly after the war in Europe had come to an end, I received orders to transfer to the Asian theater. Ellie traveled with me to San Francisco, where I was to ship out to the Philippines.

While I was in the Philippines, I received a letter from Anne which ranged, as hers often did, from personal to global affairs:

I was so very glad to get your letter which Marta forwarded to Maine, where we were over Labor Day. Charles and I drove up in the Trailer, picking up both boys from camp en route. It was great fun and made me think of living on the "Aldebaran." We left from home the same day Mme. Carrel and her nephew left for the Argentine. They had been here a great part of the summer. Mme. C was *infinitely* better than when I wrote you that hurried report to the coast. Better in body and calmer in spirit. . . .

Dear Jim—such is my life! A month has passed since I started this letter and ten days since Ansy's little sister was born—on Anne's birthday, October 2nd! (She was named Reeve.) I still can't quite believe it and feel reborn in body and spirit. It is hard to think back to the long summer and even longer winter, when I was like a bulb underground. . . . Mme. Carrel was with us about a month and her nephew also much of that time. She improved tremendously. She simply sat in the sun or under the trees all day long, sewing, and the children played at her feet. And we talked of Dr. Carrel, of his beliefs, of his work, and much of you. She was calm and peaceful, at ease, even gay at times. She was serene, and I am sure feels him to be near her when she is quiet.

As you must know, Ellie came and saw her one day . . . it was a terribly cut-up afternoon, Kay and Truman [Smith] unexpectedly came over, and I felt flattened out for the afternoon by Truman's announcement, "Well, they've split the atom. We've dropped an atom bomb on Japan—most revolutionary change in the history of man since the Birth of Christ."

Oh, Jim, why have we been given this terrible power when

we are morally so unprepared for it? I could only think of those words of a modern Quaker Saint: "An awful solemnity is upon the Earth, for the last vestige of earthly security is gone. *It has always been gone*, and religion has always said so, but we haven't believed it."

It was a staggering afternoon. Ellie and Mme. Carrel had a little time together and I know it meant much to Mme. Carrel, for she spoke afterwards of what a lovely person Ellie is. . . .

Funny, there seem to be whole periods in a woman's life when she is busy with the stage scenery—or rather, she is a kind of "property man." She pulls the chairs up, arranges the group around the fire—but doesn't contribute to it. Catholics talk about "the occasion for sin." Woman is concerned much of the time trying to make "the occasion for Joy." Not to give joy herself, but to *provide the occasion for it* for others. If she does it well, she is satisfied and it is a special kind of gift. But if she does it badly . . . !

I felt I was doing it badly most of last year, but now, looking back on the summer, remembering Mme. Carrel's happiness, looking at this lovely flower of a child that grew all that time, I can only feel grateful and joyous. And also very undeserving of this miracle. . . .

I wish you would come home now—C and Truman discuss the Atom World that faces us—continually—and I feel you would contribute to these talks. However, I also feel that your being out there will make you contribute more, not only to the talks, but to our troubled generation in this troubled era, when you come back.

They are about to bring the baby in for its six o'clock supper and I must put this down. The Boys got your letter just before I left for the hospital. They still feel they own you and love any word from you. We all miss you. There are lots of other things to say, and not time now, for the baby's routine takes all day.

279

Love from us all—in this scribbled note.

Anne

* * *

The dropping of the atom bomb on Hiroshima and Nagasaki was greeted with enthusiasm and relief by our troops in the Philippines. We had been preparing to launch what we knew must be a bloody and costly invasion of Japan's home islands. I, as a part of that invasion force, shared in their emotions, although I was amazed and more than a little worried by the scientific breakthrough that had produced the nuclear explosion. I wanted to talk about it with Lindbergh, to get his perspective on its significance for the future.

That opportunity came early in 1946, after I was released, now a major, from the Army. Ellie and I caught up with Charles in New York. He was flying between Chicago, Washington, New York, and his Connecticut home—always on the move, it seemed.

In the early postwar years he was serving simultaneously as a consultant to a secret committee, the University of Chicago Ordnance Research Project (CHORE), as a special adviser to the Air Force, and as a consultant to Pan American World Airways. It seemed to me a bewildering variety of activities, but they combined to put him in the forefront of architecting our postwar world.

We had much to talk about, starting with our wartime activities. I had heard of his visit to Germany during the last days of the fighting there, and asked him about it. He said the month he had spent there on a Navy mission to evaluate German aviation had shaken him up as much as anything he'd experienced. It had made him examine some of his cherished beliefs. He had seen the destructive effect of air bombardment, had driven a jeep through the rubble of Munich, had seen the women and children in rags, picking through the wreckage for essentials of living. Centuries of culture had been wiped out in minutes.

"I went up to Berchtesgaden and stood, looking out of the window through which Hitler had gazed at the beautiful Bavarian scene of mountains and forests. Of course Hitler was more responsible than anyone for World War II. But I was hit, too, by the realization of how we'd taken the airplane and made it an instrument of death and destruction beyond anything in history."

He described his first sight of Nordhausen, where the huge V-2 rockets had been assembled, how they'd driven their jeep through a nightmare world, brightly lit but empty of man and silent. Here lay the most technically advanced product of rocketry, designed to deliver instant, unexpected death. The V-2s traveled faster than sound. His mind had gone back to a New England home and his conversation with an eager university physicist, who had kindled his imagination with plans for a rocket to carry scientific instruments into the stratosphere. Charles had helped Dr. Robert Goddard get going seriously in the New Mexico desert by persuading Harry Guggenheim to provide him with the funds. Goddard had set Charles dreaming about space travel, the next step beyond the airplane. In the cause of war, German scientists had far outpaced Goddard and his limited means; and the rocket, like the airplane, had become a threat to mankind.

I tried to divert Charles from his gloomy thoughts by reminding him that the war was over—we could get back to research for peaceful ends now. He held up his hand and stopped me.

"I must tell you of another horror I saw at Nordhausen, worse than the rockets." The munitions factory had stood in the middle of what had been a concentration camp, a branch of Belsen. He had driven up the mountainside, above the tunnels, to an empty building. Inside, there were two furnaces, and in front of them steel stretchers—cremating ovens. As he stood there, a boy, scarcely more than a skeleton, had come up quietly and said, "Twenty-five thousand in a year and a half." The inmates of the concentration camp had been used as the labor force to assemble the rockets. As they had died off, victims of the work conditions and starvation, their corpses had been disposed of in the ovens.

The young Pole, who had survived the camp, had taken them over to what had been a large pit, now overflowing with human ashes from the furnaces. A few bones had lain scattered around. As they drove back through the forest, Charles had puzzled over such brilliant scientific achievement alongside such human degradation. Why had we allowed our pursuit of science to pervert the human spirit?

Charles went on to tell me that they now knew how close the German scientists had come to making an A-bomb. If Hitler hadn't diverted them to other things, they probably would have succeeded. We could bet our bottom dollar Stalin had his physicists working around the clock on it.

When he had been in Germany the summer before, the Russians had been trying frantically to get their hands on the German scientists who had worked on the V-2 rockets, just as the United States and Britain were. We had managed to get some of the best, but they had got some, too. The V-2, and its intercontinental successor carrying a nuclear warhead, would be a weapon against which any defense would be exceedingly difficult, if not impossible.

The future of the human race depended on how responsible we Americans were. If we developed the capacity to retaliate with a nuclear strike, should we be hit by the Russians, or anybody else, we were in a very strong position to prevent a nuclear war. No government was going to launch an attack if they knew for certain they would be devastated, too.

I asked him if he didn't think it was a little crazy to have to multiply deadly weapons in order to prevent them from being used.

Look at the alternative, he responded. Our politicians, especially Roosevelt, launched us into a war to save democracy and keep Europe free. Already we have allowed Russia to replace Germany as the totalitarian power in Europe, and the way things are going, Soviet control is reaching deep into the eastern half of the continent. If the Truman administration were to adopt the same irresponsible laissez-faire policies on our military defenses, we would be sealing, not only our own fate, but the fate of the free world.

It was this concern that was occupying most of Charles's time and energy. He was not able to talk much about these activities, as they were top secret. But we did talk in general terms, when Ellie and I spent a weekend with the Lindberghs later in the year at their Connecticut home in Darien, which they had bought the previous year. It stood on a couple of acres on a point of land running into Long Island Sound. The property was rocky, like the Maine coast, on one side. On the other was a small, white sand beach. Offshore were three small islands, a few square yards above high water, but several acres of rocks and clam grounds at low tide. You could walk to the islands when the tide was out. Charles and Anne had bought it, they said, because it reminded them of Illiec.

Once again, we walked along a rocky beach. Charles had not lost his long-limbed stride. He still had his alert, inquiring look, which he flashed when he was interested in a remark I made. His appearance had not changed very much; his hairline had receded, his face had rounded a little, and there were deeper lines around his jaws and crowfeet around his eyes. A quiet intensity had taken the place of the young man's enthusiasm, but we could still laugh, joke, and play the fool together.

Visits to the Lindberghs were sometimes enlivened by interesting guests. One of the most memorable was Igor Sikorsky,* known to the world as the helicopter pioneer. He came to dinner at the Darien home with his wife, both small of stature, both with accents from their native Russia. Sikorsky's range of interests was as wide as Charles's. Conversation went late into the evening and swung from Europe to flying boats to racial problems. Then we moved into more rarefied realms. He had written a book about the Lord's Prayer and was about to have another published about good and evil, God and the Devil. I was astonished to find a man who was regarded as a technical genius so absorbed in and eloquent about moral and spiritual matters.

During my stay in Darien in November 1946, I tried to draw Charles out on his current activities and I was amazed by the variety and complexity of what he had gotten into.

He was living in an unreal world of physics and higher mathematics, in a basement of the University of Chicago. He would sit around with professors and scientists, looking at graphs and charts and watching intricate formulas being scribbled on a blackboard. Electronic devices, computerized war games, exotic explosives, counter-counter defenses.

Pan American hoped to capture a big share of the newly created airlines market by getting in there early with established routes. That meant work for Charles, not only surveying routes, airports, passenger facilities, types of planes, but also some diplomatic dealings with governments and rival airlines. It was a healthy counterbalance, Charles said, to the rarefied atmosphere of nuclear physics in the University of Chicago basement.

---

* Igor Sikorsky, born in Russia, came to the U.S. in 1919. He built the first helicopter (1909), and the first successful multimotor plane (1913).

But in the main, Charles was dissatisfied. He had dreamed of the future of aviation and had come face to face with its destructive side. He had hoped to improve world communication with his Pan American work, but could only cringe at the thought of American tourists pouring into African game reserves or descending on Indian tribes up the Amazon. What would it do to the wildernesses, the wild animals, and the quiet, unspoiled peoples? He would go on offering his services as long as they were needed for air defense, because he believed the future security of civilization rested largely on the strength of America in the air. But he had a sense, an intuition, that there were larger challenges ahead— something to do with man's inner qualities, something to do with his relations with nature, his place on the planet.

Chapter

ELEVEN

THE FOLLOWING SPRING, in 1949, the Lindberghs decided to break away from their work and spend a couple of weeks on the *Aldebaran,* sailing down the Florida coast—the third such vacation we had spent in the gulf. This time, Charles and Anne brought the two oldest boys, Jon, now seventeen, and Land, twelve. Ellie had made plans to go north. "Anyway," she said, "another body might put the odyssey in jeopardy!"

Before we set sail from Fort Myers Beach on *Aldebaran,* Charles had a word with the two boys in my hearing. He said very seriously, "Uncle Jim is the captain, and whatever he says, goes. There may be times when things get dangerous and important decisions have to be made. Whatever decision Uncle Jim makes—that's *it*, and you are to obey 100 percent. Understand?"

"Yes, Father." They looked serious, and during the trip were very disciplined and did exactly what they were told.

Not that we had no fun. We had lots of it. Charles played

287

a memorable prank on Jon. We were up Shark River and Jon had climbed our rather tall mast to get a good look over the mangroves. Charles ducked down into the galley, came up with a bottle of molasses, stood on the cabin roof, and painted the mast with molasses as high as he could reach. Jon sat up there puzzling over how he would get down. He risked either a fast and messy descent down the mast or an even faster slide down the stays. Those thin wires were hard to grip. Finally he did come down the stays with a rush. We all had a good laugh about that.

Over the years I had watched Charles with his children. He had said once that he felt sorry for any kid who had the misfortune to be singled out as teacher's pet. The child was likely to get a false sense of security and make a lot of jealous enemies. He was always particular to give each of his children equal attention and affection. Anne expressed her affection for them warm-heartedly. Charles was no less affectionate, but he showed it in a more restrained way.

From the time they were quite young, Charles tried to get them to stand on their own feet, the boys especially. He would say, "Do the toughest thing first"—a rule he always applied to himself. And he would put up challenges and tell them what he expected from them. I remember one day on Lloyd Neck, when Jon was about eight, Charles took him out to their sheep pasture and showed him how to handle a lively ram who butted everything and everybody. He left Jon and the ram alone in the middle of the field and watched from behind a fence. Jon protected himself well until the ram got tired of butting. Charles called it time well spent. It was important to him that his boys learn to handle difficult situations.

Charles also took pains to encourage each of the children to develop their interests and talents. Jon was a keen fisherman, and so his father bought him an aluminum canoe and out he went into Long Island Sound to fish. Charles would pay him two or three cents per pound of catch and have him freeze it all. Charles took me down to the cellar once and threw open the door of a second freezer he had just bought. It was nearly packed with fish. "Those were caught by Jon," he said. "I'm paying him five cents a pound now, and it's going to ruin me!"

After a hitch in the Navy as a frogman officer, Jon went on, with his love of water and fishing, to pioneer the field of deep-sea diving and develop salmon farms in the Pacific Northwest.

Land, like his father, showed an early love for the soil, and Charles and Anne encouraged the boy's summer visits to a Western ranch. Later, Land ran the large family cattle ranch in Montana. Little Anne, who was seven at this time, grew up surrounded by dolls, and in due course became the author of a number of children's books. Scott, five, was a great animal lover. Charles made sure he had the pets he wanted and that he learned to look after them well. Scott became an authority on wild monkeys and their habitats. Reeve, the youngest, acquired her father's pioneering spirit and her mother's love for words: she has become a successful author.

I knew them all well from their earliest years, and although there were long intervals between visits to their home, being with them and watching them grow was as great a pleasure for me as my companionship with their parents. Each Christmas I, and then Ellie and I, had the fun of choosing the right gift for each one. We had married too late to have children of our own. The young Lindberghs, along with our nephews and nieces, came close to filling that void.

The letters we received from them were a source of delight to us, and from early years they reflected their later interests. Here is one from Jon, written in 1944, when he was eleven (spelling uncorrected):

Dear Uncle Jim:

I've been collecting cocoons lately and have found alot of Promethea, Ceeropsia and Pollyphemous. I keep them in a cheesecloth box through which you can see if any come out which none of mine have yet. Every night I hear the paper rattle around inside the cocoons. Early this morning we had our first thunderstorm. It started about sixthirty and lasted for fifteen or twenty minutes in which there was constant rumbling and flashes of lightning. The morning following the thunderstorm was all clouded untill noon and then turned out to be the worstest day we've had yet. I made two bird houses this morning and am going to put them out in the yard. In mothers room we have a wild cats den made up of a sleeping bag and two chairs. I'm feeling find and I hope you are too.

Sincerely yours,
Jon Lindbergh

Thank you very much for the archery set and your letter.

And one from Land in 1947, when he was ten:

How are you? We had a nice Eester. We made Eester eggs for Anne and Scott. We each got a hyacinth from Barbara. All the children had the measlas. All the children had the whooping cough but Reeve. I had the mumpes and a bad arm. But now we are a lot better. Father is making a cave in the rocks for use to play in in the summes. But in the winter the cave in snowed in. Spring in here. The flowers are up. It rains a lot here. Jon panted the boat. Father got a moder for use to us in spring. Father is making a beach for us to swim on. We would like you to come out here and swim.

Love,
Land

290

The children meant a great deal to Ellie and me. Some forty years later, Reeve, the youngest of them, in a speech at the Lindbergh Fund, told how they felt about us:

I think of Jim and Ellie's visits to our home in Connecticut during my childhood. I'll never forget how happy and free of pressure those visits were. Growing up there, I had the impression of my father and mother having to draw back from a lot of the fame that was attracted to them. There were lots of times when they felt they had to retreat from the normal kind of freedom and friendships, and Jim and Ellie really gave that freedom right back to them.

It was extraordinary to witness the wonderful spirit when Jim and Ellie were with us. My parents could always speak their minds without being quoted the next day in the newspaper. They could relax. They could explore and exchange ideas. They could just have fun.

The gift of friendship is a great one. And if you have a friend who permits you to be yourself in an unguarded and open way, when nothing else in your life really permits it, then the gift is very great indeed.

My brother Land once said to me, "If I have one friend in my whole life who is to me what Jim was to father, then I'll be satisfied." And then we thought about it, and we decided that perhaps we did have one friend like that. And it was the same one!

As we cruised through the Everglades and along the coast, Charles and Anne and I shared our thoughts. Sometimes the boys sat and listened. More often, they busied themselves with their own adventures. Since I'd last seen Charles, he'd started again as a consultant to the Air Force. One of his first priorities there was to advise on the postwar reorganization of the Strategic Air Command.

As we ate a picnic lunch, anchored off Little Hickory Island our first day out, Charles said he had come reluctantly to the conclusion that the retaliatory power of SAC bombers was the single greatest security against atomic war. No potential enemy was likely to provoke the annihilation our planes would inflict. He'd been flying out of Omaha to their bases, from Labrador to Okinawa. "You feel the fearsome power as you sit in a giant bomber, climbing to altitudes where a mountain range looks like a small ripple on the land surface, carrying a bomb load whose impact makes the explosion at Hiroshima look puny."

I wanted to know if he thought we'd ever reach the point where technology would actually make the world safe from a major war.

A lot of Americans seemed to think so, he said. Some people in the military did. They believed we had the wealth, scientific resources, and the social and political vitality to stay ahead of the Soviets.

"But you don't think so?"

"Jim, we're living not only in a nuclear age, but also in an age of ideology. We saw what power ideology gave Germany. And that's what's enabled the Soviets to go from near defeat at the hands of Hitler to become the most powerful land force in the world." Not only that, he went on, the Soviet Union was now extending its control over other countries through its Marxist doctrines. While we Americans believed in idealism and democratic restraint, Russia could be counted on to act with ruthlessness and deceit.

"We will always be on the defensive unless we commit ourselves to vigorous and positive moral policies. We need to reach beyond materialism to a philosophy springing from the character of man and the truths of God."

I didn't argue.

Anne chimed in that she thought we needed to look at the world struggle in a broader perspective. Wasn't it time that we looked beyond national borders, just as we'd had to look beyond village and tribal loyalties?

Whatever Charles's response might have been, it was interrupted by an Indian war whoop from Land, as he and Jon came charging around the trees on the shore. The yells gave way to an urgent plea, "When will supper be ready?"

We sailed down the coast and up into Shark River, just as we had on earlier trips. The intervening years had done little to spoil the wilderness of the Everglades jungle. As the boys enjoyed their share of hacking through the overhanging mangrove branches and vines, we talked on and on.

One night, after a swim in the moonlight and with the boys asleep in their bunks, we relaxed on deck, and our conversation turned to the topic that Anne had raised earlier—the need for man to accept the smallness of the planet and to live at peace with his neighbors.

As the boat rocked gently to the lapping of the waves, Charles spoke. To live in peace we needed some kind of world government, he said. The United Nations had been the best we could achieve, although it seemed an unwieldly tangle of compromise between the natural supremacy of big nations and the one-country-one-vote demand by the small ones. Man had never been able to work out a fully satisfactory political or economic organization to control society.

"A solution to instability in the world," he said quietly, "has to come at a deeper level. The quality of a civilization depends on a balance of body, mind, and spirit in its people, measured on a scale less human than divine."

Charles had developed this line of thought in a book, *Of Flight and Life,* published six months earlier.

Men were looking for something that would check the conflicting demands of governments and special interests, Charles explained. That authority either had to be imposed from the outside as it was in the Roman or the British empires, or it had to come from within. The inner control could only emerge from the acceptance of certain human val-ues—you would call them Christian values, Jim, he added—love, honesty, purity of motive, regard for others.

It did little good, he said, to attack the moral problems of our age—the excessive materialism—from the top. Over the generations we'd seen that laws and regulations attempting to do that simply did not work. We had to generate within individuals the desire to forego complicated, possession-rid-den lives, our drive for material success, for a simpler, freer life.

But how could it be done on a large enough scale to alter events? I asked.

Anne answered that there had been times in history when society had become so grim or so threatened that men were forced to look for a better way. Think of St. Francis of As-sisi, she said. The significance of his life, it seemed to her, was not just his founding of the Franciscan order, or that he preached simplicity, purity of life, even poverty for those who followed him, but that he had taken Christianity out of the church and into the streets and the marketplace and the kitchen. Ordinary people by the thousands responded to his call—they had been ready. That joyous flowering of the hu-man spirit had led to the Renaissance and the Reformation. It had all come from within.

"And do you think the world is ripe for another Renais-sance and Reformation?" I asked. "I think I do. We seem to have reached a dead end, and a lot of people are realizing it."

Charles thought so, too. But it had to be more than an intellectual desire, he said. It had to be a desire that springs from the roots of our being, until it shapes our actions in-stinctively through our conscious mind. Then we would see people as more important than things, the producer as more important than the product, peace of heart as more important than the prize of possession. That's what he had meant by a balance of spirit, mind, and body.

When we reached the Keys, Anne had to leave us at Marathon in order to go up to New York and see her publisher. The rest of us sailed on down the Keys. We had to go through the drawbridge at Marathon and blow our horn to get it raised, as our mast was tall. The bridgekeeper raised it for us, its lights flashing and bells ringing. As we came close, we saw a car approaching from the direction of Key West, traveling at least sixty miles an hour. The car skidded into the lowered traffic barrier full tilt, and we could see the barrier explode into a hundred pieces above us. We fully expected the car to be on us at any moment, but it finally came to a halt at the very edge of the bridge some fifty feet directly above us. We made our way through in stunned silence, with pieces of traffic barricade floating around us.

As we recovered our composure, Charles asked with mock solemnity, "Don't you think they should pay more attention to traffic signs in Florida, Jim?"

We sailed on to Molasses Key Light and tried trolling for the fish that swarmed around it, but every time we hooked one, a barracuda snapped off everything but its head. So we gave up and moved out to the edge of the Gulf Stream— you could see its bright, clear, almost purple water, distinct from the green of the shoal water. We all put on our diving masks and swam down to the coral rocks. Jon spotted a moray eel, its head poking out from the coral. He signaled to us and we went up to the surface.

Charles said, "I'm going to spear that moray."

We'd just read an article in the *National Geographic* about a Navy diver who'd speared a moray eel that had worked its way up the spear and nearly severed his arm.

I said, "Charles, if you do, you're going to be alone in the ocean!"

The boys and I clambered onto the dinghy as he speared the dangerous creature, a dozen feet below, then came up with it on his spear. He'd been careful to stab it sideways, so that it couldn't coil around and reach him. He held it up out of the water as it thrashed about and said, "I'm going to put it in the boat."

"Go ahead and try," I shouted. "But you'll be the only one in the boat! You're not welcome till you get rid of it!"

He had been joking, of course. He dived and managed to get the enraged eel off his spear and swam safely to the boat.

For him it had been an adventure. He used to say to me, "I'll take adventure before security, freedom before popularity, conviction before influence." It was the way he lived.

Lindbergh's *Of Flight and Life* had fascinated me and I'd brought a copy along. Between sailing and swimming, I discussed it with him.

"You summed up the progress of your thoughts over the years, Charles, in three themes. Two of them are very clear to me—first, your conviction that America should lead the world in the development of flight; and second, your opposition to our involvement in the war before we were drawn in. Your third conviction is that we are trapped by scientific materialism and that our only hope may be in balancing the awesome forces of science with a God-centered philosophy. My question is this: how is that third conviction to be implemented?"

He had gone to work on his first conviction about aviation by flying the Atlantic, stirring up public interest, pioneering a transcontinental airline, and so on. He had acted on his conviction about the impending war by doing all he could to alert democracies to the danger and then trying to stop America's involvement. "Now what practical steps, what real commitments will follow from your third conviction?"

"As usual, Jim, you hit the nail on the head. This third

296

challenge is the toughest. It is the least specific, most fundamental of the three."

Charles was direct: the solution lay in each individual, through the standards he held, not in political parties, movements, or laws, but in human values. In other words, the solution lay within ourselves. It was not an intellectual question but one of will and desire.

*   *   *

During the first week of 1950 Charles was in Washington in connection with his work as special adviser to the Air Force. His conferences at the Pentagon left him free time, and he accepted my invitation to attend some meetings, meals, and performances of plays at a Moral Re-Armament conference at the Shoreham Hotel. In addition to delegates from overseas and across the United States, a number of members of Congress attended the public meetings. The most significant feature of the gathering was the participation of people from the airlines, especially a group representing management and labor from National Airlines in Miami.

This airline was in deep trouble. Management and pilots were in a deadlock over thirty-three grievances and thirteen other issues, in what was then the longest airline strike in history. In aviation circles it was rumored that the Civil Aeronautics Board, which regulated the airlines, was considering withdrawing National's charter because the feuding could endanger the safety of the public. Charles was well aware of this situation and was startled when I told him that Ted Baker, National's president, and "Slim" Babbitt, Southeast regional vice-president of the Airline Pilots Association, were both at the conference.

"I thought those two hated each other's guts," Charles said. "Don't tell me they have joined in brotherly love!"

"Far from it. A couple of my Miami friends managed to get Baker and four officers of National to come. They did the same with Babbitt and two officers of the ALPA. We had them all register at the Shoreham, but when Babbitt heard Baker was attending, he and his men canceled their rooms and moved to the Annapolis Hotel. Babbitt said he wouldn't sleep under the same roof as that man!"

Both groups attended the sessions and heard people of opposing interests speak of their enmities and their reconciliations—French and German, Communist and anti-Communist, management and labor. From time to time Charles would ask me how it was going with the National men. "They're still here," I told him.

Toward the end of the conference, representatives of the pilot's union and management of United Airlines spoke at a luncheon about a new spirit of accord they had recently developed between them. Bill Patterson, president of United, said that averting a strike had saved them millions of dollars. That evening a play, *The Forgotten Factor*, was performed. It dramatized a bitter antagonism between a boss and union chief dissolving into a reluctant understanding.

Next day, when Charles asked me again how Baker and Babbitt were doing, I said, "Hold onto your chair, this will come as a shock. After the play yesterday, Ted Baker went to Slim Babbitt and said, 'I've been an SOB. I don't expect you to believe what I say, but I saw something which just might be an answer for us.' Babbitt said, 'And I'm just fool enough to believe you!' All of them have been sitting down together to see what they can do about the issues dividing them. If you ever pray, Charles, now is the time."

The two sides were able to eliminate all but two of the issues between them. Babbitt admitted that many of the thirty-three grievances were only his padding for negotiation purposes. On the remaining fundamental points, he outlined exactly how far the union was prepared to go, and Baker accepted their terms. Later, back in Miami, Babbitt reported to the pilots, "We got further in three hours than we had in three years. Until I get further information, I will

298

regard MRA as a wonder drug that makes real human beings out of people."

Management and union continued their negotiations and late in March they announced publicly the full settlement of their differences. D. W. Rentzel, chairman of the Civil Aeronautics Board, made a public statement, calling the settlement "a pleasant shock to the aviation industry." He went on: "To those familiar with the long history of bitter and acrimonious dispute the transformation in the attitude of the parties from one of suspicion and hostility has been little short of miraculous. In effecting a settlement of this bitter struggle Moral Re-Armament has performed an invaluable service, not only to the aviation industry, but to the country as a whole."

The dramatic outcome was not lost on Charles. Before the conference ended, he and Ellie had lunch together—I was not able to join them. They talked about the personal feud that had divided Baker and Babbitt.

"Resentment is a hard thing to let go," Ellie said.

"I suppose," Charles replied, "if I had any resentment in my life, it would be against the press." Ellie knew what was going through his mind—the ruthless publicity when their son was kidnapped; the photographer who broke into the Trenton mortuary to take pictures of his body; the men who forced their nurse's car into the curb to take pictures of young Jon. "I know they're paid to get pictures and stories," Charles said. "It's their job. But there's a place for humanity."

"You wouldn't be human, Charles, if you didn't feel bitter. But there's something you can do about it."

He laughed. "I know what you and Jim would say."

"I get upset with people, too, Charles, even with the people I love most. Jim and I make each other angry. We've simply learned how to keep adventure in our marriage by being honest, letting God take care of our feelings and then straightening things out with each other."

"Ellie, don't think I don't appreciate what's happening in National Airlines. But it would be quite something else for me to go to a newspaper editor or publisher and say, 'I'm sorry for being resentful for the way your people have treated me and my family.' In the first place, they'd just laugh at me. And, more important, do you think it would change the way the press behaves?"

"I don't know, Charles. You've never worried too much about what people thought of you. The important thing is to be free in your heart."

Ellie said Charles looked at her with a twinkle in his eye and said, "Maybe I enjoy having a resentment or two! They're like pepper. They keep life sharp and interesting. Without them, life might be too bland."

"Life would never be dull for you, Charles!"

As we moved into the 1950s Lindbergh seemed to be involved in even more activities, shuttling from one commitment to another. I caught up with him intermittently in Darien, New York, Washington, and in Fort Myers Beach, where his uncle, his mother's younger brother, lived for several years. When Charles brought his uncle down the first time, Ellie met them at the airport and asked Charles if he would like to drive the car. He said yes.

As they climbed into the car, an old, secondhand affair, Charles walked around, looked each tire over, then under the hood. Finally, he sat in the driver's seat and checked everything—the instrument panel, the brakes, the lights, the gear shift. Only then did he settle in and drive off.

When Ellie told me that, laughing, I said, "That's Charles. He does that with every car he drives, every plane he flies, every boat he takes out. He may take chances, but never leaves anything to chance." I might have added that he approached everything else the same way. He made endless drafts of his articles, until he got them exactly the way he wanted them. He turned ideas over and over in his head,

300

looking at them from all sides. When he made his flight to Paris in *The Spirit of St. Louis* he calculated every element—course, gasoline, propeller pitch, engine setting, wind, weight—down to the last ounce. The press's nickname for him, "Lucky Lindy," annoyed him. "I calculate the odds," he'd say, "so I'm prepared to make the most of whatever situation arises."

I think this patient attention to detail was as much the key to his achievements as was his intuitive brilliance. He and Thomas Edison shared the same quality. It was what drove him to persist for those five years with Alexis Carrel until he perfected the heart perfusion pump, which no one else had been able to produce.

In 1953, Charles published his full story of *The Spirit of St. Louis*. Whenever I traveled with him, he carried a briefcase or a bag bulging with papers, including the manuscript of this book. He would sit in waiting rooms, railroad stations, and airports sculpting the text, which was not just the story of his adventurous flight, but also flashbacks to his life story and its significance for him—its "values," as he called them.

Charles had written an account of his Paris flight, published under the title, *We*, in 1927. The difference between that early book and this one was a measure of growth in the maturity of the man. I was struck by the ability he had acquired to express his experiences of a quarter of a century earlier. One paragraph especially stood out for me:

It's hard to be an agnostic up here in *The Spirit of St. Louis*, aware of the frailty of man's desires, a part of the universe between its earth and stars. If one dies, all this goes on existing in a plan so perfectly balanced, so wonderfully simple, so incredibly complex that it's far beyond our comprehension—worlds and moons revolving; planets orbiting suns; suns flying with appar-

301

ent recklessness through space. There's the infinite magnitude of the universe; there's the infinite detail of its matter—the outer star, the inner atom. And man conscious of it all—a worldly audience to what if not to God?

He told me that one day, while awaiting a plane and trying as usual to remain incognito, he was working away at his manuscript when a man came up to him and said, "Excuse me, aren't you Colonel Lindbergh?"

"No."

"Oh, I beg your pardon. Bud Gurney is a friend of mine and Bud said if I ever ran into Lindbergh, to give him his best."

"You're a friend of Bud Gurney?"*

"Yes, Cliff Robertson."

Charles looked up at the actor. "Well, then, if you're a friend of Bud's, I'm Charles Lindbergh."

When Charles came down to Florida to visit his uncle in 1954 he had finished his work at the University of Chicago, but he was still involved in military aviation. As a consultant to the Air Force, he was continuing his work with the Strategic Air Command and serving on a commission to select a site for the Air Force Academy. He was also a member of a committee to develop ballistic missiles.

He told me that he was working with extremely brilliant men, physicists like Walter Bartky, Clark Millikan, and others. He was enjoying that. Their company was bracing. But he often wondered if their intellects wouldn't be better directed toward something more constructive. We'd allowed aviation to become harnessed for destructive ends, he lamented, and we had to break out of that trend.

A month earlier I had heard Charles speak on that sub-

---

* Bud Gurney was a veteran airman who became a senior United Airlines captain. He was Lindbergh's barn-storming buddy in the Midwest in the 1920s.

ject to the Institute of the Aeronautical Sciences, when they awarded him the Guggenheim medal:

Many of us here might have watched the ideas and the dreams of a quarter-century back come true. Air routes over continents and oceans spiderweb the earth. In fact, aviation has been so successful that, together with other branches of modern science, it has revolutionized the environment of man. . . . As a lawyer, my father harnessed a horse to carry on his business. As a young pilot, I unlashed my wings from fence posts, and pulled through my own propeller. But my father and I knew the feel of rain and the smell of ground, and there was time for our thoughts to wander. When night came, our muscles put our brains to sleep.

Now, modern standards require an efficiency that immobilizes the muscles and the senses while it overactivates the brain. We insulate man more and more from his old environment of earthy weather.

In aviation, our old, carefree fascination with the art of flight has metamorphosed into a responsibility for the welfare of mankind and the security of our American people. On the one hand, it has become our mission to maintain rapid intercourse between all nations. On the other, it is our duty to construct the world's greatest military force. To our skill is entrusted the terrifying power of the atom bomb.

Here, we meet the basic question of how deeply and how long man can consecrate himself to his machines without losing the human qualities essential even to effective consecration. . . .

In emphasizing force, efficiency, and speed, are we losing a humility, simplicity, and tranquility without which we cannot indefinitely hold our own, even in worldly competition?

303

These are the problems of human power, of long-term survival upon earth. We have shown what man can make of science. Now it is a question of what our scientific environment will make of man. We have measured success by our products rather than by ourselves. A materialism that overemphasizes short-term survival detracts from the humanism essential to long-term survival. We must remember that it was not the outer grandeur of the Roman, but the inner simplicity of the Christian that lived on through the ages."

Charles told me that when he had delivered that talk to the IAS, he had already been convinced that aviation, despite its hold on him, was no longer his prime concern. He saw a greater call on his thoughts and time.

Not many years ago, when he flew across the country at night, there were great stretches of velvet black between the towns and cities. So many of those spaces now were bright with dots of electric light, he said, and the cities themselves were reaching out, spinning luminous spiderwebs into the countryside. Some, like Los Angeles, had been jewels, set among mountains and orchards, sparkling in the blue air. Now they were often covered with smoke and haze, blotting out the scenery. We were all aware of the tragedy of the Midwest Dust Bowl. People had forgotten how the trees were hacked down in upper Michigan. Now the same thing was happening in the Northwest. He wondered how long those magnificent forests would last. And the worst of it was that what was happening in America was taking place on every continent.

I asked him if damage to our environment wasn't the price we had to pay for the population growth and the development of technology.

"The solution has to go deeper than questions of population control and technology. We have to reconsider the values of our Western civilization, and we have to study nature more carefully." According to him, there were basic lessons to be learned from the wilderness—the unspoiled areas of the Earth, and the creatures who had developed in them over the millennia. There was an urgency in him to do something about that. We were invading that wilderness and destroying it so quickly.

It was not long before Lindbergh finished his work with the Air Force and began devoting more of his time to conservation and wildlife preservation, pursuits that were to become his greatest concern for the rest of his life.

Chapter

TWELVE

T HE FOLLOWING YEAR, 1955, my father, who had earlier
resigned his medical practice, died. He and Mother had
been running a small winter hotel in Fort Myers Beach, which
Charles and Anne had enjoyed visiting. They were very fond
of my dad, and both wrote letters when they heard of his
death:

On a plane to San Diego
April 7th, 1955

Dear Jim,

When I came back from Englewood last night Charles told
me that your father had died. I have been thinking so much
about you. No matter how much one is prepared for death
of one's parents by age or illness, it does not lighten the flow
of tangible separation. As Ansy said to me falteringly after
Mother's death, "But where is she *now*?" It is a great wrench
and a great testing of all our powers of strength and faith.

You have much of both. You know what is in the prayer of St. Augustine—"I behold how some things pass away that others may replace them, but Thou, Oh Lord, doest never depart, Beauty of all things." Beauty follows death and there is so seldom time to let the awareness of death and its mystery and its spirit and its sense of being bathed in love fully illuminate one.

I have had to be busy, too, but I think the experience is all there inside you to learn and understand when you get time. *Do* give yourself time. One needs to mourn, in some way. Someone wrote me a new interpretation of the Beatitude: "Blessed are they who *love enough* to mourn, for they shall be comforted."

I think of your mother, too (*that* is hard—so hard) and your sister. You and Ellie will help them. You have always been such a good son to your parents.

St. Augustine's prayer continues: "To Thee will I entrust whatsoever I have received from Thee—so shall I lose nothing . . ." and "For he only loses none dear to him to whom all are dear, who cannot be lost. . . ."

But it is so hard—and everyone will lean on you and you will carry them on as you always do. But one does feel so strange, pushed up into that older generation.

Death in one sense is such a miraculous happening and so truly great and one feels so close to reality near it. (At least that is true of natural death in old age, as it was with my mother and I assume your father.) But one is so quickly pushed into the terrible urgency of busyness, that, Jim, at a moment like this it helps. You have given them such joy and pride—and Ellie has, too.

Sometime I want to show you something my old friend Professor Hocking wrote me about the "friendliness of death." The inevitable unfinishedness of life being countered by the sense of love conquering death.

Now, I can only send you this scratch note to carry my

love and thoughts to all of you—what a wonderful mother you have had. My love to Ellie.

"And life is eternal, and love is immortal, and death is only a horizon, and a horizon is nothing save the limit of our sight. . . ."

Love,
Anne

Scott's Cove
Darien, Conn.
April 19, 1955

Dear Jim,

We know what you have been going through, and Anne and I have been with you often in our thoughts these past two weeks. The loss of our own mothers, during a single winter, brings us even closer to you at this time.

It must give you great satisfaction, though, to realize that you did everything within your power to add to your father's happiness in the last decade of his life. The hotel at Ft. Myers Beach, with its diversified interests and Florida weather, did more for your family, I think, than it is possible for even you to fully appreciate.

When I was at the Beach last fall, and in your family's home, I felt that I had never been with happier or more contented people. It was really wonderful to watch your father; he seemed beyond the cares and problems of this life, enjoying his part in it at the present, yet well prepared for whatever lay beyond.

Jim, we hope to see you soon. Remember that this house is always one of your homes.

Best to you,
Charles

309

The talk that Charles and Ellie had had about the airline reconciliations continued in a lively exchange over the years, ascending at times into the heights of theology. Ellie's is essentially a simple faith, and her standards are absolute. She has no place for ifs, ands, or buts in her own life, although she has always been compassionate about others. Charles weighed one value against another; his judgments were always relative. He had a scientist's skepticism and a pragmatist's approach, at least during most of his life, so they had plenty of room for debate, which they both relished.

When Charles came down to visit his uncle during the 1950s, he and Ellie would enjoy their skirmishes:

"I don't see how you can call a standard a standard, Charles, unless it's absolute. You wouldn't settle for a relative inch in your airplane engine or your perfusion pump. Why be any less scientific when you're dealing with the standards you set for your own conduct?" (Ellie was always very direct!)

"Because, Ellie, however carefully we try to measure human behavior, we are dealing with subjective standards. What I think is absolutely honest may seem to you to be something less, and vice versa."

"That's why we need to turn to God and ask him to show us. He *does* see each one of us clearly, and if we're willing, he can cut through our excuses and let us see ourselves objectively."

Charles objected that history was full of earnest religious people who thought they were making objective, absolute judgments according to God's will—and committed the most terribly inhumane acts—the Inquisition, the Crusades, the pious slaveowners.

Ellie replied that they were probably people who applied absolute standards to others, but left themselves out. If they'd allowed God to give them an honest look at their own lives, history might have been very different. Remember, she said, what Jesus said to the mob who were about to stone the woman caught in adultery? "Let him who is without sin cast the first stone." The crowd melted away!

"Ellie, do you believe in the devil?"

"Well, there's plenty of evil in the world, and it doesn't come from God."

"So God must let the devil have his way with men. Is that being absolutely loving? Maybe God feels the need for some relative judgments in dealing with us, and in the way men deal with each other."

"Charles, I know you're trying to confuse me. There's evil in the world because God gave man a free will, and man often chooses the bad instead of the good."

"And the good comes from God and the bad from the devil? When you have two opposites like that, there must be relative ground between them. You can't expect men to be all good."

The exchange came to an end when we all realized we were hungry for dinner.

Ellie wrote to Charles one time, apologizing for being too forthright with him in their arguments. He wrote back:

This is a very long overdue letter to thank you for your most generous and nice note of March 10th, which arrived when I was in Europe and became submerged in the piles of mail and obligations that accumulated while I was away— you recall that I promised to answer it sometime, when we talked over the phone two or three weeks ago.

Ellie, you have no reason to ask forgiveness of me; it should really be the other way around, for while I thoroughly enjoyed the discussion we had at your home, a year or so ago, I would not for the world have left you worrying about anything that was said there. We just disagreed in viewpoints related to God and the Devil, and things like that; and I must say that you carried on your arguments with an ability that was hardly exceeded by its ardor. I'm sorry if I was too much on the Devil's side, but I suspect that God smiles on him, at times, at least, with more benevolence than you do.

Personally, I don't think God wants me to lose all contact with the Devil, and what bothers me is that I'm afraid that you do. If I didn't think there was a touch of sin and humor in heaven, I'd much prefer to live in hell—I feel sure I'd find plenty of old friends there. I never have quite been able to make up my mind about this. I suppose I'll have to do so suddenly, if I ever have the choice. You'll wave to me anyway, won't you?

I do respect your viewpoint, though, much as I disagree with a lot of it, and I'm afraid that in countering your well-directed thrusts, I often made statements with rather tactless bluntness. Here, I would appreciate a (relative) forgiveness.

Ellie, I've tried to keep the Devil out of this letter, but I'm afraid he's crept in anyway. Maybe you'll have to airmail him back up to Scott's Cove. But I warn you I'll be off in a week, on another trip outside the country.

The children still talk about their days in Florida, about you and Jim, and the Hotel and the beach. They surely had a wonderful time there—I only hope it didn't involve too much effort for you and Jim; I hadn't intended that, and according to their stories you did a tremendous amount for them.

This letter is long enough, and supper is almost ready. It's much too long since we've seen you and Jim up here.

Best wishes to you always,
Charles

I had some longer times with Charles during the summer of 1961. The Lindberghs rented a cottage in the mountains above Vevey, in Switzerland, for a good many summers and close by, a little higher in the mountains, was Caux-sur-Montreux, the international conference center of Moral Re-Armament. That summer Charles visited me at Caux and attended some of the meetings and plays. It was a summer I remember well. During the conference Frank Buchman, the initiator of Moral Re-Armament, died at the age of 83. Among the tributes to him that poured in from around the world was one that I felt best summarized his contribution to our age. Dr. Karl Wick, editor of the Swiss daily *Vaterland,* wrote that Buchman had "brought silence out of the monastery into the home, the marketplace and the boardroom."

Charles wrote me two letters in April and July 1961, which I received with mixed emotions and which I include here with some reluctance for two reasons. The first is that Charles expressed his disagreement with me about MRA. I was not greatly disturbed by his criticisms. I had long ago realized that the adjective "lone," which the press often used to describe him—"Lone Eagle," "Lone Hero"—was justified. He was no joiner. I'd tried to make clear to him that no one "joined" MRA—you worked together with others, of whatever faith or philosophy, who had committed their lives to their Creator's direction. But Charles was too independent to want such an association. He shied away from any association except on his own terms.

More fundamentally, insofar as I was aware, he had not up to this point put his life totally into God's hands, except perhaps on those rare occasions, such as his pioneer flight, when he had gone to the limits of his human capabilities. Despite his genuine humility, he was not one readily to relinquish the reins of his life to God or man. So he naturally resisted MRA's challenge to submit one's self to the Almighty.

Strangely enough, though, I often felt that Charles was being directed by a power greater than himself—his unconscious training for his Atlantic flight, his marriage to Anne,

313

his being led into work with Dr. Carrel, his going unscathed through combat. The only way I could express this feeling was that, like a San Francisco cable car, his life seemed to have been drawn by an unseen cable.

The second reason I present the letters with some discomfort is that in them Charles revealed his friendship toward me in very candid terms—an unusual gesture for one so restrained in expressing affection.

The first letter was written in reply to my invitation to him to visit Caux:

Anne and I received your March 27th letter, from Miami, on returning from a trip to Italy. It is grand news that you are feeling better, and that Dana Atchley's advice is bringing results. As you now know, Dana Atchley is both a wonderful person and a very outstanding diagnostician—among the top men in the world in this field. He combines understanding, sympathy, and technical ability to achieve results that border on the miraculous—and since I feel sure he would object strongly to my use of the word, I will not try to place them beyond the border though sometimes they seem to belong there.

Jim, about MRA, I think it is best to accept the fact that we do not see eye to eye. Your viewpoint and mine are vastly different both as to the ideology and as to the effectiveness of MRA. But there is no need for this to enter into our friendship. I thoroughly respect your viewpoint, much as I differ with it; and I hope that you can accept the sincerity of my difference. Friends often differ in fields of religion, as in fields of politics, and I believe that these differences can often make an even closer and more interesting relationship.

News from the children is good from all quarters of empire—from Jon and Land and families in California, from Anne and Reeve who have been with us in Italy and who

314

are now spending a week together in Paris, and from Scott who is returning to school today after driving through Austria, Hungary, Yugoslavia, Italy, France and Switzerland, in a Volkswagen. . . .

I was interested in his mention of differences "as to the ideology" of MRA, because I had always felt certain passages of his *Of Flight and Life* were some of the best expressions of MRA ideology I had seen. I could only conclude that once again he wanted to establish and preserve distance from any combined endeavor.

He wrote the second letter after he had visited Ellie and me at Caux and attended several meetings, meals, and plays:

This is going to be a difficult letter to write, because it relates to deep friendship on the one hand, and deep divergence on the other—both of long standing. Jim, I think it is essential for us to realize that your viewpoint and mine toward MRA differ both fundamentally and sincerely, and that neither the passage of time nor my visit to Caux have brought them closer together. It is because I value your friendship so highly that I write so frankly. I am most anxious that we be able to bridge, from the viewpoint of friendship, the depth of our divergence in theological and philosophical fields. . . .

I now want to tell you how much I appreciate the invitation you and Ellie gave me to visit Caux, and the extraordinary consideration and hospitality that was extended to me while I was there. The invitation means all the more to me because you knew of the divergence of our viewpoints. The visits to Caux were of great interest to me. I have never seen more dedicated people than I saw at Caux. I found myself lost in the first act of the "Hurricane"—excellent acting—a fascinating plot. I am tremendously grateful to you for giving me the opportunity of talking to the "lion hunter."

I would like to have spent hours talking to people I met and saw there.

I want to tell you too, Jim, that I think you are one of the most extraordinary people I have met in life. Wherever you go, you have the ability of adding to the quality of life, whether with a group or an individual. Everyone I know who has met you feels this. Anne and I love to be with you. The children are delighted when they hear you are coming. Uncle thinks you are wonderful, and that is a compliment few people have had from him. The evening you and Ellie came to our apartment was one of the highlights of our summer in Switzerland—even without the lion hunter. There is no one I enjoy more being with, whether it be for a swim, a meal, or a philosophical discussion. I feel that you have raised the quality of life for many people, and in most generous and fundamental ways. This is really an extra-ordinary gift, and I doubt you, yourself, can realize the extent of it.

Jim, my gratitude and best wishes go to you with this letter, which I sincerely hope will deepen our understanding and mutual respect, and thereby also deepen our friendship.

Clearly, Charles had strong views on MRA. I personally felt he was dead wrong in his evaluation, but not for a moment did our difference of opinion alter our friendship. Agreement had never been a condition of friendship for me; it had not been with Edison, Ford, Firestone, or Carrel, and it was not with Lindbergh.

*　　　*　　　*

This was a period in which Charles was reviewing his priorities and reaching out for new goals. His one continuing activity was his service to Pan American as a director and adviser. Juan Trippe, its president, and a longtime friend of Lindbergh, counted on Lindbergh's expertise in helping select their most suitable jet planes, air routes, and terminal facilities and develop cordial relations with foreign governments and competitors. This work took him to every continent except Antarctica and was enabling him to probe more deeply into his growing concern about the way civilization was affecting our planet.

What worried him most was the effect our way of life would have on the so-called "underdeveloped nations," especially those we label as primitive. He said that he'd known about "primitive man's" retreating into more and more remote areas since he was a boy in Minnesota and heard his father's tales of Indians pushed back by the rifles and axes of frontiersmen. But by World War II that retreat had become a stampede on every continent. He had grown up assuming that civilized man was superior to his primitive ancestors. Now he was not so sure. Was our intellect, which had produced our vaunted technology, really serving mankind's best interests?

Take one of the most basic of our products, our weapons, he told me. The chipped flint ax and arrowhead of our ancestors had served to provide the essentials of man's well-being—food, clothing, shelter. Today we had developed the flame-thrower, poison gas, and the atom bomb. Soon we would have the ultimate—the nuclear-tipped intercontinental ballistic missile. What progress! From man's ability to slay a tiger to his ability to make the planet uninhabitable!

Charles felt strongly that the only way to break out of the destructive cycle was to understand and accept the primitive qualities of man that we'd neglected and lost. Our intellect alone was not going to get us out by itself. We had to break away from the artificial customs and values our intellect had imposed on us in the name of civilization and find the freedoms we'd once had.

Unexpectedly, I was able to provide Charles with a means to pursue this conviction. Among the men and women from more than fifty countries who were taking part in the Caux conference was a striking figure from Kenya—the lion hunter mentioned in Charles's letter. He was a leader among the Masai people, tall, jet black, with a dignified bearing and an accent that sounded to me as if he hailed from Oxford. A warrior, he had had a British education, had hunted lions and lived a seminomadic life among his people.

I introduced him to Charles, and we had a meal together during which he invited both of us to visit his tribe who roamed the Kenya–Tanzania borderlands. I had engagements that I felt I must keep—a decision I have always regretted. Charles accepted.

When Charles and Anne came to see us in our Fort Myers Beach home, many months later, he described his stay among the Masai. He had gone in alone to the tribe and insisted that he live exactly as they did. He was given a small thatched hut, where he found a gray-haired woman awaiting him. He had been a little concerned about that—unsure of what her responsibilities included! But, she was elderly, and gentle. He won her heart by stringing together some paper clips to make her earrings. She was delighted and those earrings became the talk of the tribe.

The old woman cooked for Charles—and the meals were unusual. Milk was the main food, as the Masai were cattle herders. They would tap a vein of the animal and mix its blood and milk in a gourd, which they'd rinsed with its urine. That helped coagulate the milk and produced a kind of yogurt, which they would place near the wood fire to give it a smoky taste.

Anne made a face as Charles described the concoction. "You know Charles. He can enjoy anything, or at least appear to. He's the perfect guest."

"I *did* enjoy it," insisted Charles. "I went in there determined to savor the life of the Masai to the full. When you do that, you enjoy everything."

318

The Masai are a great people, Charles said. They were very strong and brave and full of physical presence. Although the British had tried to stop them, they still had their lion hunts in which the young men established their manhood by killing a lion with a short spear. The man I had introduced him to in Switzerland had told Charles of his own lion hunt. He had had to work his way up to the test until the elders felt he was ready. The men of the tribe went out, circled the lions, and drove them toward the eligible man. Another was selected to slow the beasts down as they charged the man with the spear. Charles had hoped to join them in one of their lion hunts, but it hadn't worked out.

"Too bad, Charles," said Anne, trying to look disappointed.

Charles went back to the Masai twice more, taking Anne with him on the third visit, in the winter of 1964–1965. They described their trip when Ellie and I visited them in Connecticut later in the year.

The two had set out in a Land Rover southward from Nairobi, and they pitched their tent on the edge of a game trail near a water hole. That evening they were witness to a procession of elephants, giraffes, and zebra. Next morning, the animals were gone, but the Masai had arrived at the water hole with their cattle.

They looked him and Anne over quietly, Charles said, just as the animals had. Then they greeted them, but as none of them spoke English and the Lindberghs were ignorant of their language, they went about their business. As Charles watched them, he envied their simple, uncluttered lives—they required none of the goods and services that complicate our city life. They had hours free to watch the beauty around them, to contemplate, to converse, to experience the sights and sounds, the feel and taste of nature.

One of the Masai elders had said to Charles earlier, "You

319

white men talk about freedom. But, don't you see, we are the ones who are much more free. We are free of all your machines and the things which shut you off from nature."

"Of course," said Anne, "they have a price to pay for that freedom." They had flies, for one thing. Flies on one's face, all the time, though one got used to them after a while. They had disease—a degree of sickness we would not tolerate. And they had frequent tribal feuds, which sometimes broke out into raids on one another. They could be very cruel.

That was true, Charles agreed. "Like us, they have their serious defects." But you didn't need to be among them long to realize the enormous vitality of the people. We needed to learn that—in our civilized world from which vitality had slipped away.

We went on to talk about the collapse of past civilizations and the threat to our own. Charles made the point that science breeds technology and technology encourages greater and greater complication. As a result, politics, big business, diplomacy, every field of human activity, become more and more difficult to control. By contrast, in primitive nature there lay basic wisdom in which complexity could flourish— be it in the development of plants or animals or of human intellect.

I protested that it had taken the advance of science to enable man to study and apply the laws of nature for the improvement of man's condition. Charles agreed that the development of man's intellect was an astonishing feature of life on our planet.

"But our sense of superiority over other creatures," he added, "and our pride in our mastery of the Earth need the humbling perspective that the wildness of nature brings to us. We now see ourselves as Earth's most destructive and wasteful creature. Wildness warns us that our survival is in danger as an overspecialized species. Our future depends

320

on our ability to combine the knowledge of science with the wisdom of wildness."

On another trip among the Masai with Ian Grimwood, Kenya's chief game warden, Charles awoke at dawn, lying beneath an acacia tree, watching birds soar above him. "As I admired their graceful flight patterns, I realized how infinitely more complex and intricate they were, compared to those of our most technically advanced airplanes. And then came the thought that where skies were most traveled, birds were less frequent. If I had to choose between the bird and the plane, I decided I would choose the bird."

What came out of his observations was a commitment to do whatever he could to help protect the wilderness left in the world and its creatures, especially those that were endangered.

He began by getting in touch with our friend DeWitt Wallace and offering an article about wildlife for *Reader's Digest*. That article was one of the first in a popular magazine to get millions of people thinking about conservation.

Each time I saw Charles after that—and it was infrequently during the late 1960s and early 1970s—he was championing a new endangered species, after studying them in their natural habitats: the blue whale after spending time in Peru's coastal waters in 1966; then the one-horned Javan rhinoceros in Indonesia, while a distinguished audience celebrated the fortieth anniversary of his transatlantic flight on Long Island, at the site of his takeoff. In his letter declining the invitation to the event, he wrote: "I devoted time to that in 1927 and 1928; I've written two books about it; it's not that era anymore and I am not that boy." Anne told me Charles remarked to her on a similar occasion, "They all want to fly me to Paris!"

In 1968, he was in the Philippines to rescue the last remaining tamarau (a water buffalo) and the monkey-eating eagle. In 1969, he was off among the equatorial coral for mations of the Pacific, which were being plundered and destroyed.

In order to make his efforts more effective, he became a member of the half-dozen leading conservation associations. He also began giving press interviews about his concerns, and in 1968 even addressed the Alaskan legislature—his first public speech since the America First days.

I asked him later what had made him change his mind about public speaking after nearly thirty years of silence. He said he had been on Maui, visiting his friend Sam Pryor, when Sam's son-in-law, Lowell Thomas, Jr., had phoned Sam from Alaska to ask if he could persuade Lindbergh to address the state legislature on the protection of wildlife. Sam said, "No, he never does anything like that."

When he hung up, Charles asked, "What was all that about?" When Sam told him, he said, "Let's go tomorrow." Sam's daughter Tay said later that Charles's appeal had saved the Alaskan wolf from extinction, through legislation passed after his visit. More than that, he had inspired Alaska to set an example in the stewardship of its magnificent wilderness.

These activities inevitably sharpened press interest in Lindbergh, and he seemed ready to use the help of newspapers and magazines to advance his causes. I wrote to him, kidding him about joining organizations and seeking publicity, and asked him if he was satisfied with the efforts of the press, especially a long article that had just appeared in the *New York Times* Sunday Magazine.

He wrote back:

I think the article was constructive, and it was written by a good friend on *The Times* (Alden Whitman). But somehow extraordinary inaccuracies creep into these press articles even when accurate information is easily available. A good example, among others, is this particular article.

While it was being written, the author asked me to let him

interview me on a television program. I declined, saying that
I had never spoken on a television program, that the publicity involved would be much too great, with resulting on-
the-street recognition, and that I already had enough
personal publicity to last me for a lifetime and several reincarnations.

He asked me if he might quote me on the latter statement, and I said he could. As you may recall, this authori-
zation resulted in a sub-headline which informed the reader
that I said I had gone through several reincarnations! Jim,
you can imagine the inquiries that arose thereafter.

Lindbergh's lifelong attitude toward the press is perhaps
best expressed in an anecdote I heard years later. His in-
spection of Strategic Air Command bases during the late
1940s took him to the Aleutian island of Adak. The commander of the base there was Colonel Robert L. Snider, a
friend of mine. Snider was out on the tarmac to greet his
arriving VIP. As they walked back toward the headquarters
hut, Charles asked, "Are there any reporters here?"

"Colonel, there aren't any reporters within a thousand
miles."

"Great!" said Lindbergh. "This is the place I've been looking for all my life!"

To the end of his days Charles avoided formal social occasions as much as he did the press. Three years after his
death, at the inaugural dinner of the Lindbergh Fund, held
at the Waldorf Hotel in New York, in May 1977, to celebrate the fiftieth anniversary of Lindbergh's flight, Anne read
part of a letter Charles had written to his close friend General Jimmy Doolittle:

Much as I appreciate your letter and the reasons for writing
it, I'm afraid that I am a pretty poor person to consult about
anniversaries in general, and dinners and ceremonies in

particular. I don't like any of them, and the longer I live, the less reason I see for them to exist. Life just seems to me to be too full of things worthwhile to spend a lot of time celebrating the past or sitting in black suits at hotel tables, eating that dreadful food and listening to speeches that are usually still worse.

I *would* like to see you, however, for I have the greatest admiration for you, and it's too long since we have been together. There are lots of things I would like to talk to you about, and I always enjoy seeing old friends (under a not-too-civilized environment). How about breaking away from those dreadful formal dinners long enough to eat a meal at my favorite Chinese restaurant in New York? There are other things there besides food. . . .

Meanwhile, my best wishes go to you, and to all my friends who like big dinners and celebrations—God bless them.

Anne had read the letter with some trepidation, since the audience was dressed in tuxedoes and dinner dresses and had just finished a "deadly formal dinner," but Charles's characteristic remarks were greeted with great applause and laughter.

*   *   *

We met at the Engineers Club during the autumn of 1969, when I had to come up to New York on business and Charles was back from a trip to Manila. I had now returned to Fort Myers Beach as a permanent business base and in 1967 had started a new real estate firm. It was a turbulent time in the country and the world: the exhausting war in Vietnam was dragging on, with ever-larger demonstrations around the country; American Indians had just occupied Alcatraz; there had been bloody riots in Northern Ireland. On the brighter side, the United States and the Soviet Union were making progress on limiting strategic arms, and some forty nations had met in Rome to try to come to grips with the dangers of ocean pollution.

Our talk got around to the remarkable successes of the American space program. Charles said he had witnessed the launching of Apollo 11, which had placed the first man, Neil Armstrong, on the moon. He watched from three miles away, down on Cape Canaveral, as the flames exploded on the launch pad and the long, thin rocket gradually lifted off, then accelerated skyward.

"Vivid scenes came back to me—Robert Goddard, with his frail little rocket wobbling upward, then toppling back into the New Mexico desert; the grim tunnels in the Hertz Mountains, filled with the ghostly shapes of the V-2s. What giant steps we had taken in those few years!"

Then, pictured on his TV screen from a quarter of a million miles away, he watched the robotlike shapes of the two astronauts actually striding on the surface of the moon. His thoughts turned to Michael Collins, the third astronaut, left alone in his space capsule orbiting the moon, awaiting the return of his friends. Charles had thought of his own isolation in the cabin of *The Spirit of St. Louis,* caught in the clouds, skimming the surface of the ocean.

"For me, the reality of the elements around me had faded for a short while. I just felt totally isolated and yet part of the universe. Out of my body, intensely aware—of what? God? My spirit? My oneness with creation?"

Charles came back from the silence into which we both had fallen. "Words can't describe these things, Jim, but remembering it later, two endeavors came together in my mind—space flight and our work at the Naval Medical Research Institute."

There at the center in Bethesda, Maryland, after World War II, Dr. Theodore Malinin and Lieutenant Commander Vernon Perry asked him to design for them an improved model of the perfusion pump he had developed for Alexis Carrel. Their objective was to freeze and then later to restore to functioning condition, not merely tissue cells, but whole organs. He wrote about this later in his book, *Autobiography of Values,* speculating on the importance of this research.

"Do you see the significance, Jim, of Goddard's and Carrel's dreams merging?"

Charles said space exploration was up against vast distances and the relatively slow speed of the fastest rockets. Even at the speed of light, journeys beyond our small solar system to our neighbors in space would far exceed the span of human life. But suppose we could preserve space voyagers alive, and wait to thaw them out in some far destination of the universe!

The science fiction of one decade was becoming the science fact of the next. Goddard and Carrel had been regarded by many of their colleagues as improbable dreamers. "Jim, when you think of how fast dreams are becoming reality, it does no harm to dream further still."

With a faraway look in his eyes, Charles was thinking aloud: the more knowledge reveals to us, the more important the mystical appears. Matter is resolved into energy, the essence of man is reduced to awareness—that alone seems to distinguish his being from the rest of the universe. And yet, are the two really separate? Are there realms of awareness waiting to be explored? There are moments when my awareness of myself merges into a greater awareness, just as the atoms of which I am composed are parts of the universe's stream of energy. As we explore these fields, who can say that man's journeying into space must be limited by concepts such as the speed of light?

Charles leaned forward and looked at me very seriously.

"These are more than idle speculations, Jim. Before too

long our exploration of these realms may have become essential to the survival of mankind, marooned on this planet. Will we discover we can reach distant galaxies, not with spaceships, but through our evolving understanding of man's qualities that make him at one with the universe? That is why I have moved from a concern with technological progress to the study of life, especially the qualities of primitive man and nature."

I felt I was back as a young man with Alexis Carrel in his flights of mysticism, or an even younger man in the electric atmosphere of a discussion between Edison, Ford, and Firestone, when they really let their imaginations fly. It would have been easy at the time to dismiss their far-out ideas as fanciful. But my life with these men had taught me better than to do that.

*   *   *

After many months during which our paths did not cross with the Lindberghs', Ellie and I received a letter from Anne, mailed from their Darien home:

I must explain that we left these parts before Christmas and headed West for Land's Ranch, where we had a marvelous week in snow and children and Christmas trees. And then flew on to Jon's family in Seattle for New Year's, and from there to Maui, where I spent the heart of the winter in our barely finished cottage on the edge of a cliff. Very wild, very beautiful and somewhat remote—twelve miles over a *very* bad road by Jeep to the nearest General Store—almost like the West Coast of Florida fifty years ago. We had an adventurous time with flood, leaks, mud (the rainy season) as well as a company of ants, cockroaches, lizards, spiders, rats, mice, and possibly mongeese, who found shelter from the storms under our roof. I don't mind sharing my roof and my crumbs with spiders and lizards—but ants, rats and cockroaches I made war on for two months—unsuccess-fully.

This is all a long drawn out explanation of why I never got to your beautiful Christmas present until a few weeks ago, when I returned to a pile of mail. Christmas cards and books accumulated here during our travels.

I always dread snow-shoeing through the mail, but there are sometimes happy surprises, and your card and those two exquisite wood-cuts of a heron (snowy egret?) and an early morning spider were—were a happy moment and broke my mood of frustrated efficiency. For a few moments I could stop and be still—wait with the listening heron and the mo-tionless web—and feel part of another and more eternal rhythm.

I do thank you, and so does Charles, who has been away so much and was not with me when I opened the mail, but saw the pictures later, for thinking of us and the heron and the spider's web in the same breath.

Charles wanted me to tell you he did not send out any books (The War Journals) this time. He felt the book was too controversial (and also too expensive!) to send around. I am happy, however, that by chance Truman [Smith] saw it and read it and was pleased by it, before he died (We were away in France.) . . .

I hope all goes well with you both. Ansy is having her second baby, the end of May. Reeve and Richard are mov-ing North—near St. Johnsbury in Vermont this summer. Jon and Barbara and their brood have just come back from Easter vacation in our cottage on Maui. Charles has just made an ecological trip over the U.S. which will be written up in the N.Y. Times Magazine soon. Scott is still studying his monkeys in the south of France. I hope to see him this sum-mer when I go abroad.

All of us would love to see you if you are near Darien,

Missoula, Seattle, Maui, Lausanne, Paris or the Dordogne!
Much love and many thoughts and thanks to you both.

The children had grown, life had moved on, and, though
the letters continued, our opportunities to see one another
naturally became less.

Life nearly came to an end for me in the autumn of 1971,
when my auto was broadsided by another at a highway in-
tersection south of Fort Myers. Before long, two letters arrived from Charles and Anne:

> Switzerland
> October 24, 1971

Dear Jim,

I have received word from Anne of Ellie's phone call saying that you were in a bad accident and are in the hospital.
This note is just to let you know that we are thinking of you
and of the wonderful times we have had together, and hoping very much that your recovery is fast and complete.

> With best wishes always
> Charles

> October 24, 1971

Dear Jim,

It was good of Ellie to call us—though of course we were
shocked to hear of that fearful accident. I am grateful you
are better. I am thinking and praying for you each day—
that your strength returns soon.

You are very dear to all our family—though we don't meet
often enough. I have seen Ansy and Scott this summer (Ansy
has a second baby—girl ("Constance"). Scott has only mon-

keys! Reeve now lives in Peacham, Vermont and is expecting her first baby in a month. I will go up to be with her 1st
November.

Much love and many thoughts
Anne

Shortly afterward, Jon Lindbergh and his family were seriously injured in a similar accident. Charles wrote me:

I received your February 13th letter when I returned to
Connecticut from Hawaii on March 3rd. I was on the East
Coast for only four days, which had to cover meetings in
New Haven and New York as well as the essential obliga-
tions that always accumulate at home when one is away—
therefore the lateness of this reply to your letter. . . .

Jim, it is grand to hear from you again and to find you
are feeling so well—at least that's the impression I get from
your letter. It makes me think of the wonderful times we
spent together in Florida, at Fort Myers Beach and to the
southward.

Jon is recovering rapidly from the car accident. He will
have no permanent effects from the brain injury. . . . Barbara, Krissy and Wendy (Jon's wife and daughters) are all
in fine shape, with no further indication of further complications or permanently noticeable scars. . . . All but Krissy
were unconscious or stunned temporarily—Jon for over half
an hour. Krissy helped to get her mother and sister out of
the wreck . . . Jon was pinned in between the seat and the
wheel . . . the local fire department arrived and cut through
the structure. . . .

The other driver was not badly injured. I am told that
the police found him, still drunk, hiding in nearby bushes.
. . . It is a miracle that Jon lived through the accident. I do
not understand why his skull was not split open and his chest
crushed. . . .

I hope you have a grand time in the South Pacific, and that you have a chance to get out and under some of the reefs. For reefs, I suggest Fiji or New Caledonia. . . .

Best to you and Ellie, always.
Charles

P.S. Thanks too for sending the page you wrote last August before the car accident. Certainly our living world, as a whole, has never been in greater danger or greater flux—if as great. Life, after developing with relative slowness through the epochs, is suddenly confronted with the full impact of the human mind through science and technology interlaced with divergent ideologies. The human population rise, the breakdown in the surface-of-the-earth environment, the advent of nuclear explosives and spatial delivery speeds all point toward still more catastrophic times ahead. Can we avoid them, or at least shape them? I do not know how there can be a greater challenge to the human intellect than what brought them on.

In response to that challenge, after his death, some of his friends created the Charles A. Lindbergh Fund, the purpose of which is to maintain a balance between technological progress and preservation of the environment.

Chapter

THIRTEEN

A year went by since Charles and I had been together at the Carrel centenary. In July 1974, Ellie and I were visiting Ellie's sister in her Middlebury, Connecticut home. After a Sunday dinner with the family, I went to our bedroom to take a nap. I stood looking out of the window at the peaceful scene—cows browsing in the sunshine in a meadow, sloping down to a lake where white sails were stirring in a boat race. Suddenly a compelling thought broke into my reverie, almost as though a voice were saying the words: "Call Charles." I was startled, especially because, as I thought about it, I was sure that the Lindberghs would have left to spend the summer, as they always did, in their Swiss chalet. But I made the call to their Darien home anyway.

Anne's voice came on the other end. She told me that Charles had been in the Columbia Presbyterian Medical Center in New York and had returned home the previous evening. He was very tired, and resting.

I had had no idea he'd been in the hospital. "Don't disturb him," I told her. "Tell him I'll be back from Florida in a couple of weeks and hope to see him. Please give him my love."

She asked for the phone number from which I was calling. We talked for a few minutes, and I hung up. A few minutes later, the phone rang. Charles was on the line and said, "Jim, can you come to dinner?"

"Charles, I've already had dinner. Anne says you're just out of the hospital. I'll be back soon and we can get together."

"No. Can you come now?"

"Are you sure?"

"Come to dinner now."

When Charles spoke with that insistence there was no more to be said. I set out on the ninety-minute drive. I was shocked to see how thin and gaunt he had become. But his voice was vibrant as he greeted me. I learned a little later from Anne that after a routine checkup early in 1972, Charles had been told that he was suffering from a form of cancer called lymphoma. It could be treated and arrested, and the treatment seemed to be successful. However, in the late spring, the disease had reappeared in a more deadly form—lymphosarcoma. Characteristically, he had told me nothing.

As Anne prepared dinner at the stove, Charles and I sat at the table in the small kitchen, and the three of us talked. He quickly dismissed my concern about his health and went on to talk about his journeys around the world, from the rainforests of Brazil to the jungles of Mindanao.

"Dinner's ready," said Anne. "Put your plates on the trays and we'll eat in the living room." As we ate, we went on talking.

Our conversation ranged over old times in many places, and with many people—to Illiec and the Carrels, the Fords and River Rouge, the swims on Martha's Vineyard, the boat trips in the Everglades.

"Many of our old friends have gone," said Charles. He talked about one of his closest friends from youth, Phil Love, their adventures in the early airmail days, and their close brushes with death. Although his voice was strong, I was afraid he was getting tired, so I got up to leave. He stopped me.

"I want to give you this." He handed me a copy of a book not yet published, written by Wayne Cole, about Lindbergh's unsuccessful battle to keep America out of World War II. Charles had inscribed the copy "To my friend Jim, in memory of old times." He made me sit down again, and we were quiet for a little while. "That was one of the strangest times in my life," he said. "It was the only major objective I failed to achieve."

"It's one experience I would just as well not live through again," said Anne. "Charles was pulled apart too many ways. And so was I." They had had many good friends in Europe who couldn't understand why Charles was so adamant about not coming to their aid.

"Do you ever regret getting into that battle, Charles?" As soon as I'd said it, I knew it was a silly question. There was that familiar flash in his eye. He grinned.

"Certainly not, Jim. I may have made mistakes, but in the light of history I think events have borne me out. Look at the divided world today. I've told Anne and the children I don't want any of them trying to defend me, in print or anywhere. I did what I felt I had to do, and that's that."

I held up my hands. "Okay, Charles! You fought the good fight. You said what you felt must be said."

"You know what stands out most vividly in those years? Not the campaign speeches, not even the years in Willow Run on the bombers. It's the months of flying in the Pacific I remember best."

Those moments in the air, he said, brought back all the memories of stunt flying, with the heightened suspense of imminent death at the hands of your opponent. That, and seeing your close companions suddenly snatched away, made all the simple pleasures of life so poignant—sunsets over the ocean, the tang of spray from breaking waves, the jokes around the mess hall with your friends.

"That was a side of war denied to us wives and mothers at home," Anne said. "What I remember most is the waiting—for letters, for news, for being with Charles again. And the efforts to be a father as well as a mother to the children in his absence."

"You didn't do too badly," said Charles, smiling at her.

We talked on about the children and their families. Then I stood up again, saying it was time Charles went to bed. He just motioned me back to my chair. "Don't hurry away, Jim. I haven't had such a good talk in a long while."

We sat quietly again until Charles, leaning far back in his chair, his legs stretched out in front of the fireplace, said, "I just had a picture in my mind of Kilimanjaro, across the Serengeti plains. What a majestic mountain that is, brooding serenely, detached from the life swarming at its foot—the elephants, zebras, lions, giraffes, buffaloes, plodding through the jungle and streaming across the grass. Jim, I wish you'd been with us on those African trips."

"No one's sorrier than I am," I told him.

"One night, without a cloud in the sky, Anne and I were camped in the Kimana swamp, with wild creatures all around. Kilimanjaro's silhouette stood out in the moonlight. Suddenly we saw a satellite cross the sky, among the stars. Two parts of my life came together—technology and aviation, symbolized by that satellite, and concern for our planet, symbolized by that mountain and the plain.

"That night my mind sailed beyond the stars to the infinity of the universe. I was back into my childhood, with the awe and fear of God. Then I was swept forward with the revelations of science—the discoveries beyond the structure of matter to the elemental force of energy, man's growing knowledge of the physical, on to his intuition of the mystical as the ultimate reality. I felt myself at one with and part of the universe—past, present, and future—part of my ancestors and my descendants, part of dinosaurs and eagles, part of the cells of my body, part of sperm and ovum, sand and stars, the atoms of the cosmos."

Perhaps the important thing in all this, he went on, was that he'd found a new perspective on life and death. Instead of seeing himself just as a man with an age of a few years, beginning on a certain date and ending on another, he saw his life more as an unbroken continuity, reaching back and forward through eons of time and space. Death was no longer an ending, but an opening.

In the stillness of the room, I heard the ticking of the clock and saw it was almost midnight. But there was one more thing on my mind, and I felt it was important that I tell him.

"Charles, I don't think I ever told you of something that happened to me at the end of the war."

He nodded for me to go on.

"Just before I left the Philippines I was standing close to a big gun when it fired. It did something to my inner ear. Later, on the way to Okinawa, the pilot took the plane down in a long, steep dive and I started in with attacks of extreme dizziness. Back in the States, they put me in a hospital. I would lie in bed, clinging to the edges of the mattress, and feel myself spinning out of control. I began to think I'd lost my ability to do anything ever again—I never knew when one of these attacks of vertigo would come on. There was nothing I could do about it.

"Anne, you'd sent me a book on St. John of the Cross, remember? I was struck that John had told himself at one point when he had lost many of his faculties, that even if he'd lost everything, even his memory, he knew that Christ would still be there. That was the acid test, I decided. Even if you couldn't remember that Christ was there, somehow you would know it still.

"There was a nurse, Betty Lyman, looking after me. I had told her quite a bit about my life and my commitment to put myself in God's hands. One day, as I came out of a spinning episode and threw the covers off, Betty said, 'Just look at your pajamas. They're soaking wet, from your neck to your feet. The room is cool. Why do you think you're perspiring so much? What's happening to you?'

" 'I really don't know.'

" 'Do you think it's fear?'

" 'Of course. If you went into one of these spells and didn't know if you'd ever stop spinning, wouldn't you be afraid?'

" 'I thought you told me a few days ago that you'd put your life completely into the hands of God.'

" 'I did.'

" 'Are you sure you did—completely?' She said it and walked out.

"I thought that over and decided she was right. Quietly, I made a decision that no matter what happened, I put my life again completely in his hands. I would trust him—and that was all. I told the nurse about it later. The next time I went into one of those spins, I gripped the sides of the bed and eventually came out of it. Betty was standing there. 'Mind if I pull the covers back?' she said. 'Look at your pajamas.' They were bone dry."

Charles looked down, his hand on his chin. "Remarkable." I said good-bye and walked to the front door with both of them. Charles grasped my hand. "Thank you for coming, Jim. Even though you had to eat two dinners."

"We want to see you and Ellie very soon," said Anne. "And thanks Jim, for that last story."

*   *   *

A few days later, I phoned the Lindbergh home from Florida and talked to young Anne. She said her mother had been trying to reach me. Her father was back in the hospital. I called Anne at the hospital immediately and learned that Charles was seriously ill. I asked her if I might be able to see him if I came up to New York.

"If you come up, Jim, we'll get you in."

I traveled up to New York and checked myself into the Biltmore. After a couple of days, Anne said that it had been arranged for me to see Charles. I was met at his door by a private nurse, who told me fifteen minutes was the maximum I could visit; he was so weak. He was indeed weak and pushed his hand under his head to support it as I came in, but his mind was clear as ever. There was in his eyes the kind of luminous depth I had seen once in Henry Ford's.

"How is the tobacco man?" was the first thing he said. He was referring to Bill Moger, a friend of mine I'd introduced him to thirty years earlier. Bill lived with his wife on the outskirts of Fort Myers. He had started a business selling handmade cigars to celebrities like President Hoover and Augie Busch, of Anheuser fame. Each cigar wrapper had the client's name printed on it. I had told Charles years before about the time Bill had said to me, "Jim, the telephone company is going to run a wire out here, so we'll have a phone."

I said, "Great, Bill, that'll increase your business. Your customers will find your name in the phone book and they'll get the word around."

"You're serious? You think they will?"

"No doubt about it."

"Then I'll go down first thing tomorrow and cancel the phone order."

His wife almost killed me. It was three years before they put a phone in.

Another time, I went out to see Bill just before Christmas, after getting back from a trip. He was busy at his little machine making cigars, with his brother and a fisherman from Sanibel helping him.

"How about going hunting, Bill?" I asked him.

"Oh, Jim, look at all those orders on that table, and look at that pile of tobacco waiting to be rolled—okay. When do we go?"

Charles, of course, had loved Bill's approach to life.

Then we talked about Theodore Malinin, who was writing a book about Alexis Carrel (*Surgery and Life*). He had called Charles several weeks before to report on the progress of the book. Charles was happy something was finally written about Carrel's scientific accomplishments. Together Malinin and Lindbergh had worked on updating the perfusion pump, first at Bethesda and later at the University of Miami where Malinin was in charge of the Surgical Research Laboratories. They also wrote a paper together on organ perfusion for the Carrel Centennial. Charles said with a twinkle that he'd given Malinin a terrible time when they were working forty-eight hour stretches. Charles would buy a bucket of Kentucky Fried Chicken and this was the only food they would eat.

The nurse came in and said, "Fifteen minutes, Mr. Newton."

"I'll let you know when I'm tired," Charles said firmly.

We talked on about mutual friends, about Charles's reconciliation with his youngest son, Scott; they hadn't seen eye to eye about a number of things for years, and had made peace with each other only days before in the hospital.

As I left, Anne asked if I would visit our mutual friend Father Joseph Durkin of Georgetown University. Durkin had written a book about Alexis Carrel. She and Charles wanted me to thank him for his messages of support and affection. When I visited Durkin he said, "To have known Lindbergh was to have touched greatness." Shortly afterward Ellie and I had a letter from Anne:

Thank you, dear Ellie, for your letters and your thoughts. I could not read all of your letter to Charles out loud to him because it made me cry—*it was so beautiful*—but I told him about it and perhaps some time I may be able to read it to him. You expressed so much and so truly.

And dear Jim, I spoke to Charles yesterday and told him of your having seen Father Durkin and having told him of our joy at having a message from him and Charles's warm expression of friendship for him. Charles was much pleased and said, "Jim is wonderful at that kind of thing, making bridges and confirming bonds between people."

Day before yesterday he had a bad day—due to a new drug that they thought might be helpful. Yesterday he was back to his (hospital) normal and I went in to see him and he was peaceful and better. Today he feels again stronger and Scott has gone in to see him.

I wanted to send you the letter of Teilhard de Chardin that I spoke of, and want you both to read. It comes from *Letters to Two Friends*:

"I found your letter yesterday upon landing. How I wish I were more than a man so that I could reassure you and could heal the person that you love so much.

"As you know, I believe that the world is an immense plastic thing subject to the influence of Spirit. We shall band together our desires so that the principle, necessarily good, which animates all things, will restore your friend's strength. This desire, this hope, this supplication for immediate and tangible well-being is our first duty, as the Gospel itself teaches us.

"But in our present Universe, as is all too clear, nothing can absolutely resist, but everything must sooner or later yield to the forces of death. Your love of Life is a healthy and magnificent power and you must jealously guard this spirit of resistance to physical diminution which helps you to bear suffering. But there is still something missing in your attitude. . . . When, by virtue of a state of things (transitory, no doubt, but inevitably linked to the state of growth of the world) death takes us, we must experience that paroxysm of faith in life that causes us to abandon ourselves to death as to a falling into a greater life. To love Life so much, and to trust it so completely that we embrace it and throw ourselves into it, even in death—this is the only attitude that can calm and fortify you; to love extravagantly what is greater than oneself. Every union, especially with a greater power, involves a kind of death of the self. Death is acceptable only if it represents the physically necessary passage toward a union, the condition of a metamorphosis."

(This also reminds me of something Jim told Charles and me of his experience in the hospital with vertigo. It is the same basic abandonment to a greater power.)

It has done me good to write you. Much love and thanks to you both.

Looking back at that day at the hospital, I am sure Charles knew his days were numbered. So did Anne, although both had hopes that his life would be spared for a few weeks, perhaps months. I kept in close touch with Anne, and a few days after we had received her letter, she phoned late one night to say, "Charles wants to come home—but I find that 'home' means Maui!"

The Lindberghs had established their cottage on the eastern coast of Maui as their legal residence. I was amazed to hear that Charles would want to set off on such a long and tiring journey in his condition.

Sam Pryor, vice-president of Pan American and longtime friend, arranged for the Lindberghs to fly on one of United's direct flights to Honolulu. Sam had wanted to arrange a special Pan Am flight, but Charles wouldn't hear of it.

Dr. Milton Howell, who was a friend of the Lindberghs and ran the Hana medical center, made plans for Charles to stay at a neighbor's cottage four miles away. When Anne had phoned him to say Charles wanted to spend his last days on Maui, Howell had objected that the medical facilities were inadequate for such serious requirements. After Charles came on the phone, Howell had surrendered.

It was decided that Jon and Scott would travel with their parents. Land would meet them in Honolulu. A hospital plane would fly them on from there to Maui.

One night when I called, Anne said, "Charles has a phone in his room and wants to talk to you."

His voice was strong. "Jim, I finally made it out of that hospital. Those doctors tried to stop me, but I got around them."

"How?"

"They tried to pressure me—in the nicest way. Said I'd worked long enough with medicine to know I should use all their facilities—they were the best. There were six doctors, and finally they admitted their machines could only keep me going artificially a little longer. I said to them, well, you're telling me there's nothing more you can do for me. So it's no longer a medical problem—it's a philosophical problem. And I want to go to Maui. I'd rather live one day on Maui than thirty in the hospital.

"The youngest doctor said, 'We won't give you a permit to leave.' You know, Jim, what I have isn't contagious. I don't need a permit. Jon took the transportation problem off my shoulders. He phoned Sam, Sam talked to the president of United, and he said, 'Just tell him to show up!' So here I am. It's a great place. Some time you must get out here, Jim. Now it's time to say good-bye."

I could barely speak, but I managed to say, "Good-bye, Charles, and a lot of love from Ellie and me."

Three days later he died.

*   *   *

When Land came down to visit us in Fort Myers Beach some months later, he told me about the flight across the Pacific and his father's last week on Maui. As we sat in my study and looked out over the gulf, I began to take in the story.

He had been waiting for them to arrive in Honolulu—Charles, Anne, Jon, and Scott. The United people were determined to protect Charles from publicity, so Land actually had to be quite persistent in finding the woman who was in charge of receiving the flight. United had placed the stretcher high up on the backs of three window seats. The only complaint Charles apparently had was that they put him in first class instead of tourist.

Before they took off from New York a young United doctor came and made a quick check of Charles—perhaps it was out of concern for the airline's liability—in any case, he told Charles that everything was going to be all right, that he'd be back on his feet in no time. "Don't try to fool me," said Charles, "I know what I'm up against. I just want to get to Maui."

As they flew across the country Charles and Anne pointed out to the boys places they'd visited, barnstorming or mapping routes. The captain wanted to circle Maui as they approached Honolulu, to give Charles a view, but Charles said no. He wanted the plane to go straight to Honolulu—the passengers had schedules to meet. As they transferred him to the ambulance plane, three pilots stood a little way off, with their caps in their hands, saying nothing. Evidently they had just come to pay their respects.

"I was shocked to see how thin he was," said Land. "He'd lost a tremendous amount of weight, but his eyes were as

344

sharp and bright as ever, and his handshake—he took my hand and gripped it." Charles obviously had called on every bit of reserve strength to finish the journey. The doctors had warned him he could die on the way, and he was going to prove them wrong.

Dr. Howell met them on their arrival at Maui and asked to talk with Charles alone. He expressed concern about the minimal medical setup, but Charles assured him that whatever happened, he, Charles, was responsible.

He didn't expect Howell to go out of his way to do anything special. He only wanted his help to spend his last days as comfortably as possible—he had much to do. He had made a checklist, as he always did when he prepared to travel. There were people he wanted to talk to, people he wanted the family to contact, letters to get off, projects that had to be finished, people to be helped.

The cottage was small, one bedroom with two beds, a bathroom, living room, and kitchen. It had a beautiful view over the ocean and along the Hana coast, and the sound of the surf was constant.

The first morning he got right down to work. His top priority was to get every detail of his burial settled. He had no use for a mortuary or any of that business. He wanted to be buried in the little Hawaiian churchyard nearby, and he wanted everything done according to the local native customs. He settled down with Dr. Howell to cover the legal problems, deal with the coroner, and all that. He insisted that Howell fill out the death certificate, everything but the date, so there'd be no trouble with the coroner. Then his friend and the manager of the adjoining Hana Ranch, John Hanchett, came in to answer questions Charles had about the design of the grave and coffin. He had very specific ideas and wanted things done simply and quickly.

Charles was in his element. He was not the least bit morbid—rather matter-of-fact. He was glad to be rid of the hos-

345

pital atmosphere, the tubes, shots, and paraphernalia. He could relax and breathe the fresh air. The family cooked his meals, though he could eat very little. He would take long naps, and called them in to talk and share meals with him.

They talked of everyday things, told jokes. One morning as Scott cooked breakfast—something he didn't ordinarily do—Land kidded him about the bacon and eggs. Charles's voice piped up from the next room, "Bring me some of that, whatever it is. It smells great." He could hardly eat, but he complimented Scott's cuisine heartily.

In all of the preparations, everyone else had more to do than Anne did, and most of the time she just sat with him. Of course she was a tremendous strength to Charles, just by being there. If he did get upset about something, she was the one who listened. He was irritated because the men who were working on the intricately designed grave had taken part of Sunday off. Charles knew it was a race—maybe a matter of hours—to get the job done in time.

Two nurses assisted him: Elizabeth from the medical center, and Rosemary, Dr. Howell's daughter-in-law. Charles would argue with them sometimes, partly in fun. The nurse would say, "Time for your sponge bath."

"No. I think sweat is good for a man. God didn't mean us to be clean all the time."

"Well, you're going to start to smell, if you don't take a bath!" They'd kid each other back and forth, and pretty soon he'd take a bath.

Charles spent a good deal of time planning his grave. He wanted it built the way the Hawaiians in that area made them. He asked Tevy, his neighbor and friend, a full-blooded native Hawaiian, to take charge of digging the grave. They went over all the details—how deep, how the walls should be made, what kind of rock to be used, where the grave should be placed in the graveyard. Charles wanted it done

346

whatever way Tevy thought was right. There was a long discussion in the family about a tree next to the gravesite; Charles felt its roots would disturb the walls and wanted it cut down. Tevy and Anne argued that it was a beautiful tree and should stay. Charles said that if Tevy thought the tree should be there, it would be there. Tevy came out of those conferences in tears. "That man, he's too strong. He talked so hard, he shook my hand so hard."

Land, Jon, and Scott helped build the grave.

"I was so glad to be able to do something for Father," Land said. "All my life it seemed as if he had been the one doing everything for me."

Tevy had his sons and grandsons and sons-in-law all out working on the grave. They did it the Hawaiian way, collecting just the right rocks—smooth black stones—and placing them in exactly the right way. John Hanchett was amazed; to the Hawaiians it was a fearsome thing to dig a man's grave before he died. They felt it condemned the man to death. Or, if he should not die, a grave could not go to waste—the man who dug it would have to be put in there. An old Hawaiian priest came out and solved the problem for them by putting in a banana plant, so that the diggers would be absolved if no human body should be laid to rest there.

Tevy was most particular about the shape, color, and texture of each rock. He made his boys take down two feet of wall at one point because he didn't like the looks of one rock. The grave was a huge hole, thirteen feet deep and thirteen feet wide, and the walls were almost two feet thick.

Charles went over every detail of the coffin, which was made by the man at the Hana ranch out of planks of local eucalyptus in the old traditional style. If there had been time he would have wanted wooden pegs instead of nails.

He preferred that the local people not dress up for the funeral service; he wanted them to come in regular work clothes. But Dr. Howell was not happy about that and pro-

347

tested that they would not understand; they would want to come in their best clothes, to show their respect. Charles had to give way.

Charles even planned the service in detail. That particular project apparently had its humorous moments. Anne stayed up half the night picking out hymns and Bible readings she thought he would like. When they went over them together, Charles said he wasn't much for songs, but how did that one go?

Anne started to sing in a high wavery voice, and after the second line, Charles said, "Stop, stop! The words are bad enough." Everybody laughed. They finally hit on the idea of having the songs sung in Hawaiian.

He even talked about the clothes he wanted to be buried in—nothing fancy—khakis, working clothes. And he asked the family to get hold of one of the old Hudson Bay blankets that he had given his mother many years before, to wrap around him.

It was not a sad time. Land told me, "We didn't come out of there—I never did—with a feeling of oh, he's dying, it's terrible. I felt that way before I came to Hawaii, but all I could think of there was, we've got to get done so he can relax, we've got to get done in time, we've got to go out there and make sure that grave is dug, and we've got to get the coffin ready, got to get that blanket from home, get that Tapa cloth from the house, and all these things done. Somehow he planted that same feeling in all of us, and there wasn't this feeling of death threatening us all the time, it wasn't a threat at all—it was the threat of running out of time, but not of death itself."

Just before the grave was finished, Scott had to leave. He didn't want to, but Charles insisted. Scott had had to hurry over from France and leave his wife in charge of his primate preserve. He had been gone for nearly a month.

The day after the grave was finished, Jon left. He, too,

didn't want to go, but he was urgently needed at home. It was agreed that Land should be the one to stay. Jon felt that his father might live on for a week or even a month, because his spirit was so good. Jon thought he could get back. But Land was sure that as soon as the grave was complete and all the preparations done, his father would relax, and then it would all overwhelm him.

Dr. Howell had said it was unbelievable how Charles had held up. One lung was almost totally gone. Only his resolve was carrying him. The day he understood that all was going to be ready, in fact, he did begin to let go. Toward the end of that day he had breathing attacks, which continued during the night. The next morning he breathed easier, but for the last two days he drifted back and forth between life and death.

But he was conscious a good deal of the time. He talked about "going over the line and coming back." He was not afraid; he just seemed in awe of death. There was a struggle going on between his body and spirit. His spirit was at peace, but his body was still fighting, as it had all through his life, obeying his discipline, his control, for survival.

He talked about dying, obviously not a great deal, but Anne got him to talk about it a little. "Charles, I wish you could tell us about what you're going through," she said. "It would help us, because we all have to face it. I will be the first to face it."

He answered, "I don't think it's anything to face. It's not what you think. I know I've been near death at least three times this week. It's not terrible—it's very easy and natural. I don't think it's the end. I think I'll go on—in a more generalized way, perhaps. And I may not be so far away either."

Charles seemed lost in wonder at the simplicity of moving from life to death. He seemed amazed that there wasn't a big break, there wasn't a wall; it was right there. He did talk about how different it was from the times he had faced death barnstorming, or as a test pilot, or during the war in the Pacific. Then, he had done all he could to avoid death. There had been no time for fear, only time to react and survive. Now here he was with time to think about it, and it just wasn't that dramatic—it seemed part of a cycle, part of being.

Reeve later told me that Anne found a note on Charles's bedside table: "I know there is infinity beyond ourselves. I wonder if there is infinity within."

Charles was Charles up to the end. On the last day, his breathing had become labored, and Dr. Howell brought in a new apparatus, which he hoped would help Charles more than the oxygen facemask. Howell had to leave to see another patient, and when the nurse tried to start up the new breathing apparatus, she couldn't get it going. As she tried to repair it, Charles immediately began analyzing the problem; he thought he knew what was wrong. She responded by turning to him and saying, "Don't be afraid. Everything's going to be all right."

Charles reared up on the bed and his eyes flashed. "I'm not afraid. I want to get this thing straightened out, and this is the way we're going to do it." Between them, they got the oxygen set-up working just before Howell returned.

When he heard about that, Charles's friend, Sam Pryor, remarked, "Typical of Charles! You might say he died fixing something."

During that night, he slipped slowly into unconsciousness. The older nurse, Anne, and Land stayed with him all night. By morning he moved on to another stage. His face was very calm, but there was no communication—nothing. After breakfast, Anne and Land sat with him, Anne at the head of the bed, holding his hand, Land at the foot. Very slowly he drifted away.

That morning the Hudson Bay blanket arrived from Land's wife and along with it a small weaving from Land's daughter and a note to Charles from Land's young son. They lined

350

the coffin with the blanket and put the weaving and the note under Charles's pillow.

There were two services. Charles had insisted that he be buried within hours of his death—quietly, before the press or sightseers could pour in. So the first service was held that day in the small church near the cottage. The minister, Rev. John Tincher, conducted it, assisted by Henry Kahula, the senior deacon and owner of the gas station in Hana, a friend of Charles and Anne. A few neighbors and Hawaiian friends came from close by.

Dr. Howell and Land and four men bore the coffin out to the grave beside the church. They lowered it in and Anne handed Land a flower to place on it. In the Hawaiian tradition, flowers were cast into the grave, and then Mrs. Howell and four Hawaiian women sang. One of the women had a voice that just soared. The sun was shining; white clouds sailed in the blue sky; birds sang in the trees and the surf pounded at the foot of the cliff. It was, said Land, the only time he felt tears come to his eyes.

The second service was held on the next day. It was to include Jon, who got back in the morning, and Sam Pryor and a few more friends who could get there. As soon as he arrived, Jon went down to the family beach with a bucket and gathered small smooth rocks to put on the grave. Then he went out to run interference with the press, who were beginning to pour in.

There had been no press at the first service. Just one reporter from a local paper, a very understanding young man who sat quietly at the back and took no pictures. But at the second service there were more than a dozen pressmen. Anne went out to meet with them and invited·them to the service. She was very gracious. The more aggressive TV reporters didn't arrive until after the service. They were annoyed because they had gotten the time of the service wrong. They jumped on Howell, and the family slipped past unnoticed

351

and spent the rest of the day at the family home at Kipa-hulu.

"As I look back on it," says Land, "I think that Father really had a marvelous opportunity to give something to all of us by the way he handled his death, which very few of us would have a chance to do. He knew he was dying, he was very uncomfortable at times, but he wasn't in great pain. We were allowed to come that close to death, to participate in it, without fear. There wasn't any fear, or strangeness, nothing horrible about it. It was a very natural thing.

"I think he was intensely interested in trying to get back to the reality of life and the reality of death, and I think he was very disturbed by the complications which had been placed by human society on both aspects of being. He wanted, somehow, to illustrate that you didn't have to complicate death any more than you had to complicate life, that it was a natural thing, that you should somehow manage to pull out of life and death both, those really essential elements that give meaning to people."

Charles had discussed the inscription he wanted on his grave. He rejected anything elaborate, and they decided on a simple, flat, granite marker with a few words from the 139th Psalm, which I think expressed his questing spirit:

If I take the wings of the morning,
and dwell in the uttermost parts of the sea. . . .

As Land finished, my mind went back to a diary entry Charles had written in 1939 after a hospital visit to a friend dying of cancer. "He did not know the hopelessness of his case. Personally, I would prefer to know if I were going to die. I would not want to be misled. It is impossible to know with certainty how one would feel under the actual test of approaching death, but I do not believe I would fear it, and

I would want to know of the meeting in advance. It is the last, and possibly the greatest, adventure of life."

My own diary entry as he had boarded the plane for Maui to meet that adventure—a voyage many feared he would not survive—read:

He's going to make it—carried on wings beyond his own—to Maui. CAL—true to the very (ultimate) crossing. The same odds. The same guiding hand—East first—Now West.

Au Revoir—friend and brother. Go with God—on the wings of the morning.

AFTERWORD

As I think about each of those five men—Thomas Edison, Henry Ford, Harvey Firestone, Alexis Carrel, and Charles Lindbergh—a host of memories and emotions sweep over me. The friendship with each of the five was a gift—I never asked to meet any of them. One by one they appeared. Nor did I receive from them a cent of payment for any work with them, except for my service with the Firestone Company.

Knowing them did much to shape my life. Edison, who never gave up, but turned a thousand failures into a triumph; Ford, with his imagination constantly grappling with new ideas; Firestone, who maintained a rock-like integrity amidst the shifting sands of business expediency; Carrel, who could lift you in a single conversation from the street to the stars; and Lindbergh, never content to pursue one great purpose, but constantly reaching for ever more challenging goals.

It is significant that the first and last of the five men each bridged in their concern the transformation of man's atti-

355

tude during this century towards life on our planet. Edison, whose inventions powered America's industrial growth, pondered in his later years how to harness the sun, wind and tide to conserve earth's dwindling resources. Lindbergh, aviation's greatest pioneer, went on to devote his energies to saving endangered species and re-discovering the forgotten qualities of primitive man, which he believed were essential for mankind's survival.

They were all such distinct personalities, and yet had certain great qualities in common. They thought and acted as pioneers; they specialized in the impossible and created the breakthroughs. They were the leading edge in their generations. They were the questers, the seekers, the explorers, with an astonishing awareness of the needs of their age and beyond. They believed.

They not only challenged my life, but they changed the life of everyone living in this century. It has been said of Thomas Edison that he "invented the twentieth century"— imagine what the world would be like without electric light or recorded sound. In most countries Henry Ford's "automobile for the millions," with Firestone's tires, has set the pattern for our dwellings, our communities, and our jobs. Without Alexis Carrel, how many decades would it have taken to develop modern surgery? And how much slower, without Lindbergh, would have been the shrinking of time and distance between continents or the awareness of man's need to protect our planet?

These five men put into our hands dynamic tools with which to shape our civilization. What have we done with them? No one would dare to say they have been an unmixed blessing. Despite the comfort, security, and convenience, despite the richness, variety, and wide horizons their inventions and their achievements have brought us, mankind today is in disarray. The earth is in danger as never before.

What use will we now make of the inheritance these men have left us? The answer is in our hands, the hands especially of the young generation. If those five men were alive today, I believe their concerns would be, first and foremost, for the young men and women whose opportunities will shape our future. And their greatest legacy to us would still be their faith, expressed by each in his own way, that we place our body, mind, and spirit at the disposal of our Creator, who will use them to fashion mankind in ways beyond our wisdom or imagination.

Index

359

Research, 122, 123, 151,
173, 178n.
Carrel's differences with
members of, 129, 163–64
Carrel's work at, 124, 125,
126, 127–28, 132, 158–59,
160, 163, 172, 204
Carrel's retirement from,
163–64, 172, 174, 175
Surgical Research Laboratory,
174
War Demonstration Hospital
at, 124
Rogers, Will, 12
Rollins College, 17
Rolls-Royce engines, 108, 109,
110, 227
Roosevelt, Franklin D., 108, 110,
111, 183, 191, 233, 283
Lindbergh and, 193–94, 211,
212, 213, 222, 232, 250, 252
Roots, John, 215, 217–18

Saint-Exupéry, Antoine de, 250,
260
Saint-Gildas, 123, 138–47, 160,
161, 162, 169, 178, 203
Carrels on, during World War
II, 182, 183, 184, 185, 190,
196, 197
German occupation of, 165,
190
St. Louis Dispatch, 71–72
San Francisco World Exhibition
of 1915, 17
Saturday Evening Post, 173
Saunterer, 22
Scarth (Edison chauffeur), 10, 27
Science, 133
Sears, Roebuck, 71, 72, 230
Seiberling, Henrietta, 88n.
Shoemaker, Sam, 84–85
Siboney, 196
Sikorsky, Igor, 284

Smith, Colonel Truman, 212,
221, 232, 246, 278, 279, 328
Smith, "Dr. Bob," 88n.
Smith, Idabelle, see Firestone,
Idabelle
Smith, Kay, 278
Smith College, 160
Smithsonian, 244
Snider, Colonel Robert L., 323
Sorenson, Charles, 108, 109,
110, 266
Soviet Union, 136, 166, 167, 174,
177, 183, 188, 283, 292
military strength of, 161, 165,
175, 222–30
nuclear weapons and, 282, 324
in World War II, 191, 192,
233, 268, 292
Spain, 89–90, 136, 166, 196
Spirit of St. Louis, The, 25, 108,
244, 301, 325
Stalin, Joseph, 166, 282
Stevens, Risë, 43
Stimson, Henry, 233
Strategic Air Command (SAC),
291–92, 302, 323
Surgery and Life (Malinin), 340
Switzerland, 94, 138

Taylor, Myron C., 82
Teilhard de Chardin, Pierre,
341–42
Tevy (Hawaiian friend of
Lindbergh), 346–47
"Texaco Program," 43
Thomas, J. W., 40, 52, 65,
67–68, 70, 76–77, 79, 90, 94
Thomas, Lowell, Jr., 322
Time magazine, 172
Tincher, Rev. John, 351
Toy Town Tavern, Newton's
experience at, 152–55, 158,
162, 167, 168, 269
Trippe, Juan, 316